MILITARY INTERVENTION

Military Intervention

From Gunboat Diplomacy to Humanitarian Intervention

Edited by
ANDREW M. DORMAN AND THOMAS G. OTTE
Security Studies Research Programme
University of Birmingham

Dartmouth

Aldershot • Brookfield USA • Singapore • Sydney

Published by
Dartmouth Publishing Company Limited
Gower House
Croft Road
Aldershot
Hants GU11 3HR
England

Dartmouth Publishing Company
Old Post Road
Brookfield
Vermont 05036
USA

British Library Cataloguing in Publication Data
Military Intervention: From Gunboat Diplomacy
to Humanitarian Intervention
I. Dorman, Andrew M. II. Otte, Thomas G.
327.117

Library of Congress Cataloging-in-Publication Data
Military intervention : from gunboat diplomacy to humanitarian
intervention / edited by Andrew M. Dorman & Thomas G. Otte.
p. cm.
ISBN 1-85521-579-9
1. Intervention (International law) 2. International relations.
I. Dorman, Andrew M., 1944- . II. Otte, Thomas G., 1967- .
JX4481.M54 1995
341.5'84–dc20 94-44042
CIP

ISBN 1 85521 579 9
Printed in Great Britain by
Ipswich Book Co. Ltd., Ipswich, Suffolk.

Contents

Contributors vii

Acknowledgements ix

Foreword - Air Vice-Marshal R A Mason CB CBE MA x

Section I - The Problem of Military Intervention

On Intervention: Some Introductory Remarks 3
Thomas G Otte

Section II - The 'Classical Period'

Chapter 1 - Of Congresses and Gunboats: Military Intervention in the Nineteenth Century 19
Thomas G Otte

Chapter 2 - Continuity and Change: the United States, Great Britain and Military Intervention in the Cold War 53
Constantine A Pagedas

Section III - The 'New World Order'?

Chapter 3 - The US National Interest and the Future of Military Intervention — 83
Wyn Q Bowen

Chapter 4 - Western Europe and Military Intervention: Unity in Diversity — 109
Andrew M Dorman

Chapter 5 - Aspects of Intervention in the South — 135
Stuart Croft and Adrian Treacher

Chapter 6 - United Nations and Military Intervention: a Study in the Politics of Contradiction — 161
Shahin P Malik and Andrew M Dorman

Section IV - Military Intervention: Continuity and Change

Military Intervention: Conclusions and Reflections — 193
Thomas G Otte

Contributors

Air Vice-Marshal R A Mason is an Honary Senior Research Fellow in the Graduate School of International Studies at the University of Birmingham.

Wyn Q Bowen is in the final year of his doctorate in the Graduate School of International Studies and a Research Associate of the Security Studies Research Programme at the University of Birmingham.

Stuart Croft is a Senior Lecturer in the Graduate School of International Studies, Assistant Dean of the Faculty of Commerce and Social Science at the University of Birmingham, and Director of the Security Studies Research Programme.

Andrew M Dorman is in the final year of his doctorate in the Graduate School of International Studies and a Research Associate of the Security Studies Research Programme at the University of Birmingham.

Shahin P Malik is in the midst of his doctorate studies in the Graduate School of International Studies and a Research Associate of the Security Studies Research Programme at the University of Birmingham.

Thomas G Otte is in the final year of his doctorate in the Graduate School of International Studies and a Research Associate of the Security Studies Research Programme at the University of Birmingham.

Constantine A Pagedas is in his final year of his doctorate at the Department of War Studies in Kings College, London.

Adrian Treacher is a Research Associate of the Security Studies Research Programme and is currently undertaking research for the British Academy on Central Asia.

Acknowledgements

We have a number of people to thank for their assistance on the production of this book. We apologise to those who we have failed to mention.

In particular, we would like to thank Stuart Croft and Erik Goldstein for their overall guidance; Air Vice-Marshal Tony Mason for kindly agreeing to provide the foreword, and Amanda Griffiths for her secretarial assistance, without which we would have failed to meet all our deadlines.

Finally, we owe a debt of gratitude to Adrian Randall, as Head of the School for the Social Sciences, University of Birmingham, for providing us with the funding for our doctoral studies during which time this book was written.

Birmingham
1994

A.M.D.
T.G.O.

Foreword

AIR VICE-MARSHAL R A MASON CB CBE MA

In 1994 military intervention remains a prominent feature of international relations but its nature, and the issues surrounding it, have undergone subtle but significant changes since the ending of east-west confrontation in 1989.

Before then, most of the states possessing the capacity, inclination and traditions of intervention beyond their own frontiers were aligned with one side or the other. With the exception of forays by nations such as Britain or France in the interests of imperial residue, regional conflicts tended to be regarded as elements in a global stuggle whatever their intrinsic regional cause or character.

Pursuit of national interest could be represented as an ideological crusade, justifying the acceptance of casualties and a necessary diversion of resources from a central war chest provided to protect the core security of the state against a direct threat. Non-aligned states made unilateral decisions about military activities in support of national interest.

In the Gulf War of 1990-91, international law, national interests, regional fears and Soviet indisposition coincided to enable the construction of a UN mandated intervention which expelled Iraqi forces from Kuwait with general international approbation.

In 1994 there are calls for further *intervention*: in the former Yugoslavia, in Rwanda, in Angola, in the Yemen, in Cambodia, in several former Soviet republics or indeed anywhere where there is evidence of disaster, disorder, massacre or any other kind of large scale suffering beyond the capacity or inclination of a regional government to resolve. Nor is it easy to sustain a distinction between *humanitarian* and *military* intervention when the protection of the former may lead inexorably to demands for the latter.

Motivation to intervene is therefore much more diffuse. National interest is likely to remain paramount, but not necessarily the defence of national security or territorial integrity. More subtle considerations of international responsibility and international stature may suffuse the projection or protection of interests far from one's own borders. The impact of the international media, however ephemeral, may also affect the disposition of a state to contribute, if not initiate, intervention.

Such diffusion is creating new dilemmas for many states. If regional conflict or instability derives from ethnic, racial, national or territorial disputes, those neighbouring countries with the greatest interests at stake may also be those whose intervention is likely to be regarded with the greatest suspicion by one or more of the contestants.

Conversely, if disinterest is to be a criterion of military intervention to resolve a conflict, sustain a peace or even, at the lowest level, protect humanitarian activities, what motivation will compel a state to allocate resources and, perhaps, incur casualties for a cause in which by definition it has little, if any, interest?

In some sense some would-be interventionists have a luxury not enjoyed by members of the old alliances for the better part of 100 years: the choice of whether to become involved or not. Indeed, the majority of old cold war confronters have moved from two generations of preparedness for unavoidable conflict at 48 hours' notice into an era of optional warfare.

The presence of the option raises new questions pertaining to military intervention: about the extent and nature of foreign interests, about the extent of support for UN activities; about roles for organizations like NATO and WEU designed for other purposes in an earlier age; about the size of defence budgets; about the structure, training, role priorities and motivation of armed forces; about national willingness to accept commitments, casualties and possibly catastrophe in pursuit of intangible objectives.

These are complex, interrelated and in some cases highly emotive questions with which, in some combination, the statesmen, politicians and military of the 1990s have little or no experience.

Questions about military intervention are not exclusive but particularly pertinent to those countries whose own stability, resources, military capacity and international stature are conducive to the role of interested or disinterested interventionalist. In an international arena bereft of familiar assumptions and parameters they are likely to preoccupy foreign and defence policy makers and analysts for some time to come. Resolution of the questions may well vary from circumstance to circumstance and from country to country but reflection prior to any decision will be enhanced by the examination and insights offered by the authors of the following chapters.

Section I
The Problem of Military Intervention

On Intervention: Some Introductory Remarks

THOMAS G OTTE

'Vive, vale. Si quid novisti rectius istis
Candidus imperti; si non, his utere mecum.'

Horace

'If you can better these principles, tell me.
If not, join me in following them'

One of the familiar observations about intervention is that there is no precise and generally acknowledged concept of intervention. The term intervention is often used in a rather broad and extremely vague way. This is partly due to the ambivalent nature of intervention which, for some, '[i]s practically the same as that of international politics in general'.[1] Already Talleyrand, the great 19th century statesman and cynic, it is said, confessed that he could see no difference between the political concepts of intervention and non-intervention. Others, like Urs Schwarz, have described intervention as a 'twilight area' where the four constitutive elements of the international system (i.e. power, self-interest, international law, and morality - or rather the lack of it) meet.[2] Indeed, the literature on intervention is so ambiguous that James Rosenau incredulously observed that '[t]he spirit of scientific explanation appears to have had no impact on it whatsoever'[3] or - worse still - that writing about intervention seems to be taken by some as 'a licence for undisciplined thought'.[4] It is one of the ironies of international studies that while interventions are frequently recurring phenomena and possibly even a 'built-in feature of the international system'[5], international theorists have not succeeded to solve the 'intervention puzzle'.

In international law, on the other hand, the concept of intervention, established by Emmerick de Vattel in the 18th century as a breach of the sovereignty of the target state, still prevails.[6] It is generally accepted that intervention aims at forcing the will of the target state and that it is, therefore, an encroachment on its independence and a break of its sovereignty. In this view '[i]ntervention is the dictatorial interference by a state in the affairs of another state for the purpose of maintaining or altering the actual condition of things'.[7] In this kind of definition, offered by traditionalist scholars of international law, intervention is seen in strictly normative terms as a deviation from the established norm of non-intervention.[8] Nonetheless, intervention, like force in general, has been and probably remains a well-established feature of international affairs and instrument of statecraft.[9] In different times it takes different forms: intervention can be overt or covert; it can take the form of economic coercion (e.g. sanctions, boycotts, embargoes) or it can coerce through the use or the threat of military force. Yet another, though less explicit form of intervention are subsidies for a regime or its domestic opponents. All too often interaction between states has therefore come to be treated as being synonymous with intervention.

Given the complex and almost amorphous nature of intervention a further delimitation and a more precise definition of the subject is needed. It seems only appropriate that a scholarly work should begin with a definition of its subject. Yet, the nature of definitions as much as the process of definition is more complicated and less straightforward than it would seem. Certainly, as the subject of what follows in this book is *military intervention* one delimitation has already been accomplished in that the main focus of the following chapters will be on overt military activity, i.e. the organized and systematic physical transgression of recognised state borders.

Yet, this first and most obvious delimitation of the subject at hand does not as yet allow for research to begin. Therefore, in order to establish a working definition that will guide the research towards some suggestive conclusions, it is necessary to first examine the *phenomenon* of intervention and not to simply define the word. The history of the social sciences and the humanities, littered as it is with failed concepts, hypotheses, and theories, suggests that while the importance of conceptualizations should not be discarded, it should not be overestimated either - certainly not at a stage when research has scarcely begun.

Consequently, the further delimitation of the subject does not aim to establish an operational, static, and a-historical definition of intervention. By contrast, acknowledging the complex nature and the fluid shape of intervention, which cannot be captured in one *a priori* definition, the subject has to be enveloped, it has to be defined by way of elimination. The approach underlying this process of delimitation is an essentially *phenomenological* one, i.e. a single phenomenon - military intervention - will be examined as to the qualities essential to its nature and as to those qualities which can be removed from it *in thought* without altering its essence. This approach, in turn, is based on the assumption that there can be no *real* definitions, definitions that capture the true nature of the subject. On the contrary, caught in Plato's cave, all the scholar can do is to develop an inevitably stipulative definition, a delimitation that aims to establish the essential features and causal links of the given subject.

However, it is worthwhile to begin this process of delimitation with some brief etymological thoughts on the term in question which may provide some useful insight into the nature of the subject at hand. The etymological root of the term *intervention* is the Latin verb *intervenere*. *Intervenere* has principally three different meanings: (1) to step between, to appear; (2) to confront, to interrupt, to hinder, to disrupt; and (3) to interfere to either hinder or to arbitrate. These three groups taken together - to step between, to disrupt, and to interfere - give a first idea of the nature of intervention: intervention is the interference by one state in the affairs of another state, thereby temporarily interrupting the normal pattern of bilateral relations between these two. The temporary nature of intervention is further emphasised by the meaning of the preposition *inter* - *between*. Thus, the first essential feature that can be established at this stage is the finite and temporary character of intervention. This first delimitation of intervention also reflects the kind of definition offered by traditionalist scholars of international law which was mentioned earlier.

As said before, force has been and probably remains an important instrument of foreign policy. But the use of force is by no means the norm in international affairs.[10] Similarly, military intervention may be a 'built-in feature of the international system'[11], but it is not the norm. Thus, military intervention represents a twofold deviation to the student of international affairs. Military intervention is, firstly, and most obviously, a deviation from the internationally acknowledged norm of non-intervention[12], but it is also a deviation from the normal pattern of the relations between the intervener and the target state.[13] In this respect military intervention is one of the higher profile forms of intervention. But this twofold deviation from established legal norms and norms of international behaviour also indicates the contradictions underlying the whole subject of intervention and its moral implications (see over).

The key to the understanding of the phenomenon of intervention, however, is to understand its objectives. The cornerstone of the Westphalian international order is the principle of state sovereignty: in other words, international relations are the relations between sovereign states.[14] But the notion of state-sovereignty also entails the decentralization of self-defence. Sovereign states are, therefore, exclusively responsible for their own security and defence - even within alliances. As a consequence, ever since the ascendance of the modern states system, it has been standard practice for all states to provide themselves with armed forces in order to either protect, or to enforce, or indeed to extend their political power.[15] Military intervention is, therefore, an act by states and it is concerned with their perceived national interests and foreign policy objectives. Its purpose is the same as that of all other forms of foreign policy: it is intended to make the target state do what the intervener wants it to do but what it might otherwise not have done.[16] Despite the essentially instrumental character of intervention it ought not be forgotten that policy formulation is not always the result of a careful, sober and rational calculation of the perceived national interests. States after all are not monolithic actors; they do not operate themselves and as any other political entity they depend on people to make them work.[17] The conduct of foreign affairs is therefore restrained by the internal context of the state concerned as much as by the nature of the international states system. Whenever states are in regular contact, they are but part of a greater whole: they exist within a system.[18] In a complex process of interaction and interdependence the actions of one state affect the perceptions and calculations of the other states, which then arrange themselves accordingly in a certain structure.[19] Even though the functions and the sovereignty of the state have been eroded by transnational trends, states remain the dominant actors in international affairs; and no viable alternative has as yet emerged to replace them.[20]

But there are still more precise conditions which have to be fulfilled for any use of force to be called intervention. The first and most important condition is the asymmetry in terms of power between the intervener and the target state, i.e. the intervener should be superior in power. Only because of this asymmetry is a ‘dictatorial interference’[21] possible at all. Historically, the great intervening parties have been the Great Powers and in the Cold War the two Superpowers in particular. One of the essential characteristics of intervention that can be established at this stage, therefore, is that military intervention is a unilateral armed act by a superior power undertaken in the pursuit of its wider foreign policy objectives.

However, the aspect of power is more ambivalent. *Power* is an essentially descriptive term characterising an asymmetrical relationship between at least two actors. Consequently, it ought to be used to define a specific relationship rather than in a general, all-embracing sense.[22] *Power* is a relationship in the sense that - in international politics - a state (or a group of states) can realize its will and achieve its objectives against the will and even the resistance of another state (or a group of other states). Amongst other things, the perception of power reflects the capability of a state to use military force unless its will is complied with.[23] Thus, it may be argued that resort to force always signifies the failure of power; had power 'worked' effectively the resort to force would have been unnecessary. It can, therefore, be further specified that military intervention is an instrument of foreign policy that is applied by a superior state when its power fails to move the target state in the intended direction.

Another condition of intervention concerns the use of force itself. For a unilateral armed act to be identified as a military intervention the use of force has to be limited with regard to the number of troops involved and the duration of the whole operation. The temporary nature of the action is an important aspect of intervention: it is 'a temporary and finite phenomenon'.[24] As was explained earlier, intervention is a deviation from the normal pattern of bilateral relations. Once an intervention has been launched the intervening power is generally anxious to return to the *status quo ante*. The return to the pre-intervention normality is essential for otherwise a new pattern of normality would be established, i.e. the longer the intervening forces remain the less unconventional they become, like e.g. the Soviet troops in Czechoslovakia after 1968.[25]

Thirdly, to repeat a point made earlier, military intervention is an instrument of foreign policy[26], i.e. it is an instrument to achieve a specific goal determined by politics, which the political decision-makers deem unattainable by usual means. The target state is a political problem for the intervener. Therefore, military interventions are unilateral armed acts which try to affect mainly - but by no means exclusively - the domestic structure of the target state and to a lesser degree its external policy.[27] A still further distinction can be made in that military intervention can be either a defensive or an offensive action. A defensive military intervention generally aims at the preservation or restoration of a régime and the maintenance of its current external policy. Historical examples of this kind of defensive action are the interventions in Spain and Naples in the 1820s in the name of monarchical conservatism and the Warsaw Pact interventions in Hungary and Czechoslovakia. The objective of an offensive intervention, by contrast, is to change the existing regime and the policy of the target state. The Anglo-French action at Suez in 1956, which tried to affect both the Nasser regime and its policies, and the Anglo-German and the Dutch actions against Venezuela in 1902 and 1908 respectively, which were concerned with the payment of Venezuela's debts, are classical examples of the offensive type of intervention.

Fourthly, one of the hallmarks of military intervention is its potential tendency to escalate the conflict between intervener and intervened. On an assumed *ladder of escalation*[28] military intervention occupies a rung of its own, above *coercive diplomacy* but well below *limited war*. As an instrument of foreign policy *coercive diplomacy* employs threats and limited force to persuade an opponent to comply with the coercer's will. Yet, 'the employment of threats and of initially limited force is closely co-ordinated with appropriate communication to the opponent'.[29] The strategy of *coercive diplomacy* - also known as *compellance*[30] or *coercive bargaining*[31] - allows for military operations to be broken up into a series of discrete actions which are subject to tight political control, thereby minimizing the risk of unintentional pressure, signalling, and strict political control.[32]

Military intervention, by contrast, is a less flexible strategy; it is not a gradual process and its goal has to be attained swiftly. While for the state employing *coercive diplomacy* the two main problems are those of credibility in intimidation and communicating to the opponent the existence of an asymmetry in motivation to create and tolerate risks[33], the position of any intervening party is certainly more clear-cut, but it is also more risky. As said before, the resort to force signals the failure of power. The logical reverse conclusion, thus, is that the principal (political) objective of a military intervention is the re-establishment of power. Unlike in *coercive diplomacy*, where power has not failed completely at the moment when this strategy is employed, the wider political objective of a military intervention does not allow for concessions to be made to the target state. Concessions made to the target state during the conflict would be an implicit acknowledgement of the failure of the intervener's power and would therefore make the complete re-establishment of power impossible, i.e. the principal objective of the intervention could not be achieved in its entirety. Many international theorists have noted that a combination of incentives and coercion - the classic *carrot-and-stick* approach - enhances the credibility of *coercive diplomacy*.[34] The instrument of military intervention, on the other hand, is usually employed when the opponent has resisted the temptation of the carrot and remains unmoved when threatened with the stick. For that reason and because of the overriding importance of the principal objective - the re-establishment of power - the immediate and generally openly declared objective has to be attained quickly and decisively. By its very nature, military intervention, unlike *coercive diplomacy*, is not a combination of signalling, increasing military pressure, and tight political control. Once employed, military force enjoys priority: military intervention, therefore, is finite, irreversible[35], and indivisible, i.e. it can not be broken up into a series of discrete actions.

For the successful employment of military intervention as an instrument of foreign policy certain conditions have to be met. Firstly, the intervener has to achieve his immediate objective by means of a swift action with a limited number of troops. And, secondly, by inflicting intolerable damage on the opponent the intervener has to impress on his mind the need for submission; this is necessary to emphasize credibly the asymmetry in terms of military power and the intervening party's capability and willingness to inflict even more damage on the target state.

But, as the intervening party's objective has to be achieved within a short period of time and as concessions cannot be made, the decision to launch an intervention potentially embraces the risk of escalation in case the intervened party resists the onslaught. If the intervening forces meet with resistance a reciprocal action will inevitably be triggered because the stakes are too high for the intervener to back down at this point.[36] If the intervened state continues to resist the further escalation into a fully fledged war is more than likely as the American experience in Vietnam or the Soviet Afghan imbroglio demonstrate[37].

Finally, another essential aspect of intervention is its legally and morally contradictory nature. The modern international system, ever since the end of the Thirty Years War, is founded on the principle of state sovereignty. The principle of state sovereignty is the pillar upon which the whole architecture of the international system rests. Intervention, therefore, defined as a *dictatorial interference* in the affairs of another state, is quite clearly illegitimate. Yet, the cornerstone of international order is not the principle of sovereignty *as such*, but the principle of self determination or nationality.[38] An intervention on behalf of self-determination would therefore seem to be legitimate, thereby raising the issue of national liberation movements.[39]

A different legitimation of intervention, and the most efficacious means to maintain some kind of stability and order, was seen in the principle of governmental legitimacy. Ever since the Holy Alliance of 1815, with its commitment to monarchical conservatism and dynastic legitimacy, formulated the notion of governmental legitimacy this principle has been applied to international conflicts to the present day. However, doubts about the legitimacy of intervention have always induced powers intent on interfering in the affairs of another state to avoid any unilateral action as far as possible and to seek at least the political support of other powers.[40] Again, the Holy Alliance, in which the three monarchical Eastern powers Russia, Prussia and Austria joined together to maintain what they regarded as the basis of international stability, i.e. the principle of dynastic conservatism, is an example of such attempts to lend greater legitimacy to an act of intervention by collective means. This tendency not to 'go it alone', it may be argued, is a reaction to the generally heterogenous nature of the international system. In an international system, in which different principles of domestic legitimacy prevail in different countries[41], collective interventions increase the intervening party's security and maintain their relative freedom of action.

But the tendency toward collective intervention also throws a revealing light on the importance of the relationship of force between the parties involved. The wider the gap in the size and power of the intervener and the intervened, the more acceptable intervention appeared (as an act in defence of the established international order) and the more acceptable an act of intervention became for other great powers since a strong action by an equal would not threaten the overall balance of power and the general peace.[42] Thus, the wider the gap in power, the smaller the risk of an intervention escalating into a war not only between the intervener and the target state, but also the smaller the risk of another great power jumping on the band-waggon and becoming involved in the ensuing conflict.[43]

Having established the essential features of military intervention or having at least sketched the shape of this phenomenon, the process of definition by delimitation has now led to a point where it is possible to formulate a more precise working definition of military intervention:

> Military intervention is the planned limited use of force for a transitory period by a state (or a group of states) against a weaker state in order to change or maintain the target state's domestic structure or to change its external policies; it is the continuation of politics with the limited addition of means of military force in order to re-establish the normal pattern of bilateral relations by forcing the opponent into compliance. Military intervention is a rigid instrument that does not leave any room for concessions to be made to the intervened and that embraces the risk of escalation.

Notes

1. cf.Hoffmann, S., 'The Problem of Intervention', in: H.Bull (ed.), Intervention in World Politics, Oxford: Clarendon Press 1984, p.7.

2. Schwarz, U., 'Great Power Intervention in the Modern World', in: A. Buchan (ed.), Problems of Modern Strategy, London: Chatto & Windus 1970 (= Studies in International Security, vol.xiv), p.176.

3. cf.Rosenau, J.N., 'Intervention as a Scientific Concept', in: Journal of Conflict Resolution, xiii/1, (1969), p.149.

4. cf.idem, 'The Concept of Intervention', in: Journal of International Affairs, xxii/2, (1968), p.173.

5. cf.Bull, H., 'Conclusion', in: idem (ed.), Intervention in World Politics, op.cit., p.181.

6. Vattel, E.de, Le Droit des Gens ou Principe de la Loi Naturelle, London, 1758, I para.31f.

7. cf.Oppenheim, L., International Law: A Treatise, vol.i, Peace, ed. by H.Lauterpacht, London: Longmans 8th ed.1955, para.134, p.305; Dahm, G., Völkerrecht, vol.i, Stuttgart: Kohlhammer, 1958, para 34, p.201f.

8. Luard, E., 'Collective Intervention', in: Bull (ed.), Intervention in World Politics, op.cit., p.157.

9. Northedge, F.S., 'The Resort to Force', in: idem (ed.), The Use of Force in International Relations, London 1974, p. 11f.; Berridge, G.R., International Politics: States, Powers and Conflicts since 1945, Brighton - New York 1987, pp.72ff.; Howard, M.E., 'Military Power and International Order', in: International Affairs, xi/3 (1964), pp.400ff.; Bull, H., The Anarchical Society: A Study of Order in International Politics, London: Macmillan, Repr.1991, pp.184ff.; Morgenthau, H.J., 'To intervene or not to intervene', in: Foreign Affairs, xlv/3, (1967), pp.425-36; Young, O.R., 'Intervention and International Systems', in: Journal of International Affairs xxii/2 (1968), p.178f; Beloff, M., 'Reflections on Intervention', in: ibid., pp.199ff.

10. Clausewitz, C. von, On War, ed. by P. Paret & M.E. Howard, Princeton, N.J.: Princeton University Press, 1989, p.605.

11. cf.Bull, H., 'Conclusion', op.cit., p.181.

12. Oppenheim, International Law, op.cit., para.134; Hoffmann, 'Problem of Intervention', op.cit., p.11f.

13. Rosenau, 'Concept of Intervention', op.cit., p.167.

14. Bull, H., Anarchical Society, op.cit., pp.24ff.; Schmitt, C., Der Nomos der Erde im Völkerrecht des Ius Publicum Europaeum, Berlin: Duncker & Humblot, 3rd ed.1988, pp.112ff. and 144ff.; Kennedy, P.M., The Rise and Fall of the Great Powers: Economic Change and Military Conflict, London: Fontana, 4th ed. 1989 (pb), p.xxiii; Holsti, K.J., Peace and War: Armed Conflicts and International Order, 1648-1989, Cambridge: Cambridge University Press s.a.(= Cambridge Studies in International Relations, vol.xiv), pp.34ff.; Hinsley, F.H., Power and the Pursuit of Peace: Theory and Practice in the History of the Relations between States, Cambridge : Cambridge University Press, Repr.1982 (pb), p.166.

15. Clausewitz, On War, op.cit., p.606f.; Howard, 'Military Power', op.cit., p.405f.

16. Hoffmann, 'Problems of Intervention', op.cit., p.9f.

17. Weber, M., Economy and Society: An Outline of Interpretative Sociology, ed.by G.Roth and C.Wittich, Berkeley, Los Angeles - London: University of California Press, 2nd ed.1978, vol.i, p.56; idem, 'Politics as a Vocation', in: H.H.Gerth & C.Wright Mills (eds.), From Max Weber: Essays in Sociology, London: Routledge & Kegan Paul, 6th ed.1967, pp.77-128, pp.84ff.; Lasswell, H.D. & Kaplan, A., Power and Society: A Framework for Political Inquiry, New Haven : Yale University Press 3rd ed. 1957, pp.3ff.; for more empirical studies see exemplary: Watt, D.C., Personalities and Policies: Studies in the Formulation of British Foreign Policy in the Twentieth Century, London, 1965; idem, How War Came: The Immediate Origins of the Second World War, 1938-9, London: Mandarin, 1990 (pb); Steiner, Z.S., The Foreign Office and British Foreign Policy, 1898-1914, London - Atlantic Highlands, NJ: Ashfield Press 1986 (pb).

18. Bull, Anarchical Society, op.cit., p.10; Schroeder, P.W., '"System" and Systemic Thinking in International History', in: International History Review, xv/1, (1993), pp.116-34; see also Hegel, G.W.F., Grundlinien der Philosophie des Rechts oder Naturrecht und Staatswissenschaft im Grundrisse, Stuttgart: F. Frommann Repr.1964 (=Collected Works, vol.vii, ed. by H.Glockner), p.441: 'In the same way as the individual is not a real person unless related to other persons, the state has no real individuality unless related to other states' [transl. TGO].

19. Bull, Anarchical Society, op.cit., pp.53ff.; Clausewitz, On War, op.cit., p.373: '[M]ajor and minor interests of states and peoples [are] interwoven in the most varied and changeable manner. Each point of the intersection binds and serves to balance one set of interests against the other. The broad effect of all these fixed points is obviously to give a certain amount of cohesion to the whole [...] The sum total of relations between states thus serves to maintain the stability of the whole rather than to promote change'.

20. Kennedy, P.M., Preparing For the Twenty-First Century, New York: Random House, 1993, p.134.

21. cf.Oppenheim, International Law, op.cit., para.134.

22. Already Max Weber pointed out that 'power' as a concept is 'sociologically amorphous' and of 'no scientific utility', see: Weber, Economy and Society, op.cit., vol.i, p.53f.; Lasswell & Kaplan, Power and Society, op.cit., p.75; see also: Morgenthau, H.J., Politics Among Nations: The Struggle for Power and Peace, New York: A.A. Knopf, 4th ed. 1967, pp.25ff.; Reynolds, C., Theory and Explanation in International Politics, London: M.Robertson, 1975, p.84; Wyllie, J.H., The Influence of British Arms: An Analysis of British Military Intervention since 1956, London : Allen & Unwin, 1984, p.6.

23. Paret, P., 'Military Power', in: Journal of Military History, liii/2, (1989), pp.239-56.

24. cf.Rosenau, 'Concept of Intervention', op.cit., p.167.

25. Wyllie, Influence of British Arms, op.cit., p.19; Schwarz, 'Great Power Intervention', op.cit., p.176f.

26. Bull, H., 'Introduction', in: idem (ed.), Intervention in World Politics, op.cit., p.5; Morgenthau, 'To intervene or not to intervene', op.cit., p.425.

27. Hoffmann, 'Problem of Intervention', op.cit., p.10, by contrast, confines the concept of intervention exclusively to attempts to affect the domestic structure of the target state.

28. Kahn, H., On Escalation, New York, 1965; Schelling, T.C., The Strategy of Conflict, London: Oxford University Press, 1960; idem, Arms and Influence, New Haven/CT - London: Yale University Press, 1966, p.104.

29. cf.Craig, G.A. & George, A.L., Force and Statecraft: Diplomatic Problems of Our Time, Oxford - New York: Oxford University Press, 1983 (pb), p.189; see also: Lauren, P.G., 'Theories of Bargaining with Threats of Force: Deterrence and Coercive Diplomacy', in: idem (ed.), Diplomacy: New Approaches in History and Policy, New York - London, 1981, pp.183-211, pp.192ff.; Berridge, International Politics, op.cit., pp.88ff.

30. Schelling, Arms and Influence, op.cit., pp.69ff.

31. Berridge, International Politics, op.cit., p.88.

32. Craig & George, Force and Statecraft, op.cit., p.192; Lauren, 'Theories of Bargaining', op.cit., p.193f.; Cable, J., Gunboat Diplomacy, 1919-1979: Political Application of Limited Naval Force, London: Macmillan, Repr.1986 (pb) (= Studies in International Security, vol.xvi), p.38f.

33. Schelling, Strategy of Conflict, op.cit., p.40; George, A.L. & Hall, D.K. & Simons, W.E., The Limits of Coercive Diplomacy: Laos, Cuba, Vietnam, Boston: Little Brown, 1971, pp.25f., 243f.

34. Craig & George, Force and Statecraft, op.cit., p.191; Lauren, 'Theories of Bargaining', op.cit., p.194.

35. Wingen, J. van & Tillema, H.K., 'British Military Intervention after World War II: Militance in a Second Rank Power', in: Journal of Peace Research, xvii/4, (1980), p.293.

36. Compare Clausewitz, On War, op.cit., p.15: '[W]ar is an act of force, and there is no logical limit to the application of that force. Each side, therefore, compels its opponent to follow suit; a reciprocal action is started which must lead, in theory, to extremes'.

37. See also: Vasquez, J.A., The War Puzzle, Cambridge : Cambridge University Press, 1993, p.242f; Yamamoto, Y. & Bremer, S.A., 'Wider Wars and Restless Nights: Major Power Intervention in Ongoing Wars', in: J.D.Singer (ed.), The Correlates of War, vol.ii, New York: Free Press, 1980, p.216f.

38. Hoffmann, 'Problem of Intervention', op.cit., p.11f; Bull, Anarchical Society, op.cit., p.36f.

39. On the other hand, though, the United Nations Charter, ch.VII, art.2, para.7, states quite clearly that nothing contained in the Charter 'shall authorise the UN to intervene in matters which are entirely within the domestic jurisdiction of any state'.

40. Schwarz, 'Great Power Intervention', op.cit., p.180.

41. Aron, R., Paix et guerre entre les nations, Paris: Calmann-Levy, 1962, here quoted from the German edition Frieden und Krieg: Eine Theorie der Staatenwelt, Francfort: S.Fischer, 1986, pp.435ff.; see also: Hoffmann, 'Problem of Intervention', op.cit., p.12f. A classic example of the heterogeneity of the international system is the *Concert of Europe*, as restored at Vienna in 1815, when there were three contending principles of domestic legitimacy: the dynastic principle, as upheld by the *Eastern Powers*, the principle of representative government, supported by Britain and France, and a third, more nationalist-democratic principle advocated by liberal and nationalist opposition movements in various countries. Other examples are the 1930s with the conflicting principles of Democracy, Fascism and Communism, and, of course, the bi-polar world of the Cold War.

42. Schwarz, 'Great Power Intervention', op.cit., p.178f.

43. Vasquez, War Puzzle, op.cit., p.240f.

Section II

The 'Classical Period'

1 Of Congresses and Gunboats: Military Intervention in the Nineteenth Century

THOMAS G OTTE

The 19th Century International Environment: the *Concert of Europe*

Like the form of international order which succeeded it, the *Concert of Europe* was conceived in a war for the mastery of the European continent. The statesmen who assembled at Vienna in 1814-5, and in particular 'the architects of the new order'[1], the British Foreign Secretary Lord Castlereagh and Prince Metternich, the Austrian State Chancellor, were determined to devise a stable international system that would contain international violence and prevent another general war in Europe. As a result, they created a territorial and political order which, although initially poised against defeated France, was above all meant to prevent the domination of Europe by a single Power. The *Concert of Europe*, as it became known, was a mechanism of consultation and cooperation among the Great Powers, Britain, Austria, Russia, Prussia, and, after the Congress of Aix-la-Chapelle, France, in order to solve international crises and to prevent or end wars. In this respect, the Vienna settlement was not merely an 'elaborate exercise in cartography'[2], redrawing the map of Europe by balancing off territory, population and resources of the major Powers. It was rather an attempt to institutionalize an equilibrium of forces, a 'balance of power', based on the willingness and ability of the Great Powers to collectively resist unilateral attempts at continental hegemony. The 'balance of power', based on a system of consultation, was indeed the key concept of post-1815 international relations.[3]

Yet, the *Concert of Europe*, in its classical form did not last long. By 1822, after the Congress of Verona, the 'conference system' devised at Vienna seven years earlier had come to an end.[4] The issue which divided the statesmen of Europe was the question of intervention. At Vienna, the Tsar of Russia, Alexander I, had also brought into being the *Holy Alliance*; based on mystical sentiments and Christian principles it was meant to usher in a new era that would transcend the pettiness of history.[5] Both, Castlereagh and Metternich, ridiculed the whole idea. The British Foreign Secretary called it 'a sublime piece of mysticism and nonsense'[6]; for Metternich it was a 'loud sounding nothing'.[7] Yet, he instrumentalized the *Holy Alliance* for his own purposes. Like the Tsar, he was concerned about the threat of liberalism to the established monarchies of Europe.[8] Thus, when revolutionary movements rose again, Metternich and the Tsar tried to combine the Great Powers into an anti-revolutionary alliance, thereby turning the *conference system* into an agency that would immediately intervene in the internal affairs of any country shaken by revolution.[9] Castlereagh, on the other hand, realised that intervention was potentially destructive within the balance of power system, for it had 'a corrosive effect upon the vital mechanism by which the balance of power equilibrium [was] sustained - alliance flexibility'.[10] Given his primary concern with the stability of the 'balance of power system' he became increasingly disaffected with the 'conference method' and automatic intervention. Yet, Britain never really withdrew from the *Concert of Europe* and the practice of consultation and cooperation survived. At times this practice took almost the form of an institution of European politics. But the *Concert of Europe* was no well-ordered organization with a permanent structure. At best it was an 'informal institution which enjoyed no more than intermittent existence'.[11] It was a decentralized system that regulated the competition and the conflicts between the established Great Powers of Europe; its maintenance, though, was a responsibility which all Great Powers had to assume collectively.

Looking at the history of the 19th century international order one can distinguish roughly three distinct periods. The first, the classical period of the *pentarchy of Europe*, lasted for about 40 years, from 1815 to 1856. But already 1848, the year of the European revolutions, marked a watershed. In its course, Prince Metternich, who had dominated the international scene after 1815, was overthrown. With his fall from power, the order of Vienna, the *Metternich system* came to an end. In the wake of the revolution a new spirit became prevalent in continental Europe; a new generation of statesmen and diplomats emerged which no longer adhered to the principles and the practice of cooperation established at Vienna. Now the clash of rival nationalisms complicated the operation of international relations. The Vienna principles were increasingly substituted by a national-liberal (Hegelian) view which saw the *Machtstaat* (power state) as the highest form of statehood, and indeed as the perfection of *Realpolitik* in the pursuit of the national interest.[12] But it was really the end of the Crimean War in 1856 which marked the end of the classical period of the *Concert of Europe*, and which opened the way for this new breed of *Realpolitiker*. Having prevented the revolutions of 1848 from escalating into a general European conflict, Russia and Britain, the latter aided by France, slithered into the first war between European Great Powers since 1815.[13] The Crimean War inaugurated an era of international anarchy in the short term and, in the longer term, of permanent alliances.[14] Caught in the undertow of the Crimean War the shattered European concert was no longer capable of containing the aggressive ambitions of individual states. Four major wars between 1856 and 1870-1 forcibly revised the map of Europe drawn up in 1815 and destroyed the old European equilibrium beyond all recognition.[15]

The end of the Franco-German War in May 1871 also marked the end of a 'territorial revolution'[16] in European affairs. The unifications of Italy and Germany had abolished the buffer zones between the Great Powers created at Vienna in 1815. Moreover, the wars between 1859 and 1870-1 had created a hyper-nationalist mood that could easily be whipped up and orchestrated by the Governments of Europe, but which also influenced the governments; these were no longer free from external pressure, be it public opinion or economic or military interests.[17] Thus, the creation of a new European balance and of a viable international system capable of sustaining it, had become more difficult. The period of unrest after 1856 was the result of the temporary 'withdrawal' of Russia and Britain from European affairs and of a slow but steady shift in the distribution of power, industrial and military, that made a change of the *status quo* inevitable.

In the changed international environment Germany emerged as the new pivot of European affairs and her Chancellor, Otto von Bismarck, became the key figure in post-1870 international politics.[18] His main concern was the inherent instability of the new European system which threatened Germany's position as a Great Power. He summed up this problem by saying that he suffered from a *cauchemar des coalitions*, a nightmare of hostile coalitions, i.e. the revival of the historic 18th century anti-Prussian alliance of France, Austria and Russia.[19] Bismarck realized that the old *concert system* was no longer an effective mechanism for the maintenance of the balance of power. His strategy, therefore, was to divert the tensions between the Great Powers away from Europe to overseas.[20] In this respect, the Congress of Berlin marked the zenith of Bismarckian diplomacy as well as a watershed in European affairs; it brought to an end a period of some 20 odd years of upheaval and ushered in a period of 34 years of relative peace and stability. But at Berlin it had also finally become clear that the traditional friendship between the three conservative Eastern Powers could no longer be relied upon. Germany's position in European affairs, therefore, had to be preserved by other means. Between 1879 (*Dual Alliance*) and 1887 (*Reassurance Treaty*) the Reich Chancellor evolved an intricate alliance system, which involved all Powers - with the exception of France - in an elaborate 'web' of secret alliances, insurance treaties, reassurance treaties, agreements and understandings, which made unilateral actions by any one of them almost impossible.[21] The *Bismarckian web*, however, unlike the *Metternich system*, was not based on a general consensus. It was a highly complicated and delicately adjusted system of checks and balances. Its main weakness was that '[i]t operated by means of secrecy, constant manoeuvre, and a high degree of disingenuousness'[22]; it was 'something of conjuring trick, a piece of conscious virtuosity'[23], carefully exploiting the differences between the other Powers by widely scattering promises so as not to carry them out. But Bismarck was as much aware of Germany's strength as of her weakness. Certainly, the new Reich was the 'semi-hegemon' of the continent[24], but it was not quite strong enough to dominate Europe. His *iron-and-blood* rhetoric aside, his policy was essentially a policy of restraint; and his *Realpolitik*, though ruthless in exploiting the weaknesses of others, was motivated by fear rather than by a desire for conquest.[25] The *Bismarck system* was a guarantee of peace, albeit one organised by Germany. With his fall from power in 1890 his system of alliance fell, too, and Europe had to seek a new guarantee of peace, one against Germany.

During the 1890s, until 1904-5, the international system was in a state of flux and constant change. In Germany a new generation of politicians, gradually brought into office after the accession of Emperor Wilhelm II to the throne in 1888, gave up Bismarck's policy of restraint and embarked upon the maladroit, boisterous, though less purposeful *Weltpolitik*.[26] In 1894 Republican France and Tsarist Russia cast aside their principles and prejudices and concluded an alliance which was to keep Germany neutral while the two partners were free to pursue their own separate interests; in effect the Franco-Russian Alliance of 1894 was therefore mainly directed against Britain.[27] Outside Europe, Japan's victory over China in 1894-5 finally established the Meji Empire as a power to be reckoned with.[28] At the same time, the crushing defeat of Spain at the hands of the United States in 1898 marked the ascendence of the United States, bolstered by her rising industrial and naval power, to a hegemonial position in the Western hemisphere.[29] With the rise of the United States and Japan to Great Power status the gradual transformation of the 'European' international system to a global one was accomplished. By 1907 this period of flux was over and a new configuration emerged: the 19th century international system had entered its third systemic form. Now, all the Great Powers, with the exception of America, had arranged themselves in two inflexible, hostile and highly armed coalitions.

The most decisive factor in bringing about this rearrangement was German *Weltpolitik*. What *Weltpolitik* was meant to achieve was probably not even clear to the rulers in Berlin themselves. On the one hand, it was thought to reverse the deterioration of Germany's international position. In addition, Prince Bülow, under whose Foreign Secretaryship *Weltpolitik* was inaugurated, hoped that a forceful foreign policy would also have a stabilizing effect on Germany's fragile political system.[30] But *Weltpolitik* also embraced the divergent nationalist views of the time and combined them to a rather vague and diffuse program of political action[31]: it was 'imperialism without an object' (Joseph Schumpeter). In the end, however, the nervousness and heavy-handedness of *Weltpolitik* and in particular the German method of not negotiating about their aims but, so it seemed, to secretly sharpen their sword 'outcircled' the German Empire.[32] The transformation of Germany from a cluster of small, insignificant and economically backward principalities to a united empire with rising industrial strength, a fast growing population and possibly the strongest, best organized and most efficient army of the day and later, after 1898/1900 and increasingly so after 1908, her naval build-up was at the heart of the Anglo-German antagonism.[33] Germany's rise implied a relative decline of Britain as a colonial, industrial and naval power. Moreover German political and economic activities in the Balkans and Asiatic Turkey intensified Russian perceptions of insecurity.[34] Thus, the perceived threat posed by Germany to the national interests of Britain, France and Russia led to the conclusion of the Anglo-French *entente cordiale* of 1904 and the Anglo-Russian Agreement of 1907 which in effect constituted a *Triple Entente*.[35] The post-1907 international system was almost bi-polar: two increasingly inflexible and increasingly hostile alliances, the Triple Alliance (Germany, Austria-Hungary, Italy) and the Triple Entente (Britain, France, Russia) were now pitted against each other. It was more unstable than both the 'Bismarckian Web' and the 'Vienna System' since it was no longer based on a general consensus between the Powers.[36] The last years before the outbreak of the Great War were marked by constantly accelerating armaments programs, offensive military planning and a growing belief in the inevitability of war.[37] While the Great Powers were still able to cooperate when two Balkan conflicts flared up in 1912/3, they were no longer capable or willing, least of all Germany, to restrain themselves or their allies in July 1914[38], when the nations of Europe 'slithered over the brink into the boiling cauldron of war without any trace of apprehension or dismay'.[39]

In conclusion it can be argued that the 19th century international system can be divided into three distinct periods with specific quasi-systemic configurations: the *Vienna System* (1815-48/56), the *Bismarck System* (1871/8-90), and the quasi-bipolar system of *ententes* (1902/7-14).

In the following three cases of 19th century intervention will be examined as to their essential characteristics. Each of these three case studies is chosen so as to represent the three distinct systemic configurations of the 19th century international system. By means of 'structured, focused comparison'[40] it will be attempted to establish the nature of military intervention in the period between 1815 and 1914. This approach combines historical (ideographic) methodology of intensive, detailed explanation of the particular with the political scientist's (nomothetic) concept of general synthetic theories. It is an essentially 'phenomenologico-qualitative' method which focuses on certain characteristic aspects of comparable historical cases.

(1) The Austrian Intervention in Naples 1820/21

The Neapolitian revolution of 1820/21 marked the climax in a series European crises and congresses.[41] Already in March 1820 revolutions had occurred in Spain and Portugal which led to the proclamation of liberal constitutions in these countries. Similarly, the Latin American colonies of Spain and Portugal - following the examples of the American and French Revolutions - were revolting against their colonial masters.[42] Now, Naples, a country with a Spanish past and governed by a Bourbon Spaniard, seemed to be in the grip of *Iberian liberalism*.

Prince Metternich, the conservative Austrian State Chancellor, was determined to intervene; to him the events in Southern Italy presented a threat to the established social and political order.[43] Moreover, a nationalist-liberal revolution in Naples, the largest Italian state, endangered the carefully contrived territorial and political fragmentation of Italy and thus Austria's position on the Italian peninsula upon which her membership of the European pentarchy depended. By virtue of her preponderant geographic position (since 1815 Austria was in the possession of Lombardo-Venetia) and strong dynastic ties with the secondary principalities Austria's position in Italy was that of a semi-hegemon. The revolution in the southern half of the Appenine Peninsula was therefore more than an ideological nuisance. It was a menace to the stability of

Austria's own dominions and of the dependent dynasties; it was a threat to one of the pillars of Metternich's European policy: Austria's predominance in Italy.[44] But there was also a legal dimension to the crisis. By taking the oath on the new constitution Ferdinand IV had broken a secret treaty with Austria, concluded in 1815, by which the Neapolitan army was placed under Austrian command and by which the restored King bound himself not to alter the political system of his kingdom without Vienna's consent.[45] Unless Austria intervened, Metternich explained to the British ambassador Sir Charles Stewart, he foresaw the 'immediate loss of certain provinces in Italy, and [that] Doctrines, under this Evil [i.e. the revolution, TGO] were disseminated, by which the whole Empire were converted and endangered, and the European System menaced with a complete overthrow'.[46]

But nothing ever worked simply with Metternich. The ever cautious Austrian chancellor wished to protect his diplomatic flanks and, therefore, avoided a simple, unilateral Austrian action against Naples.[47]

Metternich, therefore, sought the support of the Allies for an Austrian intervention at a Great Power conference which assembled on 20 October 1820 at Troppau in Austrian Silesia, and re-assembled at Laibach (Ljubljana) in January 1821. But only the three autocratic Eastern Powers - Russia, Prussia and Austria - participated fully in the congress.[48] Lord Castlereagh, the British Foreign Secretary, acknowledged the 'peculiar position of difficulty, if not danger in which the Austrian dominions have been placed by the sudden and unexpected revolution'.[49] But in his view the Neapolitan question was of concern to Austria only, and did not fall under the stipulations of the Declaration of Aix-la-Chapelle of 1818.[50]

France shared Castlereagh's objection to a conference solution of the Neapolitan question. Both Powers were represented at Troppau and Laibach by their ambassadors, a rather low rank representation compared with the three Eastern Powers who were represented by their monarchs and foreign ministers.[51] With Britain and France attending the conference as observers only, Metternich easily won the approval of Tsar Alexander I and King Frederick William III of Prussia for a unilateral Austrian intervention. On 19 November 1820 the three Powers issued a 'Protocole Préliminaire' which provided Metternich with what he wanted: the moral condemnation of the revolution and the solemn sanction of the principle of intervention. The preliminary protocol stated that

> [s]tates have undergone a change of government, due to revolution, the result of which threatens other states, *ipso facto* cease to be members of the European Alliance, and remain excluded from it until their situation gives guarantees of legal order and stability. If, owing

> to such alterations, immediate danger threatens other states, the Powers bind themselves, by peaceful means, or if need be by arms, to bring back the guilty states into the bosom of the Great Alliance.[52]

This was an 'extreme doctrine of intervention'[53], conceptualizing intervention as an instrument of statecraft contrived by the European system for cases in which a monarch was no longer capable of suppressing a revolutionary movement and had to rely on monarchical solidarity; intervention was therefore deemed to be the legitimate right of the Great Powers to be exercised against lesser nations for the upholding of the established social and political order.

Had the assembly of a conference on the Neapolitian question already indicated a rift in the Alliance, then that rift was still further widened by the extreme doctrine of intervention stated in the preliminary protocol. Neither Lord Stewart nor the French representatives, La Ferronay (the ambassador at St. Petersburg) and Caraman (the ambassador at Vienna), signed the protocol which had been drafted without their consultation.[54] While the attitude of the French was motivated by politico-strategic considerations with regard to the restoration of French influence in Italy, the British objection reflected a different concept of European politics. The British Government thought it necessary

> [t]o decline being a party to any League or Concert in the nature of a general Guarantee and to recommend to their Allies to confine their views to special cases of publick danger ... rather than to pledge themselves beforehand to interfere on every occasion when a political change may be regarded by them as irregular or unlawful ... or to hazard by anticipation the promulgation of a system of conduct to be pursued by them on all such occasions, of the prudence as well as the practicality of which understanding the most serious doubts must suggest themselves to every reflecting mind.[55]

While he principally acknowledged the legitimacy of interventions in certain circumstances, Castlereagh's concept of it was far more rigorous than the extreme doctrine formulated at Troppau: it was a minimalist doctrine of intervention. In sharp contrast to Metternich, to whom the struggle for the maintenance of the established order overshadowed all other problems, the British Foreign Secretary preferred to regard it as an international problem. He was primarily concerned with general balance-of-power considerations and insisted that any intervention must be sanctioned by reference to international matters on a case-by-case basis. Already in his famous State Paper of 5 May 1820 on the revolution in Spain he had maintained that the danger to others emerging from a change in the internal affairs of a state had to be 'direct and imminent' and 'military in character actual and existent'[56] to warrant intervention. The Troppau concept of intervention, by contrast, seemed to him to inevitably 'lead to a much more frequent and extensive interference in the internal transactions of states'[57] with possible negative implications for the general political equilibrium in European politics. Castlereagh remained at odds with the three Eastern Powers for *balance of power* reasons, but to no great avail. The congress was adjourned at the end of 1820 and re-assembled at Laibach in Carniola. The proceedings at Laibach, to which the King of Naples had also been invited, and which were consequently marked by the extreme duplicity of the Neapolitan monarch, 'might have been drawn straight from the *opera buffe*'[58] but they got Metternich the result he had worked for: Russia and Prussia sanctioned an intervention by Austria to suppress the Neapolitan revolution and to restore the Bourbon king. Now, having received the support of other Great Powers, Austria could act in the name and on behalf of the Concert of Europe; and it was only now, more than half a year after the outbreak of the revolution, that an Austrian army left Northern Italy for Naples. On 9 March the Austrians entered Neapolitan territory and attacked the 25,000 strong revolutionary army under General Pepe at the pass of Antrodoco. The revolutionary army had now either ceased to exist or was in a state of dissolution; and with the Neapolitan Parliament adjourning itself on 19 March 'until His Majesty shall be pleased to call it together again[!]'[59] the revolution had finally collapsed. On 24 March the Austrian army, having suffered almost no casualties, entered the city of Naples and on 1 April a provisional government was installed.[60]

From Metternich's point of view the Austrian intervention in Naples was a success. Through skilful diplomatic manoeuvring he had won the approval of the other Great Powers. The Congress of Troppau/Laibach gave Austria the moral legitimacy she needed for her action against Naples. Only the backing of at least the majority of the other members of the European pentarchy made the action possible at all. It was clear to Metternich that any unilateral action by Austria without prior agreement with the Allies would have alienated Russia and France, with Prussia probably falling in with the others against Austria. His success at Troppau and Laibach enabled him once again to maintain the unity of the three Eastern Powers and fill the rather vague idea of the *Holy Alliance* with the political contents of his choice. Bolstered by his diplomatic success he was able to crush the revolution in Naples, to contain - at least for a while - the danger of Italian nationalism, and to maintain Austria's predominance in Italy as one of the pillars upon which her Great Power status rested.

In the long term, however, Metternich had to pay a price for this success. By suppressing the uprising in Naples he incurred the wrath of all Italian nationalists. From now on, and more so than before, Austria was seen as a foreign suppressor, the heir to Napoleon's rule over the Appenine peninsula. Hardly 40 years later, after the war of 1859, the Habsburg Monarchy was forced to cede its Italian dominions to Piedmont-Sardinia and its long decline as a European Great Power began.

More fundamentally, however, Metternich's attempt to convert Europe to the Habsburg version of governmental legitimacy deepened the rift between the conceptions of foreign policy subscribed to by the three autocratic monarchies of the East and the one upheld by the two 'liberal' Powers Britain and France. Troppau and Laibach anticipated the split of the *Quadruple Alliance* after 1832, which placed Britain and France in more or less general opposition to the three Eastern Powers.[61]

(2) The British Intervention of Egypt in 1882

The events of 1882 were a crucial turning point in the development of the perennial Egyptian question which occupied the leaders of Europe throughout the 19th century as well as in the history of European politics. Located at the crossroads between Africa and Asia, Egypt controlled the lines of communication between Europe and the East.[62] Its strategic significance was dramatically enhanced when the Suez Canal, built by French engineers, finally opened in 1869. The whole Eastern Question and the 'geography of world-power was revolutionized by the Suez Canal'[63]; the new line of communication between the Eastern Mediterranean and the Red Sea was a more direct line than the old route around Africa and therefore economically superior to it. With the opening of the canal the land on the Nile became more important for the security of Britain and her Empire. Thus, when the opportunity arose Prime Minister Disraeli acquired the Khedive's shares in the canal in 1875.[64] In the words of Bismarck Egypt was the 'spinal cord of the Empire, which connects the backbone [i.e. India] with the brain [i.e. Britain]'.[65] Apart from Egypt's immense strategic importance, the country, although poor in resources, was also somewhat of a 'magnet for adventurers'[66]; Egypt was a miracle of fiscal and financial mismanagement and the Khedive's almost habitual bankruptcy attracted bankers from all over Europe who sought to exploit the messy finances of the Egyptian government.[67]

By 1882 the Khedive's government had run up a public debt of £98 millions; the total annual debt charges amounted to some £5 million, half the government's total revenue![68] Three years earlier, in 1879, the Anglo-

French interest in Egypt had been institutionalized with the establishment of the dual control of Egyptian finances.[69] This financial reorganization and - after a coup d'état by Khedive Ismail - the deposition of Ismail and the appointment of a new Khedive, Tewfik Pasha, by the Ottoman Sultan at the instigation of Britain, France and other European Powers had been contrived to save Khedivial rule from complete collapse under the pressure of its accumulated debts to European bankers.[70]

High taxation and the undeniable influence of the foreign community, many of them in public offices, gave rise to a growing nationalist opposition led by disconcerted Egyptian army officers and panislamist intellectuals. By 1881 this by no means homogenous movement had conquered the country and in February 1882 Tewfik was forced to appoint a new ministry in which Colonel Ahmed Arabi, the leader of the nationalist army officers, took over the War Ministry.[71] Arabi's position in the internal power struggle was further strengthened after a conflict with Tewfik during the summer of 1882. With Tewfik being powerless and anti-foreign riots, which left some 50 Europeans dead, taking place in Alexandria and other places, Arabi was now virtually a dictator.[72]

Throughout the crisis the British Government, Gladstone's second cabinet, were firmly opposed to active intervention. But events were soon forcing their hands. British reluctance to adopt a more active policy in the Egyptian question was to a large degree due to the nature of the problem. The Egyptian imbroglio was a complex web, made of various strands of problems, criss-crossing each other and yet inexorably interwoven. On the one hand, there was the dimension of Egyptian nationalism. Although condemned by Gladstone as premature and superficial - compared with Irish nationalism - and as only serving the interests of corrupt and despotic landowners of mainly Turkish descent[73] the nationalist movement manifestly threatened the lives of foreigners and the stability of the Khedive's regime. Already earlier Earl Granville, the Foreign Secretary, had explained that the only reason for an intervention in Egypt would be 'the existence of anarchy or some attack on the [Suez] Canal'.[74] Now that emergency seemed to be rapidly coming about. But still any unilateral action by Britain was, for the time being, not seriously considered by the British Cabinet; for the question of intervention concerned the other three dimensions of the Egyptian problem - the European complications.

At the core of these complications was France. The institutionalization of Anglo-French interest in Egypt through the dual control of her finances made consultation and, if possible, cooperation with France imperative. As a result of lengthy conversations between the two governments Britain and France issued a Joint Note on 8 January 1882 in which they communicated to the Khedive that they regarded his maintenance on the throne as indispensable for the welfare of Egypt and that they supported his efforts to deal with the nationalist opposition, thereby implying the possibility of a more active interference in the future.[75] But when Tewfik was forced to accept a Nationalist ministry in February, no intervention followed. The activist French Premier Gambetta had resigned on 26 January after a defeat in the French Chamber and the new ministry under Charles de Freycinet tended to avoid taking risks in overseas for fear of weakening France in Europe. To complicate matters further the new French Government, while professing their loyalty to the principle of Anglo-French cooperation in the matter, began to consort with the nationalists around Arabi and other anti-British members of the opposition; and de Freycinet himself urged the deposition of the Khedive in favour of the pro-French Hakim Pasha.[76] In addition, France now refused a more active common policy. Even though both countries agreed in May to stage a naval demonstration at Alexandria, the two governments could not decide on a common course of action; in the end, the British and French naval squadrons which were despatched to Alexandria were not to do anything at all.[77]

The main difference between London and Paris was that the British Government - in line with Gladstone's Concert of Europe policy - was anxious to internationalize the conflict and to give Turkey a mandate for intervention on behalf of all the Powers. Freycinet's ministry, on the other hand, was not disposed to take any initiative at all and only grudgingly accepted the idea of European mandate for Turkey.[78]

In the meantime, the situation in Egypt became increasingly serious. With Arabi and his military junta now firmly in control and anti-foreign riots spreading across the country action could no longer be delayed.

At this juncture the Turkish and the general European dimension of the Egyptian problem came to the fore. Although notoriously and virulently anti-Turkish on religious and political grounds, Gladstone had come to accept the idea of a European mandate for Turkey. Egypt after all was still under Ottoman Suzerainty; and it was widely expected that a British intervention in Egypt would accelerate the feared, though anticipated, break-up of the Ottoman Empire.[79] France, on the other hand, continued to oppose any Turkish action. At her suggestion an ambassadorial conference assembled at Constantinople to discuss the matter.[80] Sultan Abdul Hamid II, however, disliked the very idea of having to act under European supervision and delayed the beginning and the proceedings of the conference. Thus, when the ambassadors met on 23 June, the situation had changed dramatically. On 12 June anti-foreign riots broke out in Alexandria and Gladstone now faced a serious Cabinet revolt, sparked off by Lord Hartington, the Secretary of State for India.[81] The Foreign Secretary as well, alarmed about the safety of the Canal, accepted intervention as now inevitable. Reluctantly Gladstone yielded to the pressure when Hartington threatened to resign on 19 June.[82] Thus, the necessity to keep his administration together made the Prime Minister bow to the Cabinet majority. On 3 July, Admiral Seymour, commander of the British naval squadron off Alexandria, was instructed to destroy the forts there which Arabi's troops had been fortifying feverishly. As Gladstone informed Queen Victoria on the same day, the Cabinet 'hoped that it [i.e. the bombardment of Alexandria] would somehow [sic!] overthrow Arabi'.[83] This decision was taken in the anticipation that the ongoing ambassadorial conference at Constantinople was deadlocked; and, indeed, on 6 July Turkey refused to accept an European mandate to restore order in Egypt. On 11 July the French squadron under Admiral Conrad withdrew under orders from Paris, and Seymour's ships began a ten and a half hours' bombardment, completely destroying the forts.[84]

By now the ambassadorial meeting at Constantinople had become a futile exercise in conference diplomacy. The French Government, under pressure from Germany and the French Chamber, declined a British offer to send a joint expeditionary force to Egypt to defend the Canal. Then, on 29 July, to the delight of Granville and the dismay of Gladstone, Italy refused to accept Gladstone's invitation to participate in the military operations for fear of alienating France and because it was felt in Rome that the *Triple Alliance* with Germany and Austria-Hungary would prove worthless in a conflict that did not interest Germany directly.[85]

At this stage of the crisis the European dimension of the problem became more important. Though claiming to be disinterested in Egypt, Bismarck sought to instrumentalize the conflict for his own purposes. Since February 1882 the German Chancellor had repeatedly assured the British Government of his support for a British intervention in Egypt.[86] His main concern was that the weak Gladstone government would be pushed into action by France. A strengthened 'liberal alliance' under French leadership would have considerably weakened the value of the *Triple Alliance* since Germany and Austria would not have been able to afford Italy any effective assistance in the event of a Franco-British naval attack on Italy's long-drawn coast.[87] Thus, to increase the value of the *Triple Alliance* relations with Britain had to be improved. On the other hand, if - what Bismarck preferred - German security was to be based on the *Three Emperors League* - German policy, with regard to the Anglo-Russian antagonism, had to be poised against Britain. Either way, the tensions between Britain and France had to be kept alive. Bismarck, therefore, supported Britain throughout the crisis, though he carefully avoided estranging the French. In the end, Britain's eventual occupation of Egypt proved to be a strategical advantage for German diplomacy. For over 20 years, until the conclusion of the *entente cordiale* in 1904, Egypt remained a key factor in the Anglo-French antagonism, thereby contributing to the desired isolation of France in Europe.[88]

On 14 August the ambassadorial conference at Constantinople broke up. On the following day, a British expeditionary force under General Sir Garnet Wolseley arrived in Egypt to restore order and to protect the Suez Canal. Though greatly outnumbered, Wolseley completely destroyed Arabi's troops at Tel-el-Kebir on 13 September and entered Cairo on the 15th where the remaining enemy forces surrendered.[89] Britain was now the sole master of Egypt.

The British intervention in Egypt represents the singular case of an unintended intervention. From February 1882 onwards the policy of both France and Britain was aimed at internationalizing the Egyptian crisis. But, while London was anxious to use Turkey as a mandatory of Europe, Paris wanted above all to keep the Ottomans out of Egypt and secure a European mandate for an Anglo-French intervention. What both had in common was that neither of them wanted to 'go it alone'. But as a basis for a common policy this did not suffice. It was a comedy of errors: France, after she had initiated a more active policy under Gambetta and had pushed for a joint intervention, did not participate in the naval and military operations in Egypt at all; the British Government, by contrast, had opposed an Anglo-French intervention as much as a separate action by either of them, and yet they found themselves inexorably drawn into unilateral intervention. Throughout the crisis Gladstone and Granville were concerned about the maintenance of the Ottoman Empire, and yet, at the end of the crisis, they found themselves alone in the occupation of an Ottoman dominion. What had half-heartedly and without much planning been decided upon as an intervention to restore order in Egypt turned into the long-term occupation of the country which ended in 1922. Moreover, the unilateral intervention by Britain alienated France and destroyed the 'liberal alliance'. It also brought to a final halt Gladstone's Concert of Europe policy, and for Britain a 20 years period of isolation began.

(3) The Anglo-German Intervention in Venezuela, 1902/3

The origins of the Venezuelan crisis of 1902-3 are deep-rooted and tangled. Although it was brought about mainly by Venezuelan domestic events, it involved at its height Britain, Germany, the United States and Italy. Like other Latin American republics Venezuela had long been notorious for its political instability and its frequent revolutions. In the course of one of these revolutions Cipriano Castro toppled the government of President

Andrade and made himself President. A provincial revolutionary from the Andean region, Castro had a very parochial mind and was woefully ignorant of foreign affairs, but had a somewhat 'Napoleonic' conception of himself.[90] From the beginning, Castro's presidency was severely hampered by almost continuous civic turmoil and lack of revenues due to economic mismanagement. However, Castro's seizure of power precipitated the Anglo-German intervention of 1902-3. During Castro's revolutionary campaign and the subsequent period of continued unrest (1898-1900) foreign merchants and trading companies had sustained substantial damages to their property. Moreover, in April 1901 Castro suspended the monthly remittances for the external debt service, confiscated foreign property and restricted the activities of foreign companies.[91] With unprecedented disregard for diplomatic forms the Venezuelan Government resisted all demands by Germany, Britain, France, Italy, and Belgium on behalf of their investors to meet the country's foreign liabilities and to compensate foreign bond-holders for the damages sustained during the revolution.[92] Castro's intransigence in the matter was also influenced by the incident of the *Ban Reigh*, a British built vessel which, sailing under Columbian flag, terrorized the Venezuelan coast in order to destabilize the Castro regime.[93] Castro held Britain responsible for the *Ban Reigh*'s acts of piracy and refused to discuss any further British demands for compensation until she had satisfied Venezuela's grievances. Thus, during the first quarter of 1902, the *Ban Reigh* incident and the growing pressure from foreign powers created an impasse between Venezuela and the Powers. The British Foreign Secretary, Lord Lansdowne, therefore, came to reconsider his so far more cautious attitude in the dispute with Venezuela. On 29 July 1902, he instructed the British Minister at Caracas, William H.D. Haggard, to warn the Castro Government that unless British demands for compensation were met Britain would have to take such steps as might be necessary to secure compensation.[94] To this and to similar representations from the German Government Castro gave the same delatory reply that the *Ban Reigh* dispute had to be settled first before any further negotiations on the claims of foreign Powers could take place.[95]

At this juncture British and German interests coincided and both Governments were prepared to confer with a view to joint action. Unlike the British Government, however, Berlin had adopted a more forceful attitude after President Castro rejected the German suggestion that the outstanding compensation claims be settled by the Court of Arbitration at The Hague.[96] Yet, with regard to American 'sensitivity' towards all European activities which fell under the stipulations of the Monroe Doctrine, the German Chancellor, Prince Bülow, decided to delay any coercive action against Venezuela until the circumstances were more propitious. In September 1902 he judged the time ripe for action. The American Secretary of State, Hay, had signalled his acquiescence in coercive measures by Germany and Britain to collect debts due to their nationals, provided the two countries did not aim at territorial aggrandizement.[97] Moreover, the conclusion of the Anglo-Japanese Alliance in February 1902 and the frequently recurring rumours of Anglo-French alliance negotiations signalled the beginning of the end of Britain's *splendid isolation* and made the improvement of Anglo-German relations imperative for Berlin.[98] In the autumn of 1902 this was by no means an unattainable objective. After the end of the Boer War it appeared as if good relations between the two countries could be restored; and, indeed, this development was warmly welcomed by Arthur James Balfour, the new Prime Minister, and Lord Lansdowne, who both sought a viable *modus vivendi* with Germany.[99] In the view of both governments the Venezuelan question offered a good opportunity to improve their relations by cooperating in this matter. Lansdowne's only concern was that by allying herself with Germany over the Venezuelan affair Britain might jeopardize the friendly course of Anglo-American relations, so carefully cultivated over recent years.[100] But when Secretary Hay explained to the British Ambassador at Washington, Sir Michael Herbert, that the US had no objection to a joint Anglo-German blockade of the Venezuelan coast, all seemed clear.[101] In the course of the consultations between Britain and Germany Lansdowne, although initially opposed to the idea of a blockade, reluctantly accepted that the resort to 'ulterior measures' might prove to be inevitable. The German Government, on the other hand, ruled out the official declaration of a 'belligerent blockade' for constitutional reasons, and the landing of troops to seize Venezuelan customs-houses for logistical and - with regard to the US - diplomatic reasons.[102] In the end, Lansdowne and Count Metternich, the German ambassador to London, only agreed to deliver an ultimatum to Venezuela preceding the seizure of Venezuelan gunboats, but left the planning and the execution of the operation to the senior naval officers in the Caribbean.[103] The ultimatum was delivered on 7 December and after 24 hours had elapsed without an official Venezuelan reply diplomatic relations were severed. On the same day, British and German cruisers seized four Venezuelan gunboats at La Guara, of which three were sunk by the Germans. On 13 December, the German cruiser *Vineta* and the British cruiser *Charybdis* destroyed a fort at Puerto Cabello in retaliation for the storming of a Britsh merchant vessel by an enraged crowd of Venezuelans.[104] When Castro proposed, through the US Government, to settle the conflict through arbitration by President

Roosevelt, London and Berlin rejected the idea as belated.[105] Moreover, they were in full agreement that 'it seemed highly improbable that the seizure of the gunboats would bring the republic [i.e. Venezuela] to reason'[106], and that further action had to be taken at once 'without waiting until Washington exchanged the role of post office for one of a more active character'.[107] In consequence, Britain, Germany, and Italy, which had joined the former two Powers on 17 December, established a formal blockade on 20 December.

By now, both governments had accepted in principle the idea of arbitration either by Roosevelt or by the Hague Court of Arbitration.[108] As for President Roosevelt himself, he had little sympathy with 'the villainous monkey'[109] Castro. But the joint naval action by Britain and Germany raised his concern for US strategic interests in the Caribbean. Yet, for fear of domestic criticism the President declined the offered role of arbitrator and recommended arbitration at The Hague instead. To underline American concern about the events in the sea off Venezuela he also ordered a naval squadron to Trinidad.[110] At the same time the negotiations on the *modus procedendi* of the now accepted arbitration continued at Washington. German attempts to increase the demands on Venezuela failed because of British objections.[111] The developments in the Venezuelan Crisis had now reached a psychologically difficult stage. From the very outset of the conflict Lansdowne had been guided by the necessity of maintaining America's friendship. Thus, when the chips were down during the naval blockade, he unreservedly accepted American predominance in the Western hemisphere and signalled his willingness to compromise.[112] However, the situation was aggravated, when on 21 January 1903 three German warships destroyed the coastal fort of San Carlos in retaliation for its opening fire on the gunboat *Panther* four days earlier. Though this action was fully in line with other naval actions taken earlier and had the logic of gunboat diplomacy behind it, it created an adverse political effect. After the acceptance of arbitration the San Carlos incident seemed an unwarranted act of destruction and the result of German arrogance or - worse still - of secret German designs in South America. It created a public outcry in the United States, and both Roosevelt and Hay had pointed discussions with the German Chargé d'affaires, urging the Germans to sign the arbitration protocol.[113] In addition, the diplomats in the *Wilhelmstrasse* now found themselves under pressure from their British ally. The British public had become increasingly critical of their country's association with Germany in this matter.[114] But after the destruction of Fort San Carlos the British Government was widely seen as being involved in an 'unholy alliance' with a particularly untrustworthy power. In light of such pressure Lansdowne

> [f]eared that the position of His Majesty's Government might become intolerable if ... it was found that although our own demands had been complied with, we had broken off negotiations on account of the terms demanded by Germany for the payment of claims, the nature of which it was well known differed materially from that of our own.[115]

Under such pressure Germany was forced to give in; the protocols were signed on 13 February and the blockade was lifted on 19 February. The Hague tribunal announced its verdict - in favour of Britain and Germany - in February 1904. But for Germany it proved to be a Pyrrhic victory. In the words of the *New York Times*, Germany had in the eyes of the liberal opinion in Europe and North America 'displayed a strenuous, not to say violent, disposition, and a faculty for obstruction greater than either or both of her allies [i.e. Britain and Italy]'.[116] What had begun as an exercise to cultivate Anglo-German relations by acting in common for the protection of common interests in the periphery, in the end not only alienated Britain but also the rising Great Power United States.

Conclusion

In the 19th century, military intervention was a well-established and generally recognized instrument of statecraft in the political arsenal of the Great Powers of the day. But it was also a function of the international balance of power system. However, as the above case studies have shown, it was an instrument which could not be used indiscriminately. The Great Powers operated within an international system which was based on the principle of cooperation among them. From this fact certain rules of the 'intervention game', however unspecified, were derived.

First of all, military intervention was an instrument of Great Power politics which could not be used against another Great Power. The very '*raison d'être*' of the *Concert of Europe* was the avoidance of war between any of the Great Powers. It was a mechanism of consultation and cooperation among them - and thus dependent upon them - with a view to preventing or solving international crises. The responsibility for the maintenance of the established international order, therefore, rested with the 'pentarchy' of Europe. For this reason its members effectively abstained from intervening in the affairs of each other.

On the contrary, in the 19th century, military intervention and classical gunboat diplomacy were widely regarded to be and generally accepted as the 'civilized' way in which the Great Powers of the day dealt with the 'less civilised' and weaker nations in the periphery of Europe and in overseas.[117] In this respect Metternich's contempt for the Neapolitans, Gladstone's rejection of Arabi Pasha as yet another oriental despot, or Roosevelt's strong dislike of Cipriano Castro was more than an expression of perceived superiority, cultural or otherwise; it was also a re-affirmation of the Great Power status of their respective countries.

A further rule of intervention derived from the cooperative nature of the Great Power 'concert' was the need for an intervening power to obtain the prior consent of the other Great Powers. Military intervention was not a purely military exercise; it demanded thorough diplomatic preparation. Unlike most other 19th century statesmen Prince Metternich was acutely aware of the complex nature of intervention. His proceedings in the Neapolitan affair show that he had understood that military intervention was a political instrument, a means to achieving a political end, and that, therefore, the interests of the other Great Powers had to be taken into account. The British intervention in Egypt and the Anglo-German action against Venezuela, by contrast, failed to achieve their objectives because in neither case had the ground been prepared diplomatically. In both cases, the political decision-makers had neglected the fact that intervention is instrumental to political ends and that, therefore, political guidance is indispensable.[118] Because neither Gladstone in 1882 nor Lansdowne and Bülow in 1902 had a clear conception of what they wanted to achieve and how they wanted to achieve it, they were unable to win the support of other Great Powers for their actions.

The need to obtain the support of fellow Great Powers was inextricably linked with the question of the legitimacy of intervention. Throughout the 19th century international lawyers, and supporters of equilibrist policy in particular, pondered this question.[119] In so far as the practice of intervention with regard to the question of legitimacy is concerned two inferences can be made from the above case studies. Firstly, the wider the gap in size and power between intervener and intervened, the more acceptable was intervention to other Great Powers. Austria's crushing defeat of the Neapolitan revolutionary army, in conjunction with Metternich's skilful diplomacy, was widely accepted in the chanceries of Europe because the intervention swiftly achieved its stated objective and, thus, reduced the risk of escalation. The Anglo-German blockade of Venezuela, on the other hand, failed not only because the action was not adequately prepared on the diplomatic front, but also because the two powers were unable to convincingly project the military might in the Western hemisphere. The second inference that can be made is that intervention for the purpose of maintaining the overall balance of power was regarded as morally and legally justified as an act in defence of the established international order and the peace of Europe. The Austrian intervention in Naples was acceptable to the statesmen of Europe because Metternich succeeded to convince them that the nationalist tendencies in Italy threatened to erode Austria's position as a Great Power and was therefore a danger to the balance of power. Britain's intervention in Egypt, though neither intended nor, consequently, politically prepared, was a military success and did not affect the balance of power in Europe in a major way. On these grounds, it was, if not supported, at least not opposed by the powers of Europe. In the Venezuelan case, by contrast, Britain and Germany were unable to convince the new Great Power and regional hegemon, the United States, that their action fulfilled any international order purpose - and their action failed. It is also noteworthy that the offensive or defensive nature of intervention was closely linked with its general acceptability. In an age whose main concern was with the maintenance of international stability defensive military interventions, carried out for the purpose of maintaining or restoring the regime of the target state, were deemed legitimate, as the cases of Naples and Egypt show. Governmental legitimacy, after all, was then still seen to be a guarantee of international stability. For the same reason, offensive interventions, aiming to effect a change of the regime or the policies of the intervened state, were less likely to be supported by other Great Powers.

However, the nature of military intervention in the 19th century was yet more complex and ambivalent. It was not only a political instrument wielded by the Great Powers against lesser powers; it also had a profound effect on the relations between the members of the European 'pentarchy'. In the long term, looking at the entire period from 1815 to 1914, Castlereagh's warning against the potential, corrosive effect of intervention upon alliance flexibility[120], that vital mechanism of the equilibrist international system, proved remarkably perceptive. The Austrian intervention in Naples significantly contributed to the division of the Five Powers into two groups, the conservative-autocratic Eastern monarchies and the 'liberal', constitutional monarchies Britain and France; Gladstone's misdirected Egyptian adventure, ruthlessly exploited by Bismarck for his own purposes, isolated Britain in Europe and alienated her from France for almost a quarter of a century; and the Anglo-German action against Venezuela confirmed many in their belief that Germany was a power not to be trusted, and thus contributed to the rise of the Anglo-German antagonism.

Military intervention in the 19th century was a double-edged sword. If handled properly, with great care and deliberation, it could deliver the desired political objective in one single fell swoop; if not handled properly, it was likely to damage the intervening state's wider political interests and its standing among the other Great Powers.

Notes

1. cf.Craig, G.A. & George, A.L., Force and Statecraft: Diplomatic Problems of Our Times, New York - Oxford: OUP, 1983, p.30; see also: Webster, C.K., The Foreign Policy of Castlereagh, 1812-1815: Britain and the Reconstruction of Europe, London: G.Bell, 1950, chs.ii-v; Nicolson, H.G., The Congress of Vienna: A Study in Allied Unity, 1812-21, London: Cassell, Repr.1989 (pb), chs.i-vii; Dakin, D., 'The Congress of Vienna, 1814-5, and Its Antecedents', in: A.Sked (ed.), Europe's Balance of Power, 1815-48, London: Macmillan, 1979, pp.14-33.

2. cf.Ibid, p.31; see also: Temperley, H.W.V. & Webster, C.K., 'The Congress of Vienna, 1814-5, and the Conference of Paris, 1919', in: W.N.Medlicott (ed.), From Metternich to Hitler: Aspects of British and Foreign History, 1814-1939, London: Routledge & Kegan Paul, 1963, pp.1-24.

3. Webster, Foreign Policy of Castlereagh, op.cit., p.56; idem, 'The Council of Europe in the Nineteenth Century', in: idem, The Art and Practice of Diplomacy, London: Chatto & Windus, 1961, pp.55-69; Kissinger, A World Restored, op.cit., p.190; Crawley, C.W., 'International Relations, 1815-30', in: idem (ed.), The Cambridge Modern History, vol.ix, War and Peace in an Age of Upheaval, 1793-1830, Cambridge: CUP, Repr. 1975, p.609f.; Phillips, W.A., 'Great Britain and the Continental Alliance, 1816-22', in: A.W. Ward & G.P. Gooch (eds.), The Cambridge History of British Foreign Policy, 1783-1919, vol.ii, 1815-1866, Cambridge: CUP, 1923, p.4f.

4. Bridge, F.R., 'Allied Diplomacy in Peacetime: the Failure of the Congress "System", 1815-23', in: Sked (ed.), Europe's Balance of Power, op.cit., pp.34-53; Crawley, 'International Relations, 1815-1830', op.cit., pp.678ff.; Reinermann, A.J., 'Metternich, Italy, and the Congress of Verona, 1821-2', in: Historical Journal, xiv/2, (1971), pp.263-87.

5. See: Hurst M.(ed.), Key Treaties for the Great Powers, 1814-1914, vol.i, 1814-1870, Newton Abbott: David & Charles 1972, no.6; Grimstead, G.K., The Foreign Ministers of Alexander I: Political Attitudes and the Conduct of Russian Diplomacy, 1801-25, Berkeley - Los Angeles: University of California Press, 1969, pp.57ff.

6. cf.Kissinger, A World Restored, op.cit., p.189.

7. cf.Nicolson, Congress of Vienna, op.cit., p.253; see also: Bertier de Sauvigny, G.de, Metternich and His Times, London: Darton, Longmans & Todd, 1962, pp.129ff.

8. Sked, A., 'Metternich's Enemies or the Threat from Below', in: idem (ed.), Europe's Balance of Power, op.cit., pp.164-89.

9. Kissinger, A World restored, op.cit., pp.191ff.; Bridge, 'Allied Diplomacy in Peacetime', op.cit., pp.44ff.; Jelavich, B., The Habsburg Empire in European Affairs, 1814-1918, Hamden/Conn.: Archon Books, Repr.1975, pp.26ff.; Forsyth, M., 'Friedrich von Gentz: An Assessment', in: Studies in History and Politics, ii/2, (1981-2), pp.127-55.

10. cf.Hafner, D.L., 'Castlereagh, the Balance of Power, and "Non-Intervention"', in: Australian Journal of Politics and History, xxvi/1, (1980), p.71.

11. cf.Holbraad, Concert of Europe, op.cit., p.2.

12. Holbraad, Concert of Europe, op.cit., pp.72f.; Heller, H., Hegel und der nationale Machtstaatsgedanke in Deutschland, Berlin 1921, pp.57ff.; Kiesewetter, H., Von Hegel zu Hitler: Eine Analyse der Hegelschen Machtstaatsideologie und die Wirkungsgeschichte des Rechtshegelianismus, Hamburg: Hoffmann & Campe 1974, pp.163ff.; Rochau, L.A.von, Grundsätze der Realpolitik, angewendet auf die staatlichen Zustände Deutschlands, 2nd ed.1859, Repr. ed. by H.U.Wehler, Berlin: Ullstein, 1972, p.2f.

13. Taylor, Struggle for Mastery in Europe, op.cit., pp.65ff.; Lambert, A., The Crimean War: British Grand Strategy, 1853-6, Manchester - New York: Manchester University Press, 1986, pp.11ff.; Bourne, K., The Foreign Policy of Victorian Britain, 1830-1902, Oxford: Clarendon Press, 1970, pp.74ff.; Hearnshaw, F.J.C., 'The European Revolutions and After, 1848-54', in: Ward (ed.), Cambridge History of British Foreign Policy, op.cit., vol.ii, pp.287-358; Reddaway, W.F., 'The Crimean War and the French Alliance, 1853-8', in: ibid., pp.359-402; Grenville, J.A.S., Europe Reshaped, 1848-1878, London: Fontana, 6th ed.1984, pp.39ff.

14. Grenville, ibid., pp.201ff.; Schroeder, P.W., Austria, Great Britain, and the Crimean War: The Destruction of the European Concert, Ithaca/NY - London, 1972, pp.392ff.; Henderson, G.B., 'The Diplomatic Revolution of 1854', in: American Historical Review, xliii/1, (1937), pp.22-56; Kaehler, S.A., 'Realpolitik zur Zeit des Krimkrieges - eine Säkularbetrachtung', in: Historische Zeitschrift, clxxiv/3, (1954), pp.436-45; Craig, G.A., 'The System of Alliances and the Balance of Power, 1830-70', in: J.P.T.Bury (ed.), The Cambridge Modern History, vol.x, The Zenith of European Power, Cambridge : CUP, 1960, pp.246-73; Hildebrand, K., 'Die *Krimkriegssituation* - Wandel und Dauer einer historischen Konstellation der Staatenwelt', in: J.Dülffer et al.(eds.), Deutschland und Europa: Kontinuität und Bruch. Gedenkschrift für Andreas Hillgruber, Frankfurt - Berlin: Propyläen, 1990, pp.37-51.

15. On 1859 see: Grenville, Europe Reshaped, op.cit., pp.247ff.; Smith, D., The Making of Italy, 1796-1870, London: Macmillan, 1968; on 1864 see: Carr W., The Origins of the Wars of German Unification, London: Longmans, 1992, pp.34ff.; Sandiford, K.A., 'The British Cabinet and the Schleswig-Holstein Crisis, 1863-4', in: History, lviii/4, (1973), pp.360-83; Steefel, L.D., The Schleswig-Holstein Question, Cambridge, Ma., 1932.; on 1866 see: Carr, ibid., pp.59ff.; Derndarsky, M., 'Österreich und die deutsche Frage zwischen 1848 und 1866/71: Konzeptionelles Dilemma und situative Probleme der Donaumonarchie gegenüber Deutschland', in: J.Becker/A.Hillgruber (eds.), Die deutsche Frage im 19.und 20.Jahrhundert, Munich: E. Voegel, 1983; Faber, K.G., 'Realpolitik als Ideologie: Die Bedeutung des Jahres 1866 für das politische Denken in Deutschland', in: Historische Zeitschrift, cciii/1, (1966), pp.1-45; on 1870 see: Grenville, op.cit., pp.341ff.; Carr, op.cit., pp.144ff.; Howard, M.E., The Franco-Prussian War: The German Invasion of France, 1870-1, London: R.Hart-Davis, 1962, pp.40ff.; Kolb, E., Der Kriegsausbruch 1870: Politische Entscheidungsprozesse und Verantwortlichkeiten in der Julikrise 1870, Göttingen: Vandenhoeck &

Rupprecht, 1970; Becker, J., 'Der Krieg mit Frankreich als Problem der kleindeutschen Einigungspolitik Bismarcks, 1866-70', in: M.Stürmer (ed.), Das kaiserliche Deutschland: Politik und Gesellschaft, 1870-1918, Düsseldorf: Droste Repr.1984, pp.75-88.

16. cf.Langer, W.L., European Alliances and Alignments, 1871-90, New York: A.A.Knopf, 2nd ed.1956, p.4.

17. Hinsley, F.H., Power and the Pursuit of Peace: Theory and Practice in the History of Relations between States, Cambridge: CUP Repr., 1982 (pb), p.244ff.; Albrecht-Carrié, R., A Diplomatic History of Europe Since the Congress of Vienna, London: Methuen, 1965 (pb), pp.145ff.

18. Langer, European Alliances, op.cit., pp.31ff.; Taylor, Struggle for Mastery, op.cit., p.218f.; Eyck, E., Bismarck and the German Empire, London: Unwin, 3rd ed.1968 (pb), p.187.

19. See: Köhler, H., 'Das Kissinger Diktat - Ein Schlüsseldokument zur Aussenpolitik Bismarcks?', in: idem (ed.), Deutschland und der Westen: Vorträge und Diskussionsbeiträge des Symposions zu Ehren von G.A.Craig, Berlin: Ullstein, 1984, pp.34-43; Hildebrand, K., '"System der Aushilfen"? Chancen und Grenzen deutscher Politik im Zeitalter Bismarcks', in: G.Schöllgen (ed.), Flucht in den Krieg ? Aussenpolitik des kaiserlichen Deutschland, Darmstadt: Wissenschaftliche Buchgesellschaft, 1991, p.109f.; Gall. L., Bismarck: Der weisse Revolutionär, Frankfort-Berlin: Ullstein, Repr. 1993 (pb), p.516f.

20. The other two options under consideration at the time were: (1) the arrangement with other Great Powers at the expense of the smaller nations, and (2) localised preventive wars to eliminate potential rivals, see: Hillgruber, A., Bismarcks Aussenpolitik, Freiburg: Rombach, 2nd ed.1981, p.137f; Gall, Bismarck, op.cit., p.592f.

21. Langer, European Alliances, op.cit., p.459; Taylor, Struggle for Mastery, op.cit., pp.292ff.; Hillgruber, Bismarcks Aussenpolitik, op.cit., p.197f.

22. cf.Craig & George, Force and Statecraft, op.cit., p.38.

23. cf.Taylor, op.cit., p.278.

24. Hillgruber, Bismarcks Aussenpolitik, op.cit., pp.129ff.

25. Hillgruber, ibid., p.198f.; Pflanze, O., Bismarck and the Development of Germany, vol.i, The Period of Unification, 1815-1871, Princeton, NJ: Princeton University Press, 2nd ed.1973 (pb), pp.87ff.; Stone, N., Europe Transformed, 1878-1919, London: Fontana, 1983, pp.154ff.

26. Stone, Europe Reshaped, op.cit., pp.159ff.; Kennedy, P.M., The Rise of the Anglo-German Antagonism, 186-1914, London-Atlantic Highlands: Humanities Press, 3rd ed. 1990 (pb), pp.227ff.; idem, 'The Kaiser and German "*Weltpolitik*": Reflexions on Wilhelm II's Place in the Making of German Foreign Policy', in: J.C.G. Röhl & N. Sombart (eds.), Kaiser Wilhelm II: New Interpretations. The Corfu Papers, Cambridge: CUP, 1982, pp.143-68; Röhl, J.C.G., Germany Without Bismarck: The Crisis of Government in the Second Reich, 1890-1900, London: Macmillan 1967, pp.241ff.; Berghahn, V.R., Germany and the Approach of War in 1914, London: Macmillan, 6th ed.1986, pp.24ff.; Winzen, P., 'Prince Bülow's "*Weltmachtpolitik*"', in: Australian Journal of Politics and History, xxii/2, (1976), pp.227-42.

27. Stone, Europe Reshaped, op.cit., p.155; Kennan, G.F., The Fateful Alliance: France, Russia and the Coming of the First World War, New York, 1984; Langer, W.L., The Diplomacy of Imperialism, 1890-1902, New York: A.A.Knopf, 4th ed. 1965, pp.31.

28. Nish, I.N., The Origins of the Russo-Japanese War, London: Longmans, 2nd ed.1987, pp.21ff.

29. Sprout, H.& M., The Rise of American Naval Power, 1776 - 1918, Princeton: Princeton University Press 1939, pp.223ff.; Kennedy, P.M., The Rise and Fall of the Great Powers: Economic Change and Military Conflict from 1500 to 2000, London: Fontana, 4th ed. 1989(pb), pp.312ff.

30. Mommsen, W.J., 'Domestic Factors in German Foreign Policy before 1914', in: Central European History, vi/1, (1973), pp.3-43.; Berghahn, Germany and the Approach of War, op.cit., pp.5ff.; Röhl, Germany Without Bismarck, op.cit., p.157f.; Kennedy, Anglo-German Antagonism, op.cit., p.227.

31. James, H., A German Identity, 1770-1990, London: Weidenfeld & Nicolson, 2nd ed.1990 (pb), pp.88ff.; Hughes, M., Nationalism and Society: Germany, 1800-1945, London: Edward Arnold, 1988, pp.130ff.; Eley, G., Reshaping the German Right: Radical Nationalism and Political Change after Bismarck, Yale: Yale University Press, 1979.

32. Steiner, Z.S., Britain and the Origins of the First World War, London: Macmillan, 4th ed.1991, p.255f.

33. Kennedy, Anglo-German Antagonism, op.cit., pp.410ff.; idem, 'Strategic Aspects of the Anglo-German Naval Race', in: idem, Strategy and Diplomacy: Eight Studies, London: Fontana, 2nd ed.1989, pp.127-62.; idem, The Rise and Fall of British Naval Mastery, London: Fontana, 3rd ed. 1991, pp.255ff.; Herwig, H.H., "Luxury" Fleet: The Imperial German Navy, 1888-1918, London - Atlantic Highlands, NJ: Humanities Press, 3rd ed. 1991 (pb); Lambi, I.N., The Navy and German Power Politics, 1862-1914, Boston/MA 1984; Woodward, E.L., Great Britain and the German Navy, 1898-1912, London: Macmillan 1935; Steinberg, J., 'The *Novelle* of 1908: Necessities and Choice in the Anglo-German Naval Arms Race', in: Transactions of the Royal Historical Society, 5th ser.xxi, (1971), pp.25-44; Langhorne, R.T.B., 'The Naval Question in Anglo-German Relations, 1912-4', in: Historical Journal, xiv/2, (1971), pp.359-70.

34. Spring, D.W., 'Russia and the Coming of War', in: R.J.W.Evans & H.J.O.Pogge von Strandmann (eds.), The Coming of the First World War, Oxford: Clarendon Press, 2nd ed. 1991 (pb), pp.57-86.

35. Steiner, Britain and the Origins of the First World War, op.cit., pp.22ff.; Monger, G.W., The End of Isolation: British Foreign Policy, 1900-1907, London: T.Nelson 1963, pp.103ff.; Andrews, C., Theophile Delcassé and the Making of the Entente Cordiale, 1898-1905, London, 1968.

36. Craig & George, Force and Statecraft, op.cit., p.43f.; Langhorne, R.T.B., The Collapse of the Concert of Europe, 1890-1914, London: Macmillan, 1981, p.110f.

37. Van Evera, S., 'The Cult of the Offensive and the Origins of the First World War', in: idem et al. (eds.), Military Strategy and the Origins of the First World War, Princeton: Princeton University Press, 1991, pp.59-108; Sagan, S.D., '1914 Revisited: Allies, Offense, and Instability', in: ibid., pp.109-133; Mommsen, W.J., 'The Topos of Inevitable War in Germany before 1914', in: V.R.Berghahn & M.Kitchen (eds.), Germany in the Age of Total War: Essays in Honour of Francis L.Carsten, London: Macmillan, 1981, pp.23-46; Kaiser, D., Politics and War: European Conflict from Philipp II to Hitler, Cambridge, MA: Harvard University Press, 1990, pp.307ff.; Howard, M., 'The Edwardian Arms Race', in: idem, The Lessons of History, Oxford: OUP, 1993 (pb), pp.81-96; Bond,

B., War and Society in Europe, 1870-1970, London: Fontana, 1984, pp.72ff.

38. Stone, Europe Transformed, op.cit., pp.326ff.; Pogge von Strandmann, 'Germany and the Coming of War', in: idem/Evans (eds.), The Coming of the First World War, op.cit., pp.87-124; Fischer, F., Griff nach der Weltmacht: Die Kriegszielpolitik des kaiserlichen Deutschland, Dusseldorf: Droste, Repr.1984 (pb), pp.46ff.; Van Evera, S., 'Why Cooperation Failed in 1914', in: World Politics, xxxviii/1, (1985-6), pp.80-117; Kennedy, P.M., 'The First World War and the International Power System', in: International Security, ix/1, (1984), pp.7-40; Levy, J.S., 'Preferences, Constraints, and Chances in July 1914', in: International Security, xv/3, (1990/1), pp.151-86; Trachtenberg, M., 'The Meaning of Mobilization in 1914', in: ibid., pp.120-50.

39. cf.Lloyd George, D., War Memoirs, vol.i, London: Odhams Press, 2nd ed. 1938, p.32.

40. George, A.L., 'Case Studies and Theory Development: The Method of Structured, Focused Comparison', in: P.G.Lauren (ed.), Diplomacy: New Approaches in History, Theory, and Politics, New York : Free Press, 1978, pp.43-68, pp.49ff.

41. Bridge, 'Allied Diplomacy in Peacetime', op.cit., p.42f.; Grimstead, The Foreign Ministers of Alexander I, op.cit., p.247; Webster, C.K., The Foreign Policy of Castlereagh, 1815-22: Britain and the European Alliance, London: G. Bell, 1925, pp.259.

42. Bullen, R., 'The Great Powers and the Iberian Peninsula, 1815-48', in: Sked (ed.), Europe's Balance of Power, op.cit., pp.54-78; see also: Romani, G.T., The Neapolitan Revolution of 1820-1, Evanston/III, 1950.

43. Sked, 'Threat From Below', op.cit., p.185; Kissinger, A World Restored, op.cit., p.251f.; Webster, Foreign Policy of Castlereagh, op.cit., p.265f.

44. Kissinger, A World Restored, op.cit., p.251; Bridge, 'Allied Diplomacy in Peacetime', op.cit., p.40f.; Schroeder, P.W., Metternich's Diplomacy at Its Zenith, 1820-3, Austin, TX: Texas University Press, 1962, pp.42ff.

45. Kissinger, ibid., p.233; Phillips, 'Great Britain and the Continental Alliance', op.cit., p.34.

46. cf.Stewart to Castlereagh (private), 29 September 1820, Public Record Office, Kew, Surrey (hereafter PRO), FO 7/160.

47. cf.Kissinger, ibid., p.252; Hafner, 'Castlereagh, the Balance of Power and "Non-Intervention"', op.cit., p.77.

48. Grimstead, The Foreign Ministers of Alexander I, op.cit., p.247f.; Webster, Foreign Policy of Castlereagh, 1815-22, op.cit, pp.282ff.; Baack, L.J., Christian Bernstorff and Prussia: Diplomacy and Reform Conservatism, 1818-32, New Brunswick, NJ: Rutgers University Press, 1980, pp.78ff.

49. cf.Castlereagh to Sir George Rose [British Ambassador at Berlin] (No.14), 11 August 1820, PRO, FO 64/122.

50. Castlereagh to Sir William A'Court [British Ambassador to Naples] (private), 20 October 1820, PRO, FO 70/89; Castlereagh to Stewart (private), 16 September 1820, PRO, FO 7/160; see also: Philipps, 'Great Britain and the Continental Alliance', op.cit., p.34f.

51. Castlereagh to Stewart (private), 21 September 1820, PRO, FO 7/160.

52. cf.Phillips, 'Great Britain and the Continental Alliance', op.cit., p.37f.; Schroeder, Metternich's Diplomacy, op.cit., p.88f.

53. cf.Hafner, 'Castlereagh, the Balance of Power, and "Non-Intervention"', op.cit., p.77.

54. Phillips, 'Great Britain and the Continental Alliance', op.cit., p.38; Kissinger, A World Restored, op.cit., p.267.

55. cf.Castelreagh to Stewart (No.27), 4 December 1820, PRO, FO 7/148.

56. cf.Temperley, H.W.V. & Penson, L.(eds.), Foundations of British Foreign Policy, 1807-1902, Cambridge: CUP, 1938, p.48f.

57. British Circular Note, 19 January 1821, cf.Hafner, op.cit., p.78.

58. cf.Kissinger, A World Restored, op.cit., p.272; for a detailed account of the Laibach conference see: ibid., pp.278ff.; Webster, The Foreign Policy of Castlereagh, 1815-22, op.cit., pp.312ff.

59. cf.A'Court to Castelreagh (private), 19 March 1821, PRO, FO 70/93.

60. A'Court to Castlereagh (No.24), 25 March 1821, and (No.27), 1 April 1821, PRO, FO 70/93.

61. Phillips, 'Great Britain and the Continental Alliance', op.cit., p.41f.; Kissinger, A World restored, op.cit., p.283f.

62. Taylor, Struggle for Mastery, op.cit., pp.286ff.; Langer, Alliances and Alignments, op.cit., pp.251ff.; Hagen, M.von, England und Ägypten: Materialien zur Geschichte der britischen Okkupation mit besonderer Berücksichtigung auf Bismarcks Bündnispolitik, Bonn: Marcus & Weber, 1915, pp.8ff.

63. cf.Taylor, ibid., p.287.

64. Blake, R, Disraeli, London: Methuen, 1969(pb), pp.581ff.

65. cf.Stern, F., Gold and Iron: Bismarck, Bleichroeder and the Building of the German Empire, Harmondsworth, Mdx: Penguin, 1987(pb), p.422.

66. cf.Stern, ibid.

67. See: Feis, H., Europe: The World's Banker, 1870-1914: An Account of European Foreign Investment and the Connection of World Finance with Diplomacy before the War, Clifton, NJ, Repr.1964, pp.317ff.; Ducruet, J., Les capitaux Européennes en Orient, New York, 1964, pp.140ff.; Blaisdell, D.C., European Financial Control in the Ottoman Empire: A Study of the Establishment and Significance of the Administration of the Ottoman Public Debt, New York, 1966, pp.90ff.; Schölch, A., 'Wirtschaftliche Durchdringung und politische Kontrolle durch die europäische Mächte im Osmanischen Reich (Constantinopel, Kairo, Tunis)', in: Geschichte und Gesellschaft, i/4, (1975), pp.404-46.

68. Stern, Gold and Iron, op.cit., p.423; Langer, Alliances and Allignments, op.cit., p.262f.

69. Lowe, Reluctant Imperialists, op.cit., p.47.; Cecil, Lady G., The Life of Lord Salisbury, London 1921, vol.iii, p.331f.; Dawson, W.H., 'Forward Policy and Reaction, 1874-1885', in: Ward & Gooch (eds.), Cambridge History of British Foreign Policy, op.cit., vol.iii, pp.72-184, pp.160ff.

70. Langer, ibid., p.262.

71. Taylor, Struggle for Mastery, op.cit., p.288; Lowe, Reluctant Imperialists, op.cit., p.47f.; Steele, D., 'Britain and Egypt, 1882-1914: The Containment of Islamic Nationalism', in: K.M. Wilson (ed.), Imperialism and Nationalism in the Middle East: The Anglo-Egyptian Experience, 1882-1982, London: Mansell, 1983, pp.1-25, pp.3ff.

72. Langer, op.cit., p.272.

73. See: Steele, op.cit., p.3f.

74. cf.Dawson, 'Forward Policy and Reaction', op.cit., p.166.

75. Ibid., p.167.

76. Ibid.; Langer, Alliances and Allignments, op.cit., p.268f.

77. Taylor, Struggle for Mastery, op.cit., p.288f.; Bourne, The Foreign Policy of Victorian England, op.cit., p.139.

78. Lowe, Reluctant Imperialists, op.cit., p.97; Langer, Alliances and Allignments, op.cit., p.272f.

79. Steele, 'Britain and Egypt', op.cit., p.5f.

80. Langer, Alliances and Alignments, op.cit., p.272f.

81. Lowe, Reluctant Imperialists, op.cit., p.50; Bourne, Foreign Policy of Victorian England, op.cit., p.139f.

82. Gladstone to Granville (private), 21 June 1882, Granville Mss, PRO, PRO 30/29/125; Lowe, op.cit., p.50f.

83. cf.Gladstone to Queen Victoria, 3 July 1882, PRO, CAB 41/16/33.

84. Langer, Alliances and Alignments, op.cit., p.273f.

85. Langer, ibid., p.275; Hillgruber, Bismarcks Bundnispolitik, op.cit., p.163.

86. Bismarck to Crown Prince Frederick William of Prussia, 7 September 1882, in: J.Lepsius, A.Mendelssohn-Bartholdy & F.Thimme (eds.), Die Grosse Politik der Europäischen Kabinette, 1871-1914, Berlin: Deutsche Verlagsgesellschaft für Politik und Geschichte 1924 (hereafter GP), no.727; Mommsen, W.J., 'Ägypten und der Nahe Osten in der deutschen Aussenpolitik, 1870-1914', in: idem, Der autoritäre Nationalstaat: Verfassung, Gesellschaft und Kultur im deutschen Kaiserreich, Frankfort: Fischer, 1990, pp.140-181, p.150f.

87. Hillgruber, Bismarcks Bundnispolitik, op.cit., p.163; Rothfels, H., Bismarcks englische Bundnispolitik, Stuttgart: DVA, 1924, pp.72ff.

88. Mommsen, 'Ägypten und der Nahe Osten', op.cit., p.151f.; Lowe, Reluctant Imperialists, op.cit., p.49f.

89. Detailed accounts of the naval and military operations are to be found in: PRO, WO 106/210.

90. Hood, M., Gunboat Diplomacy: Great Power Pressure in Venezuela, London: Allen & Unwin, 1975, pp.170ff.; Liss, S.B., Diplomacy and Dependency: Venezuela, the United States and the Americas, Salisbury, NC, 1978, pp.27ff.

91. Hood, ibid., p.172f.; Pommerin, R., Der Kaiser und Amerika: Die USA in der Politik der Reichsleitung, 1890-1917, Cologne-Vienna: Boehlau, 1986, p.115f.

92. See: GP xvii, fn.p.241; Herwig, H.H., 'German Imperialism and South America before the First World War: the Venezuelan Case 1902/3', in: A.Fischer, G.Moltmann & K.Schwabe (eds.), Russland - Deutschland - Amerika: Festschrift für Fritz T.Epstein, Umbach, 1978, pp.117-30.

93. Chirol, V., 'Continental Agreements, 1900-7', in: Ward (ed.), Cambridge History of British Foreign Policy, op.cit., vol.iii, p.295f.; tel.Haggard to Lansdowne, (No.20), 14 March 1902, PRO, FO 199/162.

94. Lansdowne to Haggard, 29 July 1902, PRO, FO 80/439; Memo. Lansdowne, 17 October 1902, Joseph Chamberlain MSS, Birmingham University Library, JC 14/4.

95. 'Memorandum to Friendly Powers Concerning German Claims', 12 August 1902, PRO, FO 199/165; Bülow to William II, 1 September 1902, GP xvii, no.5,107.

96. Pommerin, Der Kaiser und Amerika, op.cit., p.116; Herwig, 'German Imperialism and South America', op.cit., p.177f.; on the German naval presence in the Caribbean see also: Haggard to Lansdowne (No.176), 25 November 1901, PRO, FO 244/611; Lansdowne to Lascelles (No.13), 14 January 1902, ibid.

97. Harbaugh, W.H., The Life and Times of Theodore Roosevelt, London-Oxford-New York: OUP, rev. ed. 1975 (pb), p.187f.

98. Mommsen, W.J., Grossmachstellung und Weltpolitik: Die Aussenpolitik des Deutschen Reiches, Berlin: Propyläen, 1993, p.160f.; Kennedy, The Rise of the Anglo-German Antagonism, op.cit., pp.251ff.; Steiner, Z.S., Britain and the Origins of the First World War, London: Macmillan, Repr.1991, p.28f.; Monger, G.W., The End of Isolation: British Foreign Policy, 1900-1907, London-New York: T.Nelson, 1963, pp.67ff.

99. Monger, op.cit., p.69f.; Rolo, P.J.V., 'Lansdowne', in: K.M. Wilson (ed.), British Foreign Secretaries and Foreign Policy: From the Crimean War to First World War, London: Croom Helm, 1987, pp.159-171; Grenville, J.A.S., Lord Salisbury and Foreign Policy: The Close of the Nineteenth Century, London: Athlone Press, 1970(pb), p.427f.

100. Lansdowne to Herbert (private), 10 February 1903, Lansdowne MSS, PRO, FO 800/144.

101. Tel. Quadt to Bülow, (No.199), 25 November 1902, GP xvii, No.5,116; Lansdowne to Lascelles, (No.318), PRO, FO 244/613.

102. Lansdowne to Lascelles, (No.318), 26 November 1902, PRO, FO 244/613; Sanderson to Buchanan (No.329A), 29 November 1902, and (No.342), 6 December 1902, ibid., tel.Rex to Metternich (No.249), 5 December 1902, GP xvii, No.5,118.

103. FO Memo, 26 November 1902, PRO, FO 244/613; Lansdowne to Lascelles (No.342), 1 December 1902, ibid.

104. See: GP xvii, No.5,120, fn.*, p.259.

105. Lansdowne to Metternich, 14 & 17 December 1902, Lansdowne, MSS, PRO, FO 800/129.

106. cf.Lansdowne to Buchanan, (No.351), 11 December 1902, PRO, FO 244/613.

107. cf.Lansdowne to Lascelles, (No.362), 18 December 1902, ibid.

108. F.H.Villiers to Lascelles, (No.369), 22 December 1902, ibid.

109. cf.Roosevelt to Hay, 30 August 1904, as quoted in Pommerin, Der Kaiser und Amerika, op.cit., p.117.

110. Harbaugh, Roosevelt, op.cit., p.188; Dülffer, J., Regeln gegen den Krieg?: Die Haager Friedenskonferenzen von 1899 und 1907 in der internationalen Politik, Berlin: Ullstein s.a., [1981], p.222f.

111. Lansdowne to Lascelles, (No.377), 31 December 1902, PRO, FO 244/613; Lansdowne to Lascelles, (No.7), 2 January 1903, PRO, FO 244/624.

112. Lansdowne to Lascelles, (No.10), 6 January 1903, ibid.; tel. Quadt to Bülow (No.13), 20 January 1903, GP xvii, No.5,131.

113. Tel. Quadt to Bülow, (No.13), 23 January 1903, GP xvii, No.5,133; Harbaugh, Roosevelt, op.cit., p.188.

114. Tel. Metternich to Bülow (private), 13 December 1902, GP xvii, No.5,122; see also: Kennedy, Rise of the Anglo-German Antagonism, op.cit., p.260f.; Morris, A.J.A., The Scaremongers: The Advocacy of War and Rearmament, 1896-1914, London: Routledge & Kegan Paul, 1984, pp.53ff.

115. cf.Lansdowne to Lascelles, (No.51), 9 February 1903, PRO, FO 244/624.

116. cf.'New York Times', 15 February 1903, as quoted in: Herbert to Lansdowne, (No.68), 26 March 1903 (copy), ibid.

117. Schwarz, U., 'Great Power Intervention in the Modern World', in: A. Buchan (ed.), Problems of Modern Strategy, London: Chatto & Windus, 1970 (= Studies in International Security, vol.xiv), p.189; Bull, H., 'The Emergence of a Universal International Society', in: idem/A.Watson (eds.), The Expansion of International Society, Oxford: Clarendon Press, Repr.1988 (pb), pp.117-126.

118. Compare Clausewitz, C. von, On War, transl.and ed. by P.Paret & M.Howard, Princeton, NJ: Princeton University Press, 1989(pb), p.607: 'Policy is the guiding intelligence and war its instrument, not vice versa'.

119. Gulick, E.V., Europe's Classical Balance of Power, New York: Norton, Repr.s.a.(pb), p.62f.; Anderson, M.S., The Rise of Modern Diplomacy, 1450-1919, London-New York: Longmans, 1993, pp.181ff.

120. Webster, Foreign Policy of Castlereagh II, op.cit., p.53f.

2 Continuity and Change: the United States, Great Britain and Military Intervention in the Cold War

CONSTANTINE A PAGEDAS

> 'The more the planet is one, the less does diplomacy seem to obey the ordinary calculations of force ...'
>
> R. Aron[1]

The Cold War Environment

The international order which emerged at the end of the Second World War was significantly different from those which preceded it. It was characterized by a bipolar global ideological conflict and, simultaneously by a dramatic change in the technology of warfare. On the military side, after the United States dropped two atomic devices on Hiroshima and Nagasaki, it was widely assumed by nuclear theorists that conventional warfare would be rendered impracticable and obsolete. During the Cold War, many had been led to believe that the basic mission of US military forces (whose military culture became oriented to major weapons systems, high technology and large wars) was the deterrence against the Soviet nuclear threat, and that other missions, such as military interventions, were only secondary.[2] As soon as the Soviet Union acquired atomic weapons in 1949, the two superpowers were locked into an arms race, devoting their energies to creating more powerful bombs carried by the most technologically advanced means of delivery.[3] Writing in the 1960's, Thomas Schelling pointed out that

> [m]ilitary force can sometimes be used to achieve an object forcibly, without persuasion or intimidation; usually, though - throughout history but particularly now - military potential is used to influence

> other countries, their governments or their people [...] For the last two decades ... this part of diplomacy has been central and continuous; in the United States there has been a revolution in the relation of military to foreign policy at the same time as the revolution in explosive power.[4]

However, it was unthinkable that the nuclear powers, for example, could use their devastating military potential in order to achieve limited political objectives. Indeed, conventional military operations were carried out more frequently than Schelling would have one believe. The Cold War was 'a mere continuation of a tradition which was well established in the nineteenth century'; in particular, military intervention was employed, though with significant altered techniques.[5] Clausewitz's dictum that 'war is simply a continuation of political intercourse, with the addition of other means' lost none of its validity in the post-war era.[6]

With regard to the political side, the means of intercourse between sovereign nations was unchanged by the Second World War. The continued anarchical nature of the system of modern states meant that military intervention remained in the arsenal of individual great power states as an instrument of policy throughout the Cold War. In the bipolar world, it was a reflection of 'the common values, rules and institutions accepted by the system of states as a whole'.[7] It also reflected the tension between the perception of war as a threat to the international system which had to be contained, and the perception of it as an instrument which states exploited for their own purposes. This instrumentality of war, acted as a positive role in the world order by enforcing international law, preserving a balance of power and sometimes, in order to bring about what the community of great power nations allowed as 'a just change'.[8]

Nevertheless, the Cold War brought about two unmistakable changes to the system of modern states. Firstly, the advent and production of nuclear weapons created a new environment whereby the superpowers, instead of confronting each other openly and directly, competed with each other surreptitiously throughout the world under the auspice of their global ideological conflict.[9] 'The possibility of war between the two major actors ... encouraged them to employ subversive tactics and, often, proxy forces on battlefields far from home territory'.[10] The risk of military intervention escalating into a wider conflict or even a nuclear war was a constant apprehension for world leaders. Schelling, who devoted much of his time to the study of the manipulation of risk, determined that a semi-uncontrollable chain of events could escalate the risk and even touch off a nuclear war. He worked out that '[i]n time of crisis or especially after the outbreak of hostilities, [there] would then be a "competition in risk taking characterized not so much by tests of force as by tests of nerve"'. This led him to conclude that '[g]eneral war need not result from a deliberate and cold-blooded decision. Events, that is, might have a momentum of their own, quite apart from the conscious intent of political leaders.'[11]

Secondly, the traditional colonial powers of Europe became unable to maintain their empires in their very weakened positions which initiated a process of swift de-colonization. This led to the creation of a plethora of new, sovereign nation-states, many of which were incapable of maintaining their own independence, or projecting power beyond their borders. On the other hand, within the United Nations, the political power of the newly-independent states gradually increased. In a sense, this global organization became a conduit for non-great power diplomacy. In the words of Raymond Aron:

> The unity of the diplomatic field is real in many ways: the big powers have the material means of acting at any point of the globe. Marshal Tito, Mr. Nehru, Colonel Nasser and the Prime Minister of Burma exchange visits and pledges of 'active neutrality'; at the United Nations, the States of Asia and America rub shoulders with the representatives of Europe and Africa. Never have so many states of so many different kinds been in regular contact. Never has the fate of each state been affected, or risked being affected, to the extent that it is today by events at the other end of the earth.[12]

These changes in warfare and international politics were reflected in the shape military intervention was to take after the Second World War which particularly affected the United States. Prior to 1945, US policy-makers tended to view their armed forces as purely instruments for war and not as tools for policy influence. Military strategy meant 'the use of engagements for the object of the war'.[13] As the world became bipolar in nature, however, the Truman Administration followed two basic principles: the first, was to contain the spread of international communism (and, if possible, roll it back); the second was to avoid a nuclear catastrophe.[14] This doctrine, presented in April 1950 and more or less carried out by succeeding administrations, was expressed in the report known as NSC-68.[15] It called for strong conventional forces to block limited challenges posed by the Soviet Union to the free world arguing that 'a defeat of free institutions anywhere is a defeat everywhere'.[16] The United States soon found itself intervening throughout the world in order to prevent weak and newly-formed governments from becoming communist.

The West's desire to check the ideological expansion of communism in the nuclear age made military intervention more frequent, yet all the more dangerous.[17] Indeed the struggle between democratic and communist ideologies was a basic feature in the Cold War.[18] The United States and the Soviet Union 'faced each other as the fountain-heads of two hostile and incompatible ideologies, systems of government and way of life, each trying to expand the reach of its respective political values and to prevent the expansion of the other'.[19] The West felt its position undermined and thus its security threatened when any nation, including small, strategically unimportant ones became communist. The growing number of nations meant that the West often had to cater to small countries, or risk them joining the Soviet camp. Very often, when these countries became 'uncaterable', a leader was quickly found who would likely take a pro-Western position and plans for a governmental overthrow were formulated. Hence, there were many times when both East and West felt that it was worth the risk to use military intervention in order to promote their national interests.

Consequently, although there was a 'transformation' in the nature of war, there was not necessarily a 'transformation' of politics. A war between the superpowers, by design or miscalculation, was ruled out for fear of its devastating consequences.[20] This unimaginable development exposed the need for the superpowers to rely on force 'in some manner short of large-scale use' in order to advance their national interests. Economic and political constraints, however, meant that the superpowers favoured relying on nuclear weapons for their defence, and in turn meant that 'the utility of military force resided primarily in the threat of its use *or in limited uses of it'*.[21] The underdeveloped world became a surrogate forum for superpower competition. Military intervention was given a specific role; it receded from its traditional meaning, and was acclimatized to the Cold War environment. Nevertheless, the Cold War, although witnessing drastic changes to the international environment in terms of nuclear weapons and new nations, retained certain fundamental aspects of the pre-war international environment which allowed states to continue to use military interventions. The changes merely altered the manner in which these operations were successfully carried out.

To illustrate military intervention as practiced in the Cold War, two case studies will be summarized and examined as to the basis for their success, or lack thereof. The first case, the United States intervention in Guatemala in 1954, is chosen to illustrate a typical military operation to topple a 'pro-communist' regime. This provides a good example of a superpower, motivated by ideology, which took forceful measures to ensure her 'sphere of influence' was not tarnished. The second case, the British and French invasion of Egypt in 1956, shows military intervention practiced by non-superpowers and end in failure (even though the military aspect of this operation was considered to be successful).

Guatemala (1954)

American intervention in Latin America has figured prominently in many accounts of the region's history in the 19th and 20th centuries. Ever since the United States issued the Monroe Doctrine in 1823, imposing itself as the hegemonial power of Latin America, this region has been perceived as a vital interest of American security. The Monroe Doctrine stated, among other things, that the US would resist, if need be by force, any foreign interference in the western hemisphere. Although there were relatively few problems enforcing this, America nevertheless found herself intervening in Latin America at the end of the 19th century and early 20th century in order to maintain political stability and protect American business investments there. To justify these actions, President Theodore Roosevelt appended to the Monroe Doctrine his own corollary in 1904. It said that

> [C]hronic wrongdoing, or an impotence which results in a general loosening of the ties of civilized society, may in America, as elsewhere, ultimately require intervention by some civilized nation, and in the Western Hemisphere the adherence of the United States to the Monroe Doctrine may force the United States, however reluctantly, in flagrant cases of such wrongdoing or impotence, to the exercise of an international police power.[22]

In the Cold War, the United States re-asserted her traditional, active political dominance over Latin America after more than two decades of 'non-intervention' which President Franklin D. Roosevelt had called the 'Good Neighbour' policy. Although this was a policy to allow the United States to turn its attention to Europe and the Far East, she never gave up her policing role in Latin America. During the Guatemalan crisis in 1954, the Secretary of State, John Foster Dulles reaffirmed this role, claiming that the 'intrusion of Soviet despotism [in Latin America] was , of course, a direct challenge to our Monroe Doctrine - the first and most fundamental of our foreign policies'.[23]

When Jacobo Arbenz was elected president of Guatemala in November 1950, Washington swiftly turned its attention to Latin America. There had been a revolution in 1944 led by Juan José Arévalo, who, as president, implemented many social reforms; however, the outdated agrarian economy and land tenure system was left in tact. In his inaugural address, Arbenz outlined his plans for developing Guatemala's 'predominantly feudal economy into a modern, capitalist one', by active government intervention which would supervise this modernization.[24]

For a long time the US companies had a large amount of capital invested in Central America; especially in the tiny country of Guatemala. Some Americans went as far as to claim that America's economic dominance of Latin America was vital to the US's economic superiority to the Soviet Union.[25] The corporate giant, the United Fruit Company, and its subsidiaries, International Railways of Central America and Electric Bond and Share enjoyed a virtual monopoly over the fruit industry, its transport in Guatemala, as well as a fleet of ships for world-wide distribution, giving them considerable power over Guatemala's economy.[26] It therefore came as no surprise that when Arbenz initiated his comprehensive, agrarian reform package, known as Decree 900, in June 1952, the United Fruit Company was outraged. By 1954, over 400,000 acres of United Fruit's holdings (or approximately one-seventh of all the arable land in Guatemala) was redistributed among Guatemala's peasants.[27]

When President Dwight D. Eisenhower and the Secretary of State, John Foster Dulles, came to power in 1953, they had minimal experience in running Latin American affairs. Their political experiences were deeply rooted in Europe and the containment of communism there. The ideological impetus of American foreign policy emanated from the very moralistic Secretary of State who has often been described as 'something of a prig, and absolutely certain of his own and his nation's goodness'.[28] He viewed communism as an 'unmitigated evil imposed by a conspiracy on helpless people, whether it came from outside as in East Europe or from within as in Asia; there could be no permanent reconciliation with Communism because "this is an irreconcilable conflict"'.[29] John Foster Dulles' brother, Allen, who had been an agent for the Office of Strategic Services (OSS) during the Second World War, was promoted to director of Central Intelligence when Eisenhower took office, and hence a very intimate triangle of foreign policy-making was established.[30]

Almost immediately, Eisenhower acquired a first impression of Latin America after the return of his brother Milton, who had been sent there on a fact-finding mission. In a cabinet meeting in March 1954, Under Secretary of State Walter Bedell Smith reported the mission's findings in a memorandum which recommended that '[t]he most important question facing the Cabinet was to make up its mind that Latin America was important to the United States ... [and that] timely action was extremely desirable to prevent Communism from spreading seriously beyond Guatemala'.[31] By May 1954, the State Department was already calling for action by the Organisation of American States (OAS) saying that '[t]he contest is of crucial importance in the global struggle between free nations and the communist forces ... what has happened is part of Moscow's global strategy'.[32]

As early as August 1953, the Bureau of Inter-American Affairs drafted a memorandum which set the tone for subsequent US-Guatemalan relations. 'Guatemala' it read 'is of special importance ... for having provided the leading example of Communist penetration in the American Republics [...] The principle subsidiary problem ... concerns the treatment of private United States interests [i.e. United Fruit]'.[33] Four alternate lines of policy were contemplated:

> a) ... the use of direct military intervention or economic sanctions on Guatemala would violate solemn United States commitments and under present circumstances would endanger the entire fund of good will the United States has built up in the other American Republics through its policy of non-intervention, respect for juridical equality, and abnegation of a position of privilege. Loss of this good will would be a disaster to the United States far outweighing the advantage of any success gained in Guatemala ...
>
> b) our secret stimulation and natural support of the overthrow of the Arbenz Government would subject us to serious hazards [...] Were it to become evident that the United States has tried a Czechoslovakia in reverse in Guatemala, the effects on our relations in this hemisphere could be as disastrous as those produced by open intervention.

The third option was complete inaction, in the hope that the regime would collapse by its own forces. Finally, though, the US Government chose to employ 'firm persuasion' tactics opting to risk covert unilateral action if it became necessary, since 'the Arbenz regime could easily and quickly be overthrown probably with less Latin American opposition than we would encounter in present conditions'.[34] In effect, it was not a matter of whether or not to intervene, but finding the most auspicious moment which would be least damaging to America's prestige. Henceforth, the United States Government embarked on a campaign to politically isolate Guatemala from the rest of Latin America while a CIA-organized coup was being developed.

Eisenhower was a President who understood the usefulness of covert operations. Therefore, extreme care went into the planning of this operation. The plans from *Project AJAX*, the CIA's successful action to overthrow Mossadegh and the return to power of the Shah of Iran, became a blueprint for future covert action. However, it was the smooth coordination between the Department of State and the CIA, spear-headed by the Dulles brothers, which was the key to the success of the operation code-named *PBSUCCESS*. John Peurifoy, who arrived as ambassador to Guatemala in October 1953, was the liaison between the CIA and State Department. In a similar role as ambassador to Greece during the Civil War, this staunch and outspoken anti-communist had actively intervened to protect the democratic elements in the Greek Government. Other Ministers in Central America were privy to the conspiracy, including Whiting Willauer in Honduras, Thomas Whelan in Nicaragua and Robert Hill in Costa Rica. Willauer later testified in 1961 before a Senate subcommittee that this 'team' of US ambassadors, headed by Peurifoy, assisted CIA operatives 'to equip and train anti-communist revolutionary forces' based in Honduras.[35] The exiled Carlos Castillo Armas was chosen by the US embassy in Honduras to lead the coup because, as a report to Washington explained, he was someone who shared the CIA's view that 'the only way to obliterate Communist influences in Guatemala is by military action carefully planned and carefully carried out'.[36]

Meanwhile, John Foster Dulles rallied the support of Latin American governments against Guatemala. American policy-makers 'considered it essential that they establish the proper international climate', for they were concerned that world opinion, and especially that of Latin America, would sympathize with the Guatemalan revolution or view the coup as 'a surrogate invasion sponsored by the United States and the United Fruit Company'.[37] At the tenth Inter-American Conference held in Caracas, Venezuela from 1 to 28 March 1954, the ground-work was laid for subsequent action against the Arbenz Government. The Secretary of State succeeded in convincing nearly all of the delegates to approve a resolution which embodied: '(1) a clear cut policy determination that the activities of the international communist movement constitute intervention in American affairs; [and] (2) a recommendation on measures for exposing, and exchanging information on the activities serving the international communist movement.'[38]

In May 1954, Washington's pretext for intervention finally arrived. President Arbenz had requested military supplies from the Soviet Union. The Soviet Government had seen this as an opportunity to gain a foothold in the western hemisphere. When the CIA discovered a 2,000 ton shipment of light artillery and small arms from Czechoslovakia, loaded on the Swedish freighter *S.S. Alfhem* in Poland and bound for the Guatemalan port, Puerto Barrios, *Operation PBSUCCESS* was put into action.

The following month, on the morning of 18 June, Castillo Armas and about 150 of his followers crossed the border from Honduras into Guatemala. The invasion itself relied more on the psychological impact rather than the use of actual military force, thanks mainly to CIA planning.[39] Since early May, radio broadcasts from the 'Voice of Liberation' were used to build up the Arbenz regime's weakness. Obsolete bombers, machine guns and other heavy armaments had been sent to Honduras and handed over to the inexperienced rebels.

There were some in Washington, however, who viewed the American Government's secret assistance of Castillo Armas' rebels as immoral. Henry Holland, the Assistant Secretary for Inter-American affairs, argued that Washington was 'indulging in the most direct unilateral political intervention', regardless of a possible communist threat in Latin America.[40] At a critical moment in the coup, on the advice of both Allen and John Foster Dulles, Eisenhower made the decision to resupply Castillo Armas with more aircraft so that Arbenz would be entirely convinced that he had no other option but to capitulate. At their Oval Office meeting on 22 June, Henry Holland pleaded with the Dulles brothers and the President not to resupply Castillo Armas for if the CIA's involvement became known, many Latin American countries would interpret this as an interference in Guatemala's internal affairs.[41] The loud strafing of the bombers, combined with the radio broadcasts, though were enough to create panic and general disorder among Guatemalans, but most importantly, it demoralized Arbenz.

During the crisis, Foster Dulles was determined to make sure that there would be no opposition in the United Nations to the US inspired coup, especially from America's European allies. On 19 June, Guatemala appealed to the UN Security Council, where America's closest ally, Great Britain saw 'no good reason to avoid accepting this item on the agenda, [since] Foreign Office officials were determined to vote against any Soviet resolution condemning Nicaragua and Honduras as "aggressors"' anyway.[42] Eisenhower and Foster Dulles, though, were adamant that this should not be placed on the Security Council's agenda at all, for if the CIA's involvement was discovered, it would have certainly caused Washington a great deal of embarrassment. On 24 June, the British Representative to the UN, Sir Pierson Dixon, was instructed to press for the idea of a UN peace commission, which did not go down well with the Americans. After a French-inspired UN resolution calling for a cessation of the hostilities was unanimously approved, Eisenhower and Foster Dulles met to discuss how to bring the US's western allies in line. Eisenhower was furious, exclaiming that 'The British expect us to give them a free ride ... on Cyprus and they won't even support us on Guatemala. Let's give them a lesson'.[43] The Secretary of State then instructed Henry Cabot Lodge, the US Representative to the UN, to avoid making a threat, but to speak frankly with Dixon and the French Representative, Henri Hoppenot, and explain that if they continued to take an independent line over Guatemala the US 'would feel entirely free without regard to their position in relation to any such matters as any of their colonial problems in Egypt, Cyprus, etc.' which Lodge noted was 'received with great solemnity'.[44] In the end, the vote was 5 to 4 against placing Guatemala on the agenda; the UK and France abstained.

On 27 June 1954, the Guatemalan president was forced to resign, turning the government over to his Chief of Armed Forces, Colonel Carlos Díaz. On 7 July, Castillo Armas was made provisional president, and in an October election, where his 'National Committee for Defence against Communism' was the only officially sanctioned political party, he received 99 percent of the vote.[45]

The 1950's were the 'glory years' for military interventions carried out by the CIA[46]; yet this 'heyday' lasted only as long as Eisenhower and the Dulles brothers were in office. The President and his Secretary of State were exceptionally adroit in winning the support of America's allies for these missions, although there was very little her allies could do to prevent them. This gave Allen Dulles flexibility when he planned these operations, and more importantly, sanctioned what the CIA was doing. The success of American military intervention in Guatemala set the standard for further US operations carried out by the CIA. In 1955, Eisenhower placed his entire faith in the Agency. He told the Doolittle Committee, which had been assigned to investigate the activities of the CIA, that

> [i]t is now clear that we are facing an implacable enemy whose avowed objective is world domination by whatever means and whatever cost. There are no rules in such a game. Hitherto acceptable norms of human [or international] conduct do not apply. We must develop effective espionage and counterespionage services and must learn to subvert, sabotage and destroy our enemies by more clever, and more effective methods than used against us.[47]

The same year, Costa Rica was invaded by forces from Nicaragua, and again the US supplied rebel forces with aircraft and artillery. More importantly, however, the Bay of Pigs invasion in April 1961, where Guatemalan-style political and military tactics were employed, ended in failure. The new Kennedy administration did not take the steps that Eisenhower and Dulles did to licit American intervention to the international society. These crucial steps were not taken because the new administration did not have the level of harmony among the President, Secretary of State and Director of the CIA, which was very much a contributing factor to the success of the previous administration's foreign policy and its furtherance by military intervention. Instead, the anxious, young President alone was confronted with 'a now-or-never choice', and one which he came to regret when he was later forced to abort the mission.[48]

For a little over 130 years, the United States had, what many have described, as a 'free hand' in the affairs of Latin America. With the coming of the Cold War, however, the American Government could not be as open or direct in promoting its national interests or protecting its economic supremacy as it had done in the past. Initially, when military intervention was contemplated by foreign-policy planners, a 'wait-and-see' approach was adopted until the moment was ripe when the intricate US-backed military coup could be carried out. Although a superpower, Washington knew that the United States still could not act alone in defiance of international disapproval. As it turned out, John Foster Dulles had to create an international environment conducive to his brother's military planning by silencing the opposition of some in Latin America, of the Western Allies in the UN, and of a few in the US Government itself. Only then, was the US Government assured of the success of military intervention.

Suez (1956)

During the Cold War, Great Britain was widely held to be a country steeped in the tradition of gunboat diplomacy and military intervention; a reputation she gained from policing her empire in the 19th and early 20th centuries.[49] Many Britons, including Anthony Eden, the Prime Minister during the Suez episode, harboured the pre-war notion that '[t]he weight of Great Britain in diplomatic bargaining is, in the last resort, proportionate to the strength of her armaments, and her influence for peace is measurable in terms of the force she can muster to prevent the overthrow of the political equilibrium by armed force.'[50] Thus, it came as no surprise that when Gamal Abdel Nasser, the President of Egypt, upset the political equilibrium in the Middle East, Eden resorted to the use of military force.

Lately, many new versions of the Suez Crisis have come out in light of the recently released documents, which challenge the line taken by many of the architects of the crisis.[51] The memoirs of both Anthony Eden, and his Foreign Secretary, Selwyn Lloyd, claim that the military intervention conducted by British and French forces successfully obtained the stated political objective, which was to separate the Israeli and Egyptian forces while not allowing the Soviets to intervene.[52] On the other hand, few historians would argue against the overwhelming evidence that *Operation MUSKETEER* 'could have quickly achieved its limited military goal, the occupation of the Suez Canal, but failed because of the unrealistic political goals of the operation, for example the overthrow of the government of Gamal Abdel Nasser, through psychological warfare, and the failure of the British to withstand diplomatic and financial pressure led by the United States'.[53] What was at stake, however, was not the re-occupation of the Suez Canal or Egypt, or even the overthrow of Nasser *per se*, but the maintenance of the balance of power in the region so that Britain could re-establish herself as a first rank power with an empire centred around the Middle East and the use of overt military intervention as a means to this end. The region was, as Lord Altricham, the Minister Resident in the Middle East during the war noted at his farewell, 'no less vital to Britain than Central and South America to the United States, or than eastern and western glacis of the Russian landmass to the Soviet Union'.[54]

Although a member of the 'Big Three' at the end of the Second World War, Great Britain emerged from it in tatters. Severely shaken by the war economically, and trying to retain some semblance of order in her empire which was on the brink of dissolution, Great Britain, after granting independence to India, chose to concentrate her efforts in the Middle East. On the whole, the British Government believed that Britain's weakened position was only temporary.[55] In August 1949, the Foreign Secretary in the Attlee Government, Ernest Bevin, pinned his hopes for British political, diplomatic and economic recovery on the Middle East. In a cabinet paper, he wrote that 'in peace and in war the Middle East is an area of cardinal importance' for it was 'a focal point of communications, a source of oil, a shield to Africa and the Indian Ocean, and an irreplaceable offensive base. Economically, it is, owing to oil and cotton, essential to United Kingdom recovery'.[56] Great Britain still had substantial amounts of capital invested in Iran and Iraq for the exploitation of oil, even after 1953, when the United States assumed a greater share following the CIA overthrow of Mossadegh over the nationalization of the Anglo-Iranian Oil Company (AIOC). The Suez Canal, therefore, which traditionally linked Great Britain with the Asian Sub-Continent and the Far East, after the war remained an indispensable life-line to the oil fields of the Middle East. If the 'jugular vein', as Bevin frequently called it, was ever cut, British influence in the Middle East would be lost, and thus her principal element for being a world power would disappear.

In 1936, Eden, then as Foreign Secretary, had negotiated an Anglo-Egyptian treaty with Egyptian nationalist politicians which aimed to achieve a complete British troop withdrawal from Egypt by 1956. These plans included the Suez Canal zone itself, finalized by negotiations in 1954. The UK, though, through the Anglo-French Suez Canal Company, retained ownership of the Canal, and therefore, there was no immediate threat to the Government's economic designs in the Middle East. This privilege was scheduled to last until 1968, when full ownership would pass to the Egyptian Government.

When General Nasser led an army officers' coup to overthrow King Farouk in 1952, Egypt embarked on a fiercely nationalistic policy. Nasser considered Egypt's central position critical for assuming the leadership of the Arab world through Egyptian economic strength and uniting Arab opinion against Israel.[57] He sought to unite what he called the 'Arab circle' surrounding Egypt, thus creating an Arab force in international politics which would also act as an arbiter between the two power blocs. As the Labour leader, Hugh Gaitskell, commented during a House of Commons debate in August 1956, 'Nasser's aggressive intentions were clear: the Egyptian President intended to destroy Israel, subvert Jordan and other Arab states and create his own Arab Empire from the Atlantic to the Persian Gulf'.[58]

Jordan and Lebanon, however, which were mandates before the Second World War, had close links with the West. Also, Turkey had acceded to the North Atlantic Treaty in 1952 and both Turkey and Iraq signed the Baghdad Pact, brokered by Britain and the US in 1955. The basis for western influence, however, was embodied in the Tripartite Declaration of 1950, in which Britain, France and the United States agreed to supply arms and war matériel to strengthen the Middle East against communist subversion and create a balance of power between the Arabs and the Israelis.[59] However, conditioned by anti-imperialist ideas, Nasser thought that Britain and France were using 'neo-colonial means, diplomatic blackmail and bullying' in order to 'maintain their privileged position in Africa and Asia', and were thus frustrating his bid to build a third force.[60]

In 1955 and 1956, Britain and Egypt gradually became diametrically opposed to each other as both governments pursued incompatible policies. Nasser's first stratagem against Britain and the West was the Czechoslovak arms deal in September 1955 (the second of its kind in two years). In exchange for cotton, Egypt acquired Soviet *MiG* fighters, *Ilyushin* jet bombers and *Stalin* tanks, thus jeopardizing the military balance the Tripartite Declaration was designed to preserve. Speaking at the opening of the UN General Assembly on 26 September, the Foreign Secretary, Harold Macmillan, told his audience that '[t]he world will not allow the USSR to become the guardian of the Suez Canal. We could make life impossible for Nasser and ultimately bring about his fall'.[61] Although

John Foster Dulles was upset by the arms deal, he tried to restrain the British from taking any drastic steps. He privately told Macmillan, foreseeing the potential dangers of overt action against Egypt in relation to Arab opinion, that '[u]npleasant events which we might instigate should have the appearance of happening *naturally*'.[62] Eventually, Britain and France, with American consent, supplied Israel with *Meteor* and *Mystére* fighter aircraft in order to preserve the balance, and to reaffirm the Tripartite Declaration. Although Nasser was not particularly popular in Egypt at the time, Britain's verbal attacks against the President in the UN succeeded only in building up pan-Arab support for him. The British Government suffered another humiliation in March 1956 when Jordan's King Hussein dismissed General Sir John Glubb as head of the Jordanian army. Seen as Nasserite propaganda beginning to influence other aspects in the Arab world, Eden, and other 'hawks' in the government, notably the 'Suez Group', began comparing Nasser to Hitler and Mussolini, casting him as Britain's greatest foe.[63] The situation further deteriorated when the US Government announced on 19 July 1956 that it would not finance the Aswan High Dam project, a keystone to Nasser's programme for Egypt's economic revitalization. Finally, the point of no return was crossed a week later when Nasser nationalized the Suez Canal Company, ending Britain's 74 year control of this vitally important waterway.

The next day, Eden sent a letter to Eisenhower explaining his frustration with Nasser:

> As we see it we are unlikely to attain our objectives by economic pressures alone [...] We ought in the first instance to bring the maximum political pressure to bear on Egypt [...] we must be ready, in the last resort, to use force to bring Nasser to his senses. For our part, we are prepared to do so [...] However, the first step must be for you and us and France to exchange views, align our policies and concert together.[64]

Foster Dulles visited London bringing the President's reply, in hopes of again calming the British Government's resentful attitude. The letter read 'I cannot over-emphasize the strength of my conviction that some such method must be attempted before action as you contemplate should be contemplated'.[65] The Secretary of State convinced London and Paris to accept the idea of a Canal User's conference, thereby taking the political initiative away from the British and the French, and in effect, Eden 'lost the chance to rally the nation behind a straightforward Anglo-French ultimatum to Egypt'.[66]

Meanwhile, military plans designed to topple Nasser were being drawn up by British and French military officials. Immediately following the seizure of the Canal, radio broadcasts from the south of France began a propaganda campaign against Nasser. At least six weeks, however, were required to organize and implement the military operation. During that time, military planners 'had to contend with supply shortages, logistics difficulties, joint command, and above all, political ambiguity and vacillation'.[67]

No attention was paid to the conference, nor to any of the more sober-minded in the British Government who advocated against the use of force. The threat or use of force was clearly condemned in the United Nations Charter. Sir Gerald Fitzmaurice, the Legal Adviser to the Foreign Office, who invoked the tenants of the Kellogg Pact of 1928 and the UN Charter, observed

> the immense change that has taken place in the climate of world opinion on the question of the use of force [...] Justification that would have been accepted without question fifty or even twenty-five years ago would by now be completely rejected [...] We are on an extremely bad wicket as regards using force in connection with the Suez Canal. Whatever illegalities the Egyptians may have committed ... these do not in any way ... justify forcible action on our part ... such a justification could only arise, if at all, from some further and much more drastic step on the part of the Egyptian Government amounting to a closure of the Canal or at any rate a definite refusal or impeding passage through it.[68]

Relentless in his desire to humble Nasser and rising Arab nationalism, Eden ignored this more considered view. The 'contest' between the Arab world and the West, as he saw it, was a perception reinforced by the reports from governors of British colonies neighbouring Egypt. A victory for Nasser, they claimed, would destroy Britain's influence in her remaining colonies in the Middle East and Africa.[69] Eden stood firmly by the instructions he had given to his cabinet in October 1955 after the Czechoslovak arms deal, not to feel 'restricted by reluctance to act without full American concurrence and support. We should frame our own policy in the light of our interests in the area and get Americans to support it to the extent we could induce them to do so'.[70]

The United States continually promoted peaceful solutions to the Suez crisis, frustrating the British Government's hostile aims. After a second conference at the end of September 1956, and the formation of the Suez Canal Users Association (SCUA), nearly all of the momentum for a military operation against Egypt was lost. Chief of the French Armed Forces, General Paul Ély, recalled that at that time, 'the Suez affair seemed ... as very probably buried and I had the feeling that any military intervention was no longer to be expected'.[71] Sir Anthony Nutting, the Minister of State for Foreign Affairs (who later resigned his post in protest of the Suez expedition) noted Eden could not contemplate the use of force unless Nasser provided a much stronger pretext and struck first.[72] Even General Charles Keightly, the Allied Commander-in-Chief for planning *Operation MUSKETEER REVISE*, 'went so far as to say that to succeed his operation would first require "some enemy action which makes British and world opinion wholeheartedly behind us"'.[73]

This led Eden, in collusion with France and Israel, to invent a pretext for military intervention. Israel, trapped between hostile Arab neighbours, was contemplating military operations against Jordan. Eden saw this as an opportunity to re-take the Canal and topple Nasser. The French Government was hoping to stop Egypt from supplying Algerian rebels with whom France was embroiled in a bloody colonial war. At two secret meetings in the Parisian suburb of Sèvres, a plan was devised for Israel to redirect her attack against Egypt by capturing the Sinai Peninsula on 29 October, justifying Anglo-French intervention. Accordingly, Israeli parachutists were dropped near the Mitla Pass, east of Suez, which supposedly posed a threat to the Canal. Britain and France issued a 12 hour ultimatum requiring Israeli and Egyptian forces to fall back ten miles on both sides of the Canal to allow an Anglo-French force to occupy the zone temporarily and act as a buffer. This was impossible for Egypt to accept since such a buffer would have cut the supply lines to her eastern front. When Egypt allowed the ultimatum to expire, Anglo-French bombing of Egyptian airfields promptly began on 1 November, while paratroops landed at the Canal on 5 November. The following day, the bulk of Anglo-French forces made an amphibious landing, capturing Port Fuad, Port Said and nearly one-third of the Canal, when a cease-fire was put into effect. General Hugh Stockwell, afterwards, remarked to the press that the entire Canal could have been captured given another 48 hours.

The actions of the British Government, however, ensured her alienation from the United States. The US Government was angry with what was happening. 'Not only had the [US] Administration concluded that Britain and France, failing to occupy the Canal zone immediately, would continue to antagonize world opinion, but the attack on Egypt was undermining American objectives in the Middle East'.[74] More importantly, the US was in the midst of a presidential election. Eisenhower did not want this episode ruining his bid for re-election. At the UN General Assembly debate on 1 and 2 November, Foster Dulles condemned the Anglo-French-Israeli actions saying '[i]f, whenever a nation feels that it has been subjected to injustice, it should have the right to use force, ... then I fear that we should be tearing the Charter into shreds'.[75] The Assembly voted 65 to 5 for a resolution calling for a cease-fire and the complete withdrawal of British, French and Israeli forces from Egypt. On 5 November, even the Soviet Union joined the US in condemning the actions of the three belligerents. Premier Nikolai Bulganin threatened rocket attacks on London and Paris and asked Eisenhower 'to join forces in the UN for the adoption of decisive measures to put an end to the aggression'.[76]

By 6 November, American pressure on the weak British pound reached a critical stage. Oil stopped flowing from the Middle East (on 4 November, Nasser had ships deliberately sunk in the Canal to block the passage of any oil going through), and Britain had expended $84 million of her foreign reserves. When the Chancellor of the Exchequer, Harold Macmillan, telephoned his American opposite number, George Humphrey, to secure support for a British loan from the International Monetary Fund (IMF) to reverse Britain's vulnerable position, he was flatly refused unless there was a cease-fire by midnight. Facing financial ruin, Eden had no other choice but to comply. The next day, with the British and French forces left stranded in the Canal zone, the UN Assembly agreed to send a UN police force to Egypt.

Military intervention at Suez was less well-co-ordinated than the American organized coup in Guatemala. Although collective intervention implies that there could have been widespread legitimacy, the Anglo-French-Israeli action was not endorsed by the United Nations, nor more importantly, by their closest and most powerful ally in the UN, the United States. The combined operation therefore lacked legitimacy.[77] Eden later bitterly pointed out in his memoirs:

> We could not help contrasting the American attitude now with our own attitude at the time of the Guatemala campaign. In that country the United States had encouraged the overthrow of a communist-influenced Government, which it considered a menace to the peace of central America. We had understood their action there and done what we could not to hamper them in the Security Council. They were now behaving in a precisely contrary manner towards us.[78]

Eden, who harboured out of date, pre-war notions of military intervention, however, did not take into account of the transformed Cold War environment. Drawing on his own personal experiences, Eden thought 'that failure to act would have brought about the worst consequences, just as ... the world would have suffered less if Hitler had been resisted on the Rhine, in Austria or in Czechoslovakia'.[79] By ignoring his legal advisers, the Prime Minister set himself up for severe disappointment. The Charter of the United Nations was specific regarding the use of force, thus when the interveners were in clear and open violation of this, they were helpless. Afterwards, General Keightly remarked that '[t]he one overriding lesson of the Suez operation is that world opinion is now an absolute principle of war and must be treated as such'.[80]

Britain still conducted military operations after Suez, but only after making sure she had the countenance of the international community. These were more defensive in nature and closely coordinated with the United States, in cases such as Jordan in 1958, where the young King Hussein invited British forces to prevent an anti-monarchist revolt. At the same time, and in a co-ordinated effort, US troops landed in Lebanon to protect the pro-Western government. In Kuwait in 1961, where 'considerable care was taken', such as getting full Cabinet support and American acquiescence, Eden's successor, Harold Macmillan specifically went to great lengths 'to avoid any Suez-type débâcle'.[81]

Conclusion

The concept of military intervention was contrived by the European powers in the early 19th century as an instrument for restoring or maintaining the balance of power. Although it was given a shake-up at the end of the Second World War, its application remained a constant feature of the post-war period. Sovereign states remained as the basic element of international intercourse. Inequalities in terms of power meant that the preservation of world order and the prevention of war could only be secured by the more powerful of these states.[82] There is no doubt, therefore, that the use of force short of war in the Cold War remained as an instrument of policy, even though the costs of resorting to limited force have expanded while the range of its purposes seemed to have contracted.[83] The prospects of a nuclear war brought about by superpower competition, however, 'have imparted to the idea of a world state an unprecedented urgency'.[84] The rapid expansion of the number of nations in the General Assembly made the United Nations, more than anything else, an overseer of international conduct, or what Hans Morgenthau called a 'world authority'.[85] The emerging political power of the underdeveloped world had a direct impact on the application of military force for political purposes. The upshot of these changes meant that there were two essentially different notions of military intervention which played a role in international relations during the Cold War. One, such as the US

Government's involvement in Guatemala, was new and slowly gaining prominence. The other, such as the British invasion of Suez, was a more traditional notion which became less practicable in the post-war environment.

America's foreign policy-making élite were well aware of the changes to the international system in the post-1945 era. The detailed planning of the overthrow of the Arbenz Government, the combination of the State Department's manoeuvres for politically isolating Guatemala and the CIA's formulation of clandestine operations to install Castillo Armas, is evidence of this. Associating Guatemala with communism, organizing Latin American opinion against her and bringing unsteady allied support in the UN round to the American side were crucial political steps the US Government took to ensure the fall of the Arbenz Government given the CIA's very weak military effort.

The unreflected continuation of the tradition of gunboat diplomacy, on the other hand, was the major contributing factor to Britain's failure at Suez. In sharp contrast to the colonial era, the backing by the United States in the UN was essential in the post-war era. With the process of de-colonization underway and post-colonial nationalism in full-swing, Suez was seen as an outdated exercise practiced by a great power in decline. Furthermore, Britain's political objectives fell by the wayside to military practicality. Having lost the initiative in July 1956 to meaningless conferences, Eden was convinced by October that there was no way out of his conundrum save open military intervention under an invented pretext, and hoping that the Americans and the United Nations would conform when presented with a *fait accompli*.[86] What the British Government did not understand was that pure military planning was no longer the basic principle of military intervention in the Cold War. Covert warfare, psychological tactics and perhaps most of all, political acumen, were some of the new ingredients which dictated their success or failure.

Notes

1. cf.Aron, R., On War: Atomic Weapons and Global Diplomacy, London, Secker & Warburg, trans. by T. Kilmarten, 1958, p.55.

2. Lord, C., 'American Strategic Culture in Small Wars', in Small Wars and Insurgencies, vol.3, no.3, Winter 1992, p.210.

3. Freedman, L., The Evolution of Nuclear Strategy, London, Macmillan, 1988, pp.63-75.

4. cf.Schelling, T.C., Arms and Influence, New Haven, Conn., Yale University Press, 1966, p.vi.

5. cf.Morgenthau, H.J., 'To Intervene Or Not To Intervene', in Foreign Affairs, vol.45, no.3, 1967, p.426.

6. cf.Clausewitz, C.von, On War, ed. and trans. by M. Howard & P. Paret, Princeton, N.J., Princeton University Press, 1976, pp.605ff.

7. cf.Bull, H., The Anarchical Society: A Study of Order in World Politics, London, Macmillan, 1991, p.187.

8. Ibid., p.188f.

9. Morgenthau, 'To Intervene Or Not To Intervene', op.cit., p.428.

10. cf.Little, R., Intervention: External Involvement in Civil Wars, London, Martin Robertson, 1975, p.7; Wyllie, J.H., The Influence of British Arms: An Analysis of British Military Intervention Since 1956, London, George Allen & Unwin, 1984, p.16.

11. cf.Trachtenberg, M., History & Strategy, Princeton, N.J., Princeton University Press, 1991, p.16f., quoting Schelling, Arms and Influence, op.cit., p.94.

12. cf.Aron, On War, op.cit., p.55.

13. cf.Clausewitz, On War, op.cit., p.128, p.177; Gizewski, P., 'Use of the Military Instrument Short of War', in: C.G. Jacobsen (ed.), Strategic Power: USA/USSR, London, Macmillan, 1990, p.382.

14. These two objectives are somewhat paradoxical. Containing communism was thought to increase the risk of nuclear war, whilst the US would have to accept the spread of communism if priority was given to avoiding this risk. See Craig, G.A. & George, A.L., Force and Statecraft: Diplomatic Problems of Our Time, Oxford, Oxford University Press, 1983, p.118f.

15. Commentaries on NSC-68 by American bureaucrats such as P. H. Nitze and R. R. Bowie, Directors of the States Department Planning Staff, 1950-3 and 1953-7, and C. Kaysen, Deputy Assistant to the President for National Security Affairs, 1961-3, can be found in E.May (ed.), American Cold War Strategy: Interpreting NSC-68, New York, Bedford Books of St. Martin's Press, 1993, pp.99-120.

16. cf.Gaddis, J.L., Strategies of Containment: A Critical Appraisal of Post-War American National Security Policy, New York, Oxford University Press, 1982, p.91; see also Etzold, T.H. & Gaddis, J.L., (eds.), Containment: Documents on American Foreign Policy and Strategy, 1945-1950, New York, Columbia University Press, 1978, pp.383-442; Williams, P., 'The United States Defence Policy', in J.Baylis et al., Contemporary Strategy: Theories and Policies, London, Croom Helm, 1975, p.203; Freedman, The Evolution of Nuclear Strategy, op.cit., pp.69-71; Gizewski, 'Use of the Military Instrument Short of War', op.cit., p.385.

17. Beloff, M., 'Reflections on Intervention', in The Journal of International Affairs, vol.22, no.2, 1968, p.199.

18. The competition between two opposing ideologies is not entirely new. In the middle of the nineteenth century, the reactionary Holy Alliance, especially Russia, counterbalanced the 'liberal' tendencies of Great Britain.

19. cf.Morgenthau, 'To Intervene Or Not To Intervene', op.cit., pp.428f.

20. See Hinsley, F.H., Power and the Pursuit of Peace: Theory and Practice in the History of Relations between States, Cambridge, Cambridge University Press, 1982, p.348; Freedman, L., 'Escalators and Quagmires: Expectations and the Use of Force', in International Affairs, vol.67, no.1, 1991, p.22.

21. Author's emphasis, cf.Gizewski, P., 'Use of the Military Instrument Short of War: The United States', op.cit., p.383.

22. Annual Message, 6 Dec. 1904, in F.Israel (ed.), The State of the Union Messages of the Presidents, 1790-1966, (3 vols.), New York, Chelsea House & Robert Hector, 1966, vol.II, p.2,134, as quoted in Dimbleby, D. & Reynolds, D., An Ocean Apart: The Relationship Between Britain and America in the Twentieth Century, London, Hodder & Stoughton, 1988, pp.30f.

23. cf.Dulles, J.F., radio and television address, 'International Communism', 30 June 1954 as quoted in Immerman, R.H., The CIA in Guatemala: The Foreign Policy of Intervention, Austin, Texas., University of Texas Press, 1982, p.10.

24. cf.Ibid., p.63; see also idem, 'Guatemala as Cold War History', in Political Science Quarterly, vol.95, no.4, Winter 1980-1, pp.629-53.

25. Matthews, H.L., 'The United States and Latin America', in International Affairs, vol.37, no.1, January 1961, p.9.

26. At its height, United Fruit provided more than 80 per cent of the nation's electricity, owned all but 29 miles of Guatemala's railroad tracks, it was *the* leading banana grower in Central America (four times the amount of its nearest competitor, the Standard Fruit Company of New Orleans), and exported almost one-third of all bananas from Latin America bound for the United States and Europe. See Gordon, M., 'A Case History of US Subversion: Guatemala, 1954', in: J.L.Fried (ed.), Guatemala in Rebellion: Unfinished History, New York, Grove Press, 1983, p.49; Immerman, CIA in Guatemala, op.cit., pp.72ff.

27. The Guatemalan Government's offer to compensate United Fruit was $1,185,500, which was based on tax records. Later, the US Government formally submitted to the Guatemalan Government on behalf of United Fruit a bill for $15,854,848, most of which was to go toward 'severance damages'. Ibid., p.81.

28. cf.Ambrose, S., Rise to Globalism: American Foreign Policy Since 1938, New York, Penguin, 5th rev. ed., 1988, p.134.

29. cf.Ibid., pp.134f.

30. Before the Second World War, both Dulles brothers worked for the prestigious Wall Street law firm of Sullivan and Cromwell. They were responsible for many of United Fruits' lucrative Latin American contracts. See Immerman, CIA in Guatemala, op.cit., p.124.

31. Minutes of cabinet meeting, 5 Mar. 1954, Dwight D. Eisenhower Papers as president, 1953-1961 (Whitman File), Cabinet Series, Dwight D. Eisenhower Library, Abilene, Kansas, USA, as quoted in Immerman, CIA in Guatemala, op.cit., p.18.

32. Foreign Relations of the United States (FRUS), 1952-1954, Vol.IV: The American Republics, Washington D. C. Government Printing Office, 1983, pp.1,107-10, 1,149-54, 1,156-63, 1,170-2; Young, J.W., 'Britain's Latin America Dilemma: The Foreign Office and the Overthrow of "Communist" Guatemala, June 1954', in The International History Review, vol.8, no.4, November 1986, p.575.

33. cf.FRUS, 1952-1954, IV, pp.1,074-86.

34. At that time the world's attention was focused on the armistice in Korea. cf.ibid.

35. cf. Internal Security Subcommittee, US Senate Committee on the Judiciary, 87th Congress, 1st Session, Hearings on Communism in the Caribbean, part 13, 27 July 1961 as quoted in Gordon, 'A Case History of US Subversion', op.cit., p.47; See also Immerman, CIA in Guatemala, op.cit., p.140.

36. cf.Immerman, ibid., p.143.

37. cf.Ibid.

38. The US delegation sent powerful speakers to the conference such as UN Ambassador Henry Cabot Lodge and the Ambassador to Venezuela, Fletcher Warren, among a team of others in order to promote Dulles' proposal, commonly known as the Declaration of Caracas. Argentina and Mexico abstained, while Guatemala voted against this resolution. cf.FRUS, 1952-1954, IV, pp.45-64.

39. Immerman, CIA in Guatemala, op.cit., pp.161-8; idem, 'Guatemala as Cold War History', op.cit., pp.647ff.

40. FRUS, 1952-1954, IV, pp.1,168-9.

41. FRUS, 1952-1954, IV, p.1,177.

42. cf.Young, 'Great Britain's Latin America Dilemma', op.cit., p.581.

43. Ibid., p.584.

44. FRUS, 1952-1954, IV, pp.1,184-5.

45. Peurifoy was very instrumental in dealing with the junta which Díaz formed including, most notably, Colonel Elfego Monzón. The ambassador 'convinced' Díaz to resign from the junta in favour of Monzón, however, with Castillo Armas expecting the presidency, Peurifoy again mediated. In the end, Monzón was appointed head of Castillo Armas' armed forces. See Immerman, CIA in Guatemala, op.cit., pp.174ff.

46. Ambrose, Rise to Globalism, op.cit., pp.153ff.

47. cf.Ibid., p.132.

48. cf.Schlesinger Jr., A.M., A Thousand Days: John F. Kennedy in the White House, London, Andre Deutsch, 1965, p.217.

49. Cable, J., Gunboat Diplomacy: Political Applications of Limited Naval Force, London, Chatto & Windus, 1971, pp.9ff.; Wingen, J.van & Tillema, H.K., 'British Military Intervention after World War II: Militance in a Second-Rank Power', in The Journal of Peace Research, vol.17, no.4, 1980, p.291.

50. cf.Chaput, R., Disarmament in British Foreign Policy, London, George Allen & Unwin, 1935, p.372, as quoted in Garnet, J., 'The Role of Military Power', in Baylis et al., Contemporary Strategy, op.cit., p.55.

51. The major works are Carlton, D., Britain & the Suez Crisis, London, Basil Blackwell, 1988; Kyle, K., Suez, London, Weidenfeld and Nicolson, 1991; Lucas, W.S., Divided We Stand: Britain, the US and the Suez Crisis, London, Hodder & Stoughton, 1991.

52. Gorst, A., & Lucas, W.S., 'Suez 1956: Strategy and the Diplomatic Process', in The Journal of Strategic Studies, vol.11, no.4, 1988, p.391; See Eden, A., Full Circle, London, Cassell, 1960; Lloyd, S., Suez 1956: A Personal Account, London, Jonathan Cape, 1978.

53. cf.Gorst and Lucas, 'Suez 1956', op.cit., p.392; *Operation MUSKETEER* is the general term used for referring to the military intervention in Egypt in 1956. There were other versions of the plan, such as *MUSKETEER REVISE* (the plan actually used for the invasion), and *MUSKETEER WINTER* plan. See idem, p.391, footnote 1.

54. cf.Hurewitz, J.C., 'The Historical Context', in W.R.Louis & R.Owen (eds.), Suez 1956: The Crisis and its Consequences, Oxford, Oxford University Press, 1991, p.22.

55. For example, see Bullock, A., Ernest Bevin, vol.iii, Foreign Secretary 1945-1951, London, Heinemann, 1983, p.111.

56. cf.Northedge, F.S., 'Britain and the Middle East', in R.Ovendale (ed.), The Foreign Policy of Britsh Labour Governments 1945-1951, Bath, Leicester University Press, 1984, p.149.

57. Nasser wrote an article for Foreign Affairs in 1955 arguing that Israel's foreign policy was 'expansionist' and aimed to prevent any Arab 'strengthening in the area'. Idem, 'The Egyptian Revolution', Foreign Affairs, vol.33, no.1, January 1955, p.211; Hillal Dessouki, A.E., 'Nasser and the Struggle for Independence', in Louis & Owen (eds.), Suez 1956, op.cit., p.35.

58. cf.Ovendale, R., The Origins of the Arab-Israeli Wars, London, Longman, 1984, p.152.

59. The emphasis of the Tripartite Declaration was on the balance of local powers rather than in the supply of arms. See Kemp, G., 'Strategy and Arms Levels, 1945-1967', in J.C.Hurewitz (ed.), Soviet American Rivalry in the Middle East, New York, Frederick A. Praeger, 1969, pp.21-36.

60. cf.Hillal Dessouki, 'Nasser and the Struggle for Independence', op.cit., p.33f.

61. cf.Kyle, Suez, op.cit., p.76.

62. Author's emphasis, cf. FRUS, 1955, Vol.XIV: Arab-Israeli Dispute, Washington D. C., Government Printing Office, 1989, pp.542-9, as quoted in Kyle, Suez, op.cit., p.77.

63. Eden's conviction of Nasser as a 1930's-type dictator (an issue over which he resigned as Foreign Secretary) can be found in Eden, Full Circle, op.cit., pp.430ff; see also Nutting, A., No End of a Lesson: The Story of Suez, London, Constable, 1967, pp.31 ff.

64. cf.Eden to Eisenhower, 27 July 1956, as quoted in Carlton, Britain & the Suez Crisis, op.cit., Appendix I, p.114.

65. cf.Eisenhower to Eden, 31 July 1956, as quoted in ibid., p.115.

66. cf.Ibid., p.42.

67. cf.Bowie, R.R., International Crises and the Role of Law: Suez 1956, London, Oxford University Press, 1974, p.53.

68. cf.Kyle, K., 'Britain and the Crisis, 1955-1956', in Louis & Owen (eds.), Suez 1956, op.cit., p.114.

69. Ibid., p.118.

70. cf.Reynolds, D., Britannia Overruled: British Policy and World Power in the 20th Century, London, Longman, 1991, p.204.

71. cf.Carlton, Britain & the Suez Crisis, op.cit., p.49.

72. Ibid.; Nutting, No End of a Lesson, op.cit., p.63.

73. cf.Kyle, 'Britain and the Crisis', op.cit., p.119f.

74. cf.Lucas, Divided We Stand, op.cit., p.276.

75. cf.Ibid., p.279.

76. cf.Ibid., p.290.

77. For a detailed discussion of this point, see Luard, E., 'Collective Intervention', in H.Bull (ed.), Intervention in World Politics, Oxford, Clarendon Press, 1986, pp.157-79.

78. cf.Eden, Full Circle, op.cit., p.566.

79. cf.Ibid., p.559.

80. cf.Kyle, 'Britain and the Crisis', op.cit., p.130.

81. cf.Wyllie, The Influence of British Arms, op.cit., p.62.

82. Calvocoressi, P., World Politics Since 1945, London, Longman, 6th ed., 1991, p.120.

83. Bull, The Anarchical Society, op.cit., p.194.

84. cf.Morgenthau, H.J., Politics Among Nations: The Struggle for Power and Peace, New York, Alfred A. Knopf, 4th ed., 1966, p.483.

85. Ibid.

86. Neustadt, R.E., Alliance Politics, New York, Columbia University Press, 1970, p.63.

Section III

The 'New World Order'?

3 The US National Interest and The Future of Military Intervention

WYN Q BOWEN

Introduction

The outcome of the 1992 American Presidential election and the foreign policy approach pursued by the US in the first nine months of Bill Clinton's Presidency have been dictated by two coincidental phenomena: the disappearance of the overwhelming threat once posed to US national interests by the former Soviet Union, and the emergence of a domestic social and economic agenda in dire need of government attention. The interaction of these two phenomena over the period since the Gulf War has resulted in the division of American society along familiar lines, similar, although far from identical, to those witnessed in the US following the momentous foreign policy successes of the First and Second World Wars.

This division is between those in the media, the public and Congress who favour a major retrenchment of the US at a time of a sharply reduced external threat and severe domestic hardship and those favouring a limited retrenchment of the US. This second group recognize the need to concentrate resources on contemporary domestic problems, but at the same time identifying the need to keep the US on an internationalist footing perceiving America to be inextricably involved in the world as its sole superpower. Although this portrait of the contemporary political environment in the US is in very general terms it nonetheless illustrates that there exist diverging views pertaining to the national interest of the US beyond the basic consensus regarding the imperative of ensuring the 'physical survival and constitutional integrity' of the United States.[1] Consequently, there is intense debate in the US regarding the means by which national interests should be protected and promoted.

For example, an advocate of an internationalist role for the US will view the American national interest in broad terms, extending far beyond the territorial homeland, to include: the need and desirability of protecting allies; the securing of resource supplies; and the promotion of democratic and free market economic ideals around the world to secure America's global interests in general. In contrast, a neo-isolationist would advocate a foreign policy which views the national interest in very narrow, territorial, domestic terms, attaching little, if any significance, to a global involvement for the US beyond the protection and sustenance of American society, the American economy, and US nationals.

The concept of the national interest is similar, therefore, to other social science concepts, such as power and democracy, because it is intrinsically evaluative in nature and, as a direct result of this characteristic, it is open to numerous, divergent definitions and, therefore, to contentious debate.[2] This debate is an on-going process in the US but in the latter half of 1993 it has intensified because of the earnest public, media and Congressional concern regarding the Clinton administration's foreign policy. In particular, the different elements of the US polity have widely debated the relationship of Bill Clinton's military intervention policy to the US national interest at this time of domestic and global change and upheaval.

It is not only in the realm of military intervention in which Bill Clinton is suffering a neo-isolationist assault upon his internationalist orientated foreign policies. For example, in the area of international trade there exists the traditional division between those internationalists in favour of the North American Free Trade Agreement (NAFTA) and a successful completion to the Uruguay round of the General Agreement on Trade and Tariffs (GATT) and those vehemently opposed to such agreements. The issue is so significant that Vice President Albert Gore appeared on television with the isolationist Ross Perot to argue over whether the prospects of the US joining NAFTA would have positive (Gore) or negative (Perot) results for the US.[3]

Although President Clinton was elected to address domestic issues and has primarily been preoccupied with these issues since his inauguration in January 1993, he has simultaneously emphasized the need for the US to remain fundamentally involved at the international level, so that it can head the collective global effort to promote peace, freedom, democracy and free market economics around the globe. In doing so Bill Clinton clearly recognizes America's unprecedented power and influence in the post-Cold

War world and hence, its inextricable involvement around the globe. These twin desires (that is, to remain globally involved but also to concentrate the application of American efforts and resources upon the domestic agenda) have driven the Clinton administration, over its first nine months in office, to favour an internationalist foreign policy coupled with a multilateral emphasis on deliberations regarding military intervention.

In concentrating on the need and the desirability of a multilateral approach to international crises over this period, however, the Clinton administration has failed in three respects: to develop a new rationale for the American national purpose beyond the water's edge; to identify American national interests in the post-Cold War world; and consequently, to identify how and why the US will militarily intervene in the future. These omissions have contributed significantly to US foreign policy failures in Bosnia, Somalia and in Haiti and, in addition, they have resulted in significant public, media and Congressional pressure for the US to avoid becoming entangled overseas. As a result the Clinton administration has been under great pressure to formulate a foreign policy rationale explicitly dictating when, how and why the US will use military force overseas, an imperative when the American domestic agenda demands immediate attention and effective action from the Clinton administration.

It is argued in this chapter that if the Clinton administration fails to draw up an explicit rationale to dictate the future application of US military force abroad and continues to pursue an *ad hoc* foreign policy, fraught with the potentiality of humiliation at the hands of foreigners and policy back-tracking, then pressures within America could result in an increase in significance for those forces favouring a major retrenchment of the US. This could lead the Clinton administration to withdraw from its international roles and obligations to some degree, or even to the election of a neo-isolationist President in 1996. Consequently this would be accompanied by a negative impact upon real US interests situated around the world such as markets and oil supplies.

It is also the aim of this chapter to highlight the inextricable linkage of foreign and domestic policy-making within the US in this vastly altered strategic environment of the post-Cold War era. This was a fact President Clinton recognized in his inaugural address in January 1993 when he stated that 'there is no clear division today between what is foreign and what is domestic'.[4] This is not to say, however, that the interrelation of domestic and foreign policy issues is a new phenomenon peculiar only to the early 1990s.

The End of Containment and the Rise of the Domestic Agenda

Prior to the end of the 1980s the doctrine of Containment established a 'rationale for global US involvement'.[5] This identified the need to combat and contain the perceived Soviet threat to US national security, and provided the US with its primary 'rationale for possessing military strength' and hence, periodically using it through military intervention to protect US national interests.[6] For example, it was Containment policy that provided the primary rationale for US military intervention in Korea (1950-53), in Vietnam, in the Dominican Republic (1965) and in Grenada (1983).

US success in the Cold War, however, undermined the assumptions that had guided American national security policy for 'nearly half a century', by removing from the American military-political strategic equation the perceived fundamental threat to US national interests.[7] Consequently this left the US without a sense of purpose which had permeated American politics and society since the beginning of the Cold War.[8] In a recent article in *Foreign Affairs* Norman Ornstein described this situation by quoting Oscar Wilde, who said that there were 'two great tragedies in human existence: one is never to get one's dearest desire, the other is to get it'.[9] Here Ornstein obviously referred to US success in the Cold War and the doctrinal void and the lack of a concrete sense of purpose beyond the territorial US that this created in US national security policy-making.

Having lost this fundamental rationale, the US was confronted with the problem of having to redefine its national interest in terms of its domestic, foreign, and national security policies. The New World Order (NWO) rhetoric of George Bush which accompanied the swift, and hence popular, US led victory in the Gulf War initially brought to Bush's foreign policy Wilsonian hopes of creating an effective, collective, global security system 'administered by international institutions, and resting on the commitment of leading states to the maintenance of peaceful international relations'.[10] President Bush hoped this NWO would replace the Cold War order, and ultimately dictate US foreign and national security policy just as the Cold War had dictated the rationale of US foreign policy prior to December 1989.

The idealism of this proposed NWO disguised, however, the true nature of the post-Cold War, politico-strategic environment in which the removal of the superpower nuclear stalemate had effectively released the 'long suppressed' ethnic, nationalistic and other regional tensions.[11] Thus, the Cold War had the dual effect of containing the perceived Soviet threat to US national interests and it also suppressed regional ethnic, nationalistic and religious tensions and conflicts around the world. The Gulf coalition and the successful collective security effort to expel Iraq from Kuwait, in the name of the NWO, had the effect of papering over these problems, and hence can be regarded as the period of calm before the storm between the Cold War, or the era of the 'long peace' as John Lewis Gaddis depicted the Cold War,[12] and post-Cold War eras.

Although President Bush's NWO envisioned a 'new partnership of nations that transcended the Cold War', which was based upon 'consultation, cooperation, collective action'[13] and the assumption that aggression against the territorial integrity of a state was not to be tolerated, he failed to specifically define America's role in an increasingly troubled and conflict ridden world and to define exactly when, how, and why the US would resort to military intervention to protect which specific national interests. This failure coincided, in the Spring of 1991, with the emergence of an increasingly pressing and problematical domestic economic and social agenda in the US. Subsequently, it was this coincidence of phenomena which President Clinton inherited, with all its political and strategic connotations, in January 1993.

In the year preceding the November 1992 Presidential election, American 'industrial production was static, retail sales were slow' and in December 1991 unemployment had risen to '7.1% compared to 6.9% in November 1991 and 5.3% at the beginning of the recession eighteen months earlier'.[14] The US was experiencing low levels of consumer and business confidence and the government was saddled with a federal deficit which had more than tripled the national debt since 1980, to $3.1 trillion.[15] The economic gloom was reflected in a New York Times/CBS opinion poll in January 1992 which recorded that 'eight in ten Americans' believed the economy to be in 'bad shape'.[16] In addition to the prolonged recession and the nation's staggering national debt, the country's domestic problems included a poor quality education system, an insensitive and ineffective health care system, a major drugs problem, a rising incidence of crime, and high levels of poverty.[17] The disappearance of the Cold War threat has, therefore, resulted in, and interacted with, America's rediscovery of its urgent domestic agenda, which had been relegated for so long to a secondary position subordinate to the all unifying national policy of Containment.[18]

David Gergen noted in late 1991 that as a result of the lack of order on American streets, the worsening economic recession and the consequent increasingly 'pessimistic, inward and nationalistic' feeling within the US few outside the White House continued to talk of 'creating a NWO'.[19] In the aftermath of the Cold War, and the subsequent lack of a unifying national purpose such as containment for American society, the average American was not able to understand why the government was 'ever ready to respond to overseas crises with will, wallet and even American lives', but 'so seldom seemed ready' or able to deal with such 'human crises at home as unemployment, lack of affordable health care and a stagnating economy'.[20] The Gulf War was particularly significant in this respect, because a large portion of the American public viewed the US as having 'unlimited resources to defend the oil and sovereignty of Kuwait and Saudi Arabia' but could not 'find the means to defend the health and welfare of American working families'.[21] Hence, the pressing domestic agenda created an increasing desire on behalf of most Americans to put these domestic economic and social issues first by redirecting American emphasis and resources away from military elements of national security to other perceived important areas.[22]

The lack of well defined American national interests and role in the post-Cold War world, therefore, occurred at a time when the average American citizen was far more concerned with his family's immediate economic and social well-being than he was with the future direction of US foreign policy and America's role in the post-Cold War era. In a New York Times/CBS national poll conducted in October 1992, 43% of voters deemed the economy and jobs to be the major issues which the next administration had to deal with, 21% believed it to be the budget deficit, 19% chose health care, while only 8% believed the major issue facing the US was foreign policy.[23] From mid-1991 until the end of 1993, the debate concerning US public and political priorities has, therefore, been dominated by the 'interaction of this public mood with the end of the Cold War'.[24] This interaction has resulted in the rise of two opposing camps that cross the party divide in the US advocating divergent perceptions of the US national interest. Firstly, there are those who favour a major retrenchment of the US and hence, a narrow definition of the national interest. Secondly, there are those who favour a more limited retrenchment of the US and hence, a wider definition of the national interest in the face of the disappearance of the Soviet threat and the rise of the domestic agenda. Furthermore, this debate concerning US political priorities has been instrumental in the conduct of the Clinton administration's foreign policy and its approach to military intervention overseas.

The 1992 Presidential Election

The 1992 Presidential campaign was characterised by this conflict between these two opposing views. The sentiment offered by those in the US who advocated a policy of major retrenchment for the US typified by Patrick Buchanan's 'America First' campaign challenge to George Bush for the Republican Party nomination (in early 1992), and Democrat Tom Harkin's contribution of the 'Come Home America' theme to the Democratic primary election campaign at approximately the same time.

In campaigning for the Republican Presidential nomination Pat Buchanan demanded 'a new patriotism' from Americans where they would begin to put the 'needs of America first', and for 'a new nationalism, where in every recognition be it arms control or trade, the American side seeks advantage and victory for the US'.[25] He argued that the US drastically reduce its global commitments by terminating the provision of foreign aid and withdrawing US forces from Europe. In doing so he attacked President Bush for apparently wanting to be 'President of the world' while he [Pat Buchanan] was merely 'running for President of the USA'.[26] As for promoting the establishment, enhancement and maintenance of democracies around the world Pat Buchanan was reported as saying that 'how other people rule themselves is their own business' and 'to call it a vital interest of the US is to contradict history and common sense'.[27]

In introducing the theme of 'Come Home America' to the 1992 election race Senator Tom Harkin (Democrat/Iowa)[28] was highly critical of the Bush administration for believing that 'the real threats to national security' were 'half way around the world when' they were really 'half way down our street'. Harkin, who had opposed intervention in the Gulf,[29] proposed that the '$416 billion spent in subsidizing Western Europe would be better spent at home',[30] and stated that he would reduce defence spending 'by 50% over ten years'.[31] Senator Harkin's neo-isolationist tendencies were mirrored by another Democrat nomination hopeful, Jerry Brown (a former Governor of California), who said, that as President he 'would not give a penny for foreign aid until every farmer, businessman and family were taken care of'.[32]

The advocates of major retrenchment in the US were, and still are, best typified by Texan billionaire Ross Perot, who campaigned for the Presidency obtaining 19% of the vote in the process[33] and in doing do showed no interest or concern with keeping the US on an internationalist footing in the post-Cold War era. Prior to the 1992 election year, Ross Perot had opposed US involvement in the Gulf, describing the oil states of the Middle East as 'just sand, snakes, scorpions and oil'.[34] In campaigning for the Presidency, he advocated charging Germany and Japan (he called them free riding allies) '$50 billion each' to pay for the US troops placed on their soil.[35] He proposed a ban on foreign lobbyists in Washington, incessantly assailed free trade policies and launched an attack on corrupt government practices proposing a policy to clean up Washington.[36]

Such advocates of major retrenchment identified the US national interest primarily in North American, territorial, and domestic terms. As a result of this narrow definition of the national interest, members of this group advocated, that in a time of pressing domestic, social, and economic hardship, and the end of the Soviet threat, foreign policy, and American international commitments in general, should be relegated on the list of American public priorities. This should be done, it was argued, to allow America to concentrate on the amelioration of its domestic problems.

Thus, during the 1992 election year there existed, on both sides of the political spectrum, a major retrenchment philosophy at a time of domestic hardship and reduced external threat to the US. The two candidates chosen by the Republican and Democratic parties (George Bush and Bill Clinton) to compete for the Presidency of the US in 1992, however, both advocated a centrist and limited retrenchment philosophy for the future national policy of the US, and hence, favoured a wider interpretation of the national interest. Both George Bush and Bill Clinton were noted during the 1992 campaign as favouring an assertive, internationalist, free-trade orientated and activist vision of America's future role in the world. This was despite the overwhelming preoccupation of the electorate with the state of the American economy and American society and both candidates' primary emphasis upon solving these domestic problems. Both candidates recognized that even during a period of severe domestic hardship, the national interest remained intrinsically tied to the international arena because of the inextricably interdependent nature of the world, for example, through trade, resource supplies, communications, and weapons proliferation. In addition, they recognized that the US is the only remaining true Superpower and hence, is condemned to be the paramount character on the world stage whether the US fails to play a major role on this stage, or otherwise.[37] Both men campaigned, however, on election platforms which placed a primary emphasis upon adequately addressing America's domestic problems. They simultaneously recognized, however, the imperative that the US must remain fundamentally involved in world affairs to ensure the persistence of global stability, security and peace in the post-Cold War era, and in so doing, promoting US national interests around the globe.

The 1992 Presidential election campaign was widely seen as a battle for the centre with neither George Bush or Bill Clinton espousing radical policies on either the domestic or foreign policy fronts. The question, therefore, arises why did Bill Clinton win the Presidency over George Bush when both men were deemed so centrist? This has primarily been explained by George Bush's inadequate prescriptive proposals for domestic problems and his lack of a vision for America's role in the post-Cold war era.[38] It was Bill Clinton's seemingly sounder vision of a post-Cold War role for America and his more committed policy to solve the domestic problems of the US, however, which ensured a Democratic election victory in November 1992.

Although Bill Clinton focused primarily on the need to pursue an activist approach towards solving the domestic problems which most concerned the electorate with the resulting need to redirect American resources and efforts towards solving America's health care, education, welfare, criminal, drug, investment and tax problems, he did stress the importance of keeping the US on a global footing. He insisted that the US could not continue without a plan to lead the world and hence, advocated an assertive and internationalist approach towards foreign policy, thereby promoting a wide and globalist definition of the US national interest.

Clinton linked domestic needs with foreign policy by identifying the importance to domestic issues of ensuring the continued security and stability of the world. This entailed the promotion of free trade, free markets, human rights and American participation in international organisations.[39] In addition, Bill Clinton identified the domestic and foreign policy link by initially pledging to support the creation of a UN military force. He promised that a Clinton administration would support US interests around the globe but would 'share the burdens [of global security], where possible, through multilateral efforts to secure the peace' such as through NATO and a new UN rapid deployment force.[40] Thus, Bill Clinton's preference for a foreign policy based upon multilateralism was evidently part of his election campaign in which he justified a continued role for the US in the promotion of global stability and security. He emphasized the need to share the costs on a collective basis with the other members of the international community, so that the whole burden of this task did not land upon the US at a time when the electorate would not tolerate such expense.

Together with this multilateral emphasis, Clinton stated in April 1992 that he would 'maintain the forces the US needs to win and win decisively, should the necessity arise'[41] but at the same time he emphasized that this could be done with a 'less militarised foreign policy'.[42] This centrist stance on security issues dates back to Clinton's founder membership of the Democratic Leadership Council, a group of pro-defence Democrats that blamed the Democratic Party's Presidential losses on the 'vulnerability of the party' to Republican Party charges of weakness in foreign and national security policies.[43]

In addition, Clinton further stressed his commitment to internationalism by advocating a 'democracy based foreign policy' and a willingness to remain involved in world affairs to promote such values as democracy, human rights and free market economics. To reinforce this stance during the election campaign, Bill Clinton urged President Bush to 'consider seeking UN authorisation for air strikes to protect relief efforts in Bosnia'.[44]

Thus, although the US election was dominated by the debate over domestic national priorities at a time of social and economic hardship, it could be argued that in voting for Bill Clinton the American public, demonstrated a belief that an 'active, interdependent role for America, working with the UN and other transnational organisations' was in the national interest despite the increased attention which the 'long repressed domestic problems' of the US demanded.[45] Alternatively, it could be argued that the American electorate merely voted on a narrow domestic agenda in which Bill Clinton was the most attractive choice for President. Whatever the motivation of the US electorate to vote Bill Clinton into power, the 19% of the vote which the isolationist Ross Perot received was enough to caution the new President in his foreign policy dealings by illustrating the extent of American domestic support for a degree of retrenchment and for a concentration of resources and time on domestic, economic and social issues.

The Clinton Administration and Military Intervention

Prior to September 1993 the Clinton administration's policy towards military intervention paid inadequate attention to the necessity of tying acts of military intervention/non-intervention to the US national interest. However, through a trial and error foreign policy of painful losses and humiliations abroad, US military intervention policy under the Clinton administration since mid-September 1993 has begun to show signs of being pulled more into line with the US national interest. This has been evident through a spate of administration foreign policy speeches and action on the ground in Somalia, during September and October 1993.

The Clinton administration has consistently stated that the US must remain as world leader to 'build a world of security, freedom, democracy, free markets and growth'.[46] According to Bill Clinton, US leadership does not mean, however, that the US seeks to 'act alone', to 'act rashly' or to do things 'which could draw the US into a conflict not of its own making and not of its own ability to resolve, but simply concerted action that the international community can and should take to deal with these issues'.[47] In pursuing these goals, the Clinton administration has stressed the need for other countries to share more of the responsibilities that they ought to share. Thus, Clinton's desire to limit the application of resources to world crises in order to court the American public by concentrating US time, effort and resources on the pressing domestic agenda, interacted with his parallel desire to continue leading the world. This theme emerged in the 1992 election, and placed a marked multilateral emphasis on Clinton's foreign policy. For example, in Bosnia, where the US is involved with NATO and the UN and where the Western European Union and the EC are also involved; in Somalia with the UN; and in Haiti with the UN and the Organisation of American States (OAS).

This multilateral emphasis has been driven by the perceived need to reduce the nation's expenditure on global commitments and defence, but not to abandon them at a time of reduced threats to American interests and, more importantly, at a time when domestic problems demand concerted action.

It has been argued that multilateralism, and the related concept of collective security, theoretically assume that 'all nations perceive international problems the same way and are prepared to run the same risks for vindicating their view'.[48] This view conflicts with the post-Cold War world, however, with its resultant nationalistic and ethnic fragmentation. In such a world 'universal causes are hard to come by'.[49] This situation, and the Clinton administration's pursuit of a multilateral foreign policy, has complicated the US position over Bosnia, Somalia and Haiti and consequently has resulted in criticism of Bill Clinton's handling of these affairs in relation to US national interests.[50]

In pursuing a multilateral approach to US foreign policy, and seeking coalitions and international consensus wherever possible in addressing international crises, Bill Clinton has risked removing from his calculations what should be the primary rationale for US foreign and national security policy and hence, for US military intervention: the national interest. For example, in November 1992 President Bush committed 20,000 troops to Somalia on a humanitarian operation on behalf of the UN in order to stave off the impending starvation of thousands of Somali people caught in that country's civil war. Since the inauguration of the Clinton administration, however, the rationale for this UN mission has altered dramatically from being a humanitarian mission into being an effort to 'disarm warring factions', to apprehend 'criminal elements'(notably General Aideed), to establish a national police force, a prison system and a judicial system.[51] Furthermore US involvement in Somalia has been over-personalized and politicized with the emphasis on UN policy on hunting down the Somali warlord General Aideed. In its eagerness to pursue a multilateral foreign policy, the Clinton administration recommitted US troops to this task at the request of the UN, but failed to explain to the American electorate why the US should become involved in an altered, non-humanitarian operation concerned with the internal politics of Somalia - a distant country to which Americans have no special ties.[52]

The Clinton administration's emphasis upon multilateralism in its foreign policy and rationale for military intervention has resulted in the failure of the administration to formulate an all-purpose national vision to dictate how and why the US will militarily intervene in the affairs of other nations. In an age of US multilateralism there exists the risk, as in Somalia, that American lives and resources will be put in jeopardy when the US national interest is not clearly and precisely defined along with a national vision to guide US foreign policy. Prior to 1989 the Soviet threat provided this vision and, hence, justified the expense of American resources and lives on countering this threat. The omission of such an all-embracing vision has potentially very damaging consequences for the US, none more serious than the potential loss of US standing and credibility on the world stage. Certain Clinton administration statements concerning the Bosnian conflict are a testament to this potentiality. In the absence of well defined national interests and a national vision, Secretary of State Warren Christopher has been consistently inconsistent in his description of the impact of the Bosnian conflict on American national interests. Prior to the Secretary of State's failed attempts to develop a Western policy consensus over Bosnia and to promote the US preference for arming the Bosnian Government and using air strikes on Serbian artillery positions, Warren Christopher described the Bosnian situation as a 'conflagration that could envelop all of Southern Europe and perhaps rage beyond'. Thus, implicitly recognizing a perception that the Bosnian war could threaten the stability of the European continent which has been a vital interest of the US since the beginning of the Cold War. On other occasions since then, however, Warren Christopher has stated that the Bosnian conflict does 'not affect American vital interests'[53] and that it was a 'humanitarian crisis a long way from home in the middle of another continent'.[54]

Such inconsistency in identifying the US national interest in the UN operation in Somalia has resulted in the death of US servicemen and the televised sight of their bodies being dragged through the streets of Mogadishu. This has inevitably generated Congressional and public pressure for the Clinton administration to limit its actions on the international stage, bring US troops home for their own protection and hence, to define the US national interest in narrow, domestic terms at a time of major domestic economic and societal decay in America. To diffuse such pressures and reduce criticism of his foreign policy, which jeopardizes the President's power to define the nation's foreign policy interests, Bill Clinton could define the American national purpose in line with redefined US national interests. If Bill Clinton does nothing, he risks the rise in influence of those in the US advocating major retrenchment and a limited definition of the US national interest. This would subsequently entail the jeopardizing of real US interests around the globe, such as: oil supplies, markets for American goods and services, the provision of protection for allies, non-proliferation, and so forth.

The Future of US Military Intervention and the National Interest

It appears that it has been the *ad hoc* emergence of events and not the American national interest that has dictated where, how and why the US has militarily intervened abroad throughout the first nine months of the Clinton administration. Piecemeal and *ad hoc* foreign policy, however, results in contradiction and confusion, and it is in this situation which the Clinton administration found itself in September 1993. To avoid future inconsistency in foreign policy, Bill Clinton needs to articulate a coherent foreign policy vision incorporating an identification of US values, interests and priorities in the world. The country may be beset with domestic social and economic problems, and the related desire to see foreign commitments reduced, but this should not prevent the US from articulating a basic set of principles to dictate the future application of US military force overseas. Consequently, President Clinton would need to identify American 'strategic interests, he has to identify American humanitarian interests, and he has to express clear goals for the US that may be tied to military action'.[55] Once these goals have been established, they could be used to dictate the future rationale of US military intervention. That is, justifying military intervention, or non-intervention, on a case by case basis. Subsequently, if the US was able to reinforce this policy with action in the field then President Clinton's foreign policy dilemmas could be checked significantly. In addition, by minimizing such 'foreign distractions' through the definition of a 'clear course' for the US abroad, and by putting an end to reacting inconsistently to world events, as and when they occur, President Clinton would be in a stronger position to address his domestic agenda more successfully.[56]

Clear-cut and successful foreign policy breeds popularity with both the US electorate and Congress. This is a message President Clinton would wisely take on board if he is to deflect criticism of his handling of foreign policy, avoid calls for increased isolationism which he is totally averse to, and create more breathing space in dealing with the nation's domestic problems. For example, Bill Clinton's standing with Congress and the Pentagon was significantly boosted by his retaliatory strike on Baghdad in June 1993 to punish Iraqi involvement in an alleged attempt to assassinate former President Bush. This improved opinion of the Clinton Presidency in Washington was the product of a swift and tough retaliation and was compared with President Reagan's 1986 strike on Libya in retaliation for that country's support of international terrorism.[57] In addition, in September 1993 Bill Clinton was given an approval rating of 50% in a survey among Americans shortly after the President had played host to the Israeli-Palestinian peace ceremony and after he had appeared with three former Presidents of the US to promote the case for US participation in the North American Free Trade Agreement.[58]

Furthermore, a national vision must dictate under what circumstances the US will either unilaterally or multilaterally intervene at times of international crises. The best way to achieve this would be by distinguishing between the major strategic interests of the US and other lesser interests. Such major interests would for example include: the preservation of access to Persian Gulf oil and the US security commitment to South Korea in the event of North Korean aggression. Desirable interests of the US could include the promotion of democracy, human rights, and free market economics around the globe. With a division of US national interests along such lines, the US could intervene unilaterally when its vital strategic interests are at threat, and intervene multilaterally, on the other hand, when US desirable interests are threatened and when the US shares a compatible interest with other states in acting to alter an international situation.

In a spate of foreign policy speeches, statements and actions in the field during September and October 1993, the Clinton administration actually began to show signs of moving in just such a direction. That is to say, certain Clinton administration foreign policy announcements and policy changes towards Somalia reflected a long overdue appreciation on behalf of the Clinton administration of the need to formulate a rationale for continued US internationalism and that this rationale should be inextricably tied to the US national interest.

In September 1993, the US Permanent Representative to the UN, Madeline Allbright, Anthony Lake, President Clinton's national security advisor, Secretary of State Warren Christopher and President Clinton, in his 27th September speech to the UN General Assembly, spelled out what they believed should be the future direction of US foreign policy including some general guidelines regarding how, why and when the US should, unilaterally or multilaterally, militarily intervene overseas in the future.

Similar to previous Clinton election speeches and administration statements, the September policy speeches all mirrored the continued need for the US to remain engaged with the world. In the words of Anthony Lake, this was to be done in order to 'increase our security, update our security arrangements and promote democracy abroad'.[59] In reiterating the need for the US to 'remain engaged' in the world and 'to lead' in the post-Cold War era, President Clinton stressed that although 'domestic renewal' was an 'overdue tonic' in the US this should not be pursued through isolationism and protectionism, two philosophies he described as 'poison'.[60]

Bill Clinton depicted the overriding American foreign policy purpose in traditional American terms, as the need to 'expand and strengthen the world's community of market-based democracies'.[61] The rationale behind this purpose according to Anthony Lake is dictated by the belief that the US will be 'more secure, prosperous and influential' and the 'broader world will be more humane and peaceful' if democracy and market economics 'hold sway in other nations'.[62]

In contrast to the Cold War doctrine of containment, which identified the need to contain the expansion of what Anthony Lake called the 'big red blob' (communism), he announced a new doctrine of 'enlargement' through which the US will pursue a policy of enlarging the world's 'blue areas of market democracies'.[63]

Both Bill Clinton and Anthony Lake stressed that in the future the US will act both unilaterally and multilaterally on the international stage and that the US will 'not hesitate to act unilaterally when there is a threat to our core interests or those of our allies'[64] or multilaterally when this 'advances our interests'.[65] The fundamental point which emerged from both Bill Clinton's and Anthony Lake's speeches with regard to US military intervention was that in the future it will be the US national interest which dictates when the US intervenes 'in partnership with others', for example, with the UN, NATO or the OAS; and when the US intervenes unilaterally.[66] In addition to the above, President Clinton laid down a set of guidelines to be fulfilled before the US will commit forces to peacekeeping operations. These include the identification of a 'real threat to international peace'; a clear statement of the operation's objectives; the identification of an 'exit point' for US forces; and a prior determination of the mission's cost.[67]

There was much talk, therefore, about vital and lesser US interests and how these need to be related to whether the US military intervenes on a unilateral, or multilateral, basis in the future. Beyond this and the doctrine of enlargement, however, the Clinton administration has still failed to develop a coherent and detailed national purpose dictating why, how, and when the US will apply military force abroad, to achieve what objectives and in the name of what interests. Anthony Lake has stated: 'We should act multilaterally where doing so advances our interests and we should act unilaterally when that will secure our purpose. The simple question in each instance is this: what works best?'[68] Whilst Bill Clinton has stated:

'We will often work in partnership with others and through multilateral institutions such as the UN. It is in our national interest to do so. But we will not hesitate to act unilaterally when there is a threat to our core interests or to those of our allies.'[69]

Both statements fail to offer a concrete rationale for future US military intervention or a guide to America's reaction to world crises as and when they arise. These failures have resulted from the lack of a definition of what actually constitutes America's core interests and what actually constitutes America's desirable interests.

Anthony Lake has recognized the fundamental problem that the Clinton administration faces and he identified the compelling need for the US to 'define a purpose' by calling for a 'national dialogue' in which 'those who see the value of American engagement in the world' should 'steady our ranks', and 'rally the American people' around that purpose.[70] In saying that if the US does not 'make a convincing case for our engagement at a time of high deficits and pressing domestic needs', Lake illustrated that the US will probably experience increased Congressional calls for more retrenchment accompanied by 'drastic reductions in our military, intelligence, peacekeeping and other foreign policy accounts'.[71] This would severely damage America's ability to lead the world and promote security, stability and international peace, in an era in which it is the only nation capable of doing so.

The post September 1993 US policy in Somalia appears to reflect a more rational approach towards international crises. The US has stopped the controversial manhunt for the Somali warlord General Aideed and instead it has tried to get him to participate in national reconciliation talks. The US announced a deadline for the withdrawal of US troops from Somalia (end March 1994) which it implemented. The Clinton administration, as a result of public and Congressional pressures for retrenchment and criticism of US involvement in Somalia, has appreciated, therefore, that the US has no national interests involved in this crisis.

However unfortunate US policy failures in Bosnia and Somalia have been, they provide vital lessons and pointers for the future application of US military force overseas. They could prove potentially invaluable in the development and the definition of the future nature and limits of US military intervention and how this is related to the nation's national interests and hence, whether the nation's interests involved in particular crises abroad warrant the commitment of US forces and US resources.[72]

US policy towards the crisis in Haiti is the most recent case in point concerning the future potentiality of US military intervention and illustrates the inherent problems of trying to conduct US foreign policy without a stated national purpose beyond America's shores. The Clinton administration's handling of the Haiti crisis prior to November 1993 has been severely complicated by the lack of an international purpose and the repercussions of failed policy and failed US involvement in Somalia.

The US domestic environment has fundamentally affected the potentiality of US military intervention in the UN operation to restore the democratically elected leader Jean Bertrand Aristide to power in Haiti. Domestic concern was added to by televised scenes of unrest and violence in Port au Prince (Haiti) and the prevention of US and Canadian UN troops from landing on Haiti as part of the UN mission to restore Aristide to power by 30 October 1993. Domestic demands for US non-involvement in Haiti and hence, a more retrenched American approach to international crises, reached a peak when Senator Jesse Helms (Rep/N.Carolina) attempted to restrict Bill Clinton's ability as Commander in Chief to send troops to Haiti if needed and severely threatening, therefore, his foreign policy prerogative. However, his resolution was defeated by 81 votes to 19 and the Senate adopted a compromise vote 98 to 2 instead, asking, although not requiring, President Clinton to seek approval from law-makers before committing American ground forces.[73]

Despite the failure of this resolution the Clinton administration's foreign policy powers did suffer detrimentally. In the first place, Congressional calls for a more retrenchist national policy could jeopardize the future success of Bill Clinton's foreign policy. In the second place, both the Haiti and Somalia crises will inevitably have sent a message to all the potential destabilizers of regional and global peace and stability that in order to prevent the US from acting abroad either unilaterally or multilaterally all that has to be done is to threaten the safety of US troops. This will subsequently generate public and Congressional pressures to avoid US involvement in overseas crises.

Damage to the Clinton administration's foreign policy credibility in Haiti is particularly tragic in the development of a future rationale for US military intervention for several reasons. First, the UN and OAS mandated operation to restore the ousted Aristide to power (by 30 October 1993) was the product of Bill Clinton's own policy, a policy which he did not inherit from George Bush, in contrast to the Somalia and Bosnian crises. Second, the crisis in Haiti directly affects US national interests, i.e., the negative domestic impact of the Haitian refugee flow into the US, the safety of US nationals, and the domestic impact of the role of the present Haitian regime in the international drugs trade. Third, this crisis is taking place in America's backyard, within its own, traditional sphere of influence, and not on a distant continent where the US has few, if any interests.

Conclusion

In the future the US must discriminate in its foreign policy and ask itself the question, when contemplating military intervention either unilaterally or multilaterally, whether the price in American resources, time and lives is worth paying. If the decision is taken to militarily intervene the US must explicitly and unreservedly explain its rationale to the American public and to Congress and intervention must take place with a genuine commitment and a 'reasonable chance of success'.[74] The contemporary domestic situation in the US resembles the situation in which America found itself during the early post-World War Two era. There exists a division in American society between those who would like to see the US retrench and distance itself from the rest of the world following a major foreign policy victory and those who highlight the need for the US to pursue an internationalist foreign policy.

During the late 1940s, however, the emergence of a single, major, external threat to American well-being and to US interests throughout the world united the country around the perceived need to contain the Soviet threat. This national purpose dictated US foreign, national security and military intervention policies for the best part of four decades. In the present domestic environment the existence of two opposing camps with divergent definitions of the national interest is where the similarities between the two eras come to an end. In contrast to the late 1940s, the US now finds itself with a pressing domestic agenda which demands attention. In addition, this domestic agenda has coincided with the disappearance of a single, overwhelming threat to the American well-being and the emergence instead of a diffuse array of post-Cold War instabilities, none of which appear to directly threaten US national security.

The resultant situation has been one in which it has been difficult for the Clinton administration to rally the country around an internationalist policy, particularly due to the failure of both the Bush and Clinton administrations to develop and articulate a foreign policy doctrine. In the absence of such a national purpose beyond America's shores the US now lacks guidelines dictating when, why and how the US should militarily intervene abroad. The result of this has been a negative public and Congressional reaction to US policy in Bosnia, and in particular, in Somalia where US national interests and purposes have not been spelled out clearly. This is an intolerable situation if, as in Somalia, US servicemen lose their lives because the President has not clearly and objectively articulated to the American people what exactly the US is hoping to achieve by its involvement in such crises.

If the Clinton administration continues its present inconsistent approach to foreign policy and fails to define a national doctrine and a more explicit rationale through which the US could militarily intervene overseas, it is likely that the domestic consensus which brought Bill Clinton to power will crumble, accompanied by a shift of the electorate towards a more isolationist philosophy. This could have a subsequent negative impact upon true American interests which the internationalist orientated President Clinton believes are situated throughout the globe.

The Cold War has effectively been over for four years and apart from the so-called doctrine of engagement, merely the most recent manifestation of the free market, democratic philosophy which underscores the US national purpose, the US still finds itself without a foreign policy *raison d'être* in the post-Cold War era. Admittedly the US doctrine of containment took several years to formulate, and put into practice, but the process promises to take much longer this time around. However, the Clinton administration has begun to address the issues and problems involved by talking about core and lesser national interests and the potentiality of militarily intervening to protect these interests on either a unilateral or multilateral basis. The next step should be for the Clinton administration to explicitly define those national interests which it deems vital and those it deems desirable.

If the US were to intervene multilaterally to protect such desirable interests in conjunction with Bill Clinton's four point prerequisite plan for peacekeeping operations, and intervened unilaterally only when the above vital interests were threatened then the US could, in Hans J.Morgenthau's words, 'intervene less and succeed more'.[75] Consequently, domestic public and Congressional pressures for major retrenchment and for the US to limit its foreign policy dealings would be weakened because the US would be in possession of a foreign policy purpose identifying precisely when, why and how the US will contemplate using force overseas and on what basis.

The longer it takes to develop such a rationale the more US influence and prestige on the international stage will be placed in jeopardy and the more disenchanted the US electorate and Congress will become with the Clinton administration's attempts at trying to lead both the US and the world simultaneously. If the US fails to develop such a rationale then this disenchantment could well promote an increasingly retrenchment orientated Congress with the possible consequence of pushing the Clinton administration towards a more limited definition of the national interest, or at the extreme, the election of an isolationist President in 1996, such as Ross Perot.

A major retrenchment definition of the US national interest and how this could dictate military intervention in the future would radically differ from that of an internationalist definition which the present Clinton administration is advocating. For example, unilateral intervention would probably only take place to protect US nationals and to prevent a direct attack on the US mainland. Beyond this unilateral military intervention to protect, for example, treaty bound allies (that is, if the US would keep treaty obligations etc.) would by no means be guaranteed. Multilateral intervention on the other hand, to promote altruistic interests such as the promotion of democracy, human rights and market economics, would be increasingly unlikely the more narrowly defined the US national interest is.

If the Clinton administration fails to set priorities for its foreign policy involvements over the next three years and the US continues to approach military intervention on an inconsistent and *ad hoc* basis then domestic issues and problems, and public and Congressional concern with these issues, could result in the election of a more retrenchist administration in 1996. This is a potentiality which poses grave implications for the future peace and stability of the world and for the securing of US vital interests in the future.

Notes

1. Brown, S., On the front burner: issues in US foreign policy, Boston, MA, Little, Brown and Co., p.2.

2. See: Gallie, W.B., 'Essentially Contested Concepts', in Proceedings from the Aristotelian Society, vol.LVI, 1955-56.

3. 'American Survey - The Great NAFTA Bazaar', in The Economist, 13th November 1993.

4. cf.Parry, G., 'The interweaving of foreign and domestic affairs', Government and Opposition, vol.20, no.2, Spring 1993, pp.143-151.

5. cf.Wallop, N., 'America needs a Post-Containment doctrine', in Orbis, vol.37, no.2, Spring 1993, pp.188-9.

6. Ibid., p.188.

7. Hendrickson, D.C., 'The end of American history: American security and national purpose and the New World Order', in Rethinking America's security - beyond Cold War to New World Order edited by G. Allison and G.F. Treverton, New York, W.W.Norton and Co., p.395.

8. Smith, G., 'What role for America?', in Current History, vol.92, no.573, April 1992, p.180.

9. cf.Ornstein, N., 'Foreign policy and the 1992 Election', in Foreign Affairs, vol.71, no.3, Summer 1992, p.2.

10. cf.Falk, R., 'In search of a New World Order', in Current History, vol.92, no.573, April 1992, p.145.

11. cf.Ibid., p.148.

12. Ibid., p.148.

13. cf.Gardner, R.N., 'Practical Internationalism', edited by Allison and Treverton, op.cit., p.272.

14. cf.Prowse, M., 'US jobless figure hits highest level in five years', in The Financial Times, 11 January 1992.

15. Greenwold, J., 'Why the Gloom?', in The Times, 13 January 1992.

16. cf.Prowse, M., op.cit.

17. Hunter, R.E., 'Starting at Zero: US foreign policy for the 1990s', in US Foreign Policy after the Cold War, edited by B. Roberts, Cambridge, MA, MIT Press, p.5.

18. Ibid., p.3.

19. cf.Randal, S.J., 'United States Foreign policy in the NWO: a historical reflection', in International Journal, vol.XLVIII, no.1, Winter 1992-93, p.12.

20. cf.Woodford, H., 'The Democratic Challenge', in Foreign Policy, no.86, Spring 1992, p.101.

21. cf.Ibid., p.101.

22. Smith, W.Y., ‘US national security after the Cold War’, in the Washington Quarterly, vol.15, no.4, Autumn 1992, p.26.

23. Norris, P., ‘The 1992 US Elections’, in Government and Opposition, vol.28, no.1, Winter 1993, p.67, table 3.

24. cf.Yankelovich, D., ‘Foreign Policy after the election’, in Foreign Affairs, vol.71, no.4, Fall 1992, p.2.

25. cf.‘Down Pat’, in The Economist, 14 February 1991 p.45.

26. cf.Walker, M., ‘Patrick Buchanan taxes Bush with being hooked by the Japanese connection’, in The Guardian, 15th January 1992.

27. cf.Ornstein, N., op.cit., p.9.

28. Ibid., p.8.

29. ‘Bush’s Small World’, in The International Herald Tribune, 14 January 1992.

30. cf.‘Bashing Foreigners in Iowa’, in The Economist, 21 September 1991, pp.48-49.

31. cf.‘Candidates on Issues: Defense’ in The Christian Science Monitor, 13 February 1992.

32. cf.Ornstein, op.cit., p.9.

33. Norris, op.cit., p.51.

34. cf.‘Campaign Basics: Ross Perot’, in The International Herald Tribune, 3 July 1992.

35. Ibid.

36. ‘Perot poll scares the White House’, in The Times, 23 April 1992.

37. Steel, R., Pax Americana, London, Hamish Hamilton, p.325.

38. See Omestad, T., ‘Why Bush Lost’, in Foreign Policy, no.89, Winter 1992-93.

39. Ornstein, op.cit., p.10.

40. cf.Gerlach, J.R., 'A UN Army for the NWO ?'in Orbis, vol.57, no.2, Spring 1993, p.224.

41. cf.Omestad, op.cit. p.80.

42. cf.'American Foreign Policy?', in The International Herald Tribune, 29-30 May 1993.

43. Omestad, op.cit., p.80.

44. cf.Ibid., p.80.

45. cf.Ornstein, op.cit., p.14.

46. cf.Tonelson, A., 'Superpower without a sword', in Foreign Affairs, vol.72, no.3, Summer 1993, p.167.

47. cf.'A grave disappointment to us all' in The International Herald Tribune, 7 May 1993.

48. cf.Kissinger, H., 'Foreign policy is about the national interest', in The International Herald Tribune, 25 October 1993, p.5.

49. cf.'A grave disappointment to us all', op.cit.

50. Kissinger, op.cit., p.5.

51. Kirkpatrick, J., 'Clinton does have a foreign policy agenda: just ask Boutros Ghali', in The International Herald Tribune, 28-29 August 1993.

52. Ibid.

53. cf.Cohen, R., 'Confused, *ad hoc*, and unexplained', in The International Herald Tribune, 28-29 August 1993.

54. cf.'Clinton's Washington is retrenching' in The International Herald Tribune, 9 June 1993.

55. cf.Lewis, A., 'In this moment of truth, Clinton must lead' in The International Herald Tribune, 8-9 May 1993.

56. 'American Foreign Policy?', op.cit.

57. Fletcher, M., 'Retaliatory Strike raises Clinton standing at home', in The Times, 28 June 1993.

58. Fletcher, M., 'Clinton lifted by foreign triumphs', in The Times, 16 September 1993.

59. cf.Lake, A., 'Speech to John Hopkins SAIS, 22 September 1993', OFFICIAL TEXT, US Information Service, pp.1-2.

60. cf.Clinton, W.J., 'Address to the 48th Session of the United Nations General Assembly 27 September 1993', PRESS RELEASE, US Mission to the UN.

61. cf.Clinton, op.cit., p.6.

62. cf.Lake, op.cit., p.4.

63. cf.Ibid., p.13.

64. cf.Clinton, op.cit., p.7.

65. cf.Lake, op.cit., p.12.

66. Clinton, op.cit., p.7.

67. Ibid., p.13.

68. cf.Lake, op.cit., p.12.

69. cf.Clinton, op.cit., p.7.

70. cf.Lake, op.cit., p.13.

71. cf.Ibid, p.13.

72. Kissinger, op.cit., p.5.

73. 'Compromise Leaves Clinton's authority undiminished', in The International Herald Tribune, 22 October 1993.

74. 'American foreign policy - otherwise engaged', in The Economist, 30 October 1993, pp.23-26.

75. Morgenthau, H J., 'To intervene or not to intervene', in Foreign Affairs, vol. 45, no. 3, April 1967, pp.425-436, p.436.

4 Western Europe and Military Intervention: Unity in Diversity

ANDREW M DORMAN

Introduction

Historians may well conclude that the end of the Cold War and the collapse of the Soviet Union created more problems than they solved. Within the Soviet Union and in the other states of the former Warsaw Pact there has been a resurgence in ethnic discord and a rise in nationalism which continues to pose considerable problems for the states concerned. Further afield the end of the Cold War has brought little respite for the bulk of the world.[1] This has led the United Nations Secretary-General, Boutros Boutros-Ghali, to observe that '[p]overty, disease, famine, oppression and despair abound ...'[2]

Consequently the states of Western Europe are now confronted by a new set of security problems. No longer are defence planners primarily concerned with the narrow military threat posed by the Soviet Union and its successors. In the short term at least, states such as Britain and France no longer face the threat of a direct conventional attack upon their homelands.[3] Instead, a more amorphous concept of security has developed.[4] This is one of the reasons that has led Jacques Delors to conclude:

> [w]e cannot limit our horizons to the new Europe. All around us, naked ambition, lust for power, national uprisings and

> underdevelopment are combining to create potentially dangerous situations, containing the seeds of destabilization and conflict, aggravated by the proliferation of weapons of mass destruction.
>
> The Community must face this challenge. If it is to be worthy of the European ideal it must square up to the challenges of history and shoulder its share of the political and military responsibilities of our nations, which have always left their mark on history.[5]

The previously reticient attitude of the West European powers to the deployment of their military forces outside the NATO region has given way to the commitment of significant military forces in a variety of operations both within and outside Europe. These have included the Gulf War, and the subsequent operation to relieve the Kurds in Northern Iraq, Somalia, and deployments in Cambodia, Mozambique, Croatia and Bosnia.[6]

This chapter seeks to show that military intervention is no longer viewed within Western Europe as an archaic form of state action within the international system. Instead a variety of West European leaders are beginning to view it as an increasingly important tool of modern state action. Furthermore, there is a growing divergence of interests between the various West European states, which is likely to result in a growing number of military interventions based on a somewhat disjointed policy and compromised goals leading to an increased risk of failure. This might, however, be tempered by the influence of the United States upon the decision-making process of a number of key West European states and its membership of various regional and global organizations. In addition, the role of domestic public opinion, influenced by the media, will have an increasing effect upon the key decision-makers within the states themselves, and thus ultimately upon state action.

For the purposes of this chapter, Western Europe has been defined in terms of those states to the west of the former Iron Curtain including the Scandinavian countries and Greece. The chapter has four parts. The first two sections deal with the requirement to intervene and the analytical approach taken. The third section evaluates Western Europe in terms of four groups of states. These have been termed the *Old Sheriffs*, the *Young Guns*, the *Extras* and the *Fringe*. The fourth section attempts to identify the potential movements of individual states between these groups and looks towards the future expansion of the groupings eastwards.

The requirement to intervene

There are five principal reasons why the West European states, either individually or collectively, will continue to resort to the use of military intervention.

Firstly, Western Europe contains a number of former colonial powers, each with a long history of using military intervention. A history of colonization has left Britain and France in particular, with vestiges of their empires which continue to require their support whilst others still retain an interest in their former colonies. An example of this occurred in 1991 when the French and Belgians flew troops into the former Belgian colony of Zaire in order to organize the evacuation of Western nations and help suppress rioting.[7]

Secondly, the dependence of Western Europe upon other states for the supply of essential raw materials including oil has received renewed interest with the collapse of the threat from the Soviet Union. A number of academics have argued that the significant participation of a number of West European states in the recent Gulf War was directly attributable to this interest.[8] This has led the Western European Union Secretary-General, Willem van Eekelen, to argue that the movement of defence policy within Europe towards the protection of its wider interests will result in a greater linking of foreign and defence policy. This would be in line with the Clausewitzian argument of military force becoming the extension of foreign and economic policy.[9]

Thirdly, there will continue to be internal and external political pressures for the use of military intervention. The United States has historically called upon its West European allies for joint action when its own interests have been involved.[10] If the strong West European commitment to providing military personnel is to remain, then as the United Nations (UN) continues to expand both the scale and realm of its operations, the requisite force contributions from Western European will rise. In addition, the role of internal politics has an increasing influence as foreign and domestic policy become more entwined. In particular, domestic public opinion coloured by the media has an important role to play *vis-à-vis* the humanitarian intervention element within military intervention.[11]

Fourthly, the threat posed by the spread of ballistic missiles and weapons of mass destruction encourage the use of preventative military action. Concern has already been expressed in this area, notably in Britain's 1993 Defence Estimates.[12]

Fifthly, there is a growing fear from the ramifications of ethnic unrest in the states bordering Western Europe. Europe's experience of World War 1 has heightened this fear particularly in the Balkans.[13] Thus the current approach to the situation in Bosnia, for example, is very much one of containment and the enforcement of a *cordon sanitaire*.

The Analytical approach taken

Within Western Europe there is a relative galaxy of rival inter-governmental organizations for the coordination of policy. The Conference on Security and Cooperation in Europe (CSCE), the North Atlantic Treaty Organization (NATO), the Western European Union (WEU) and the European Union (EU) have all been suggested as potential frameworks for future consolidated action. However, such an institutional approach is beset with problems.

The CSCE has undertaken a number of steps to facilitate joint decision-making. This has included the creation of a permanent secretariat and Office of Free Elections in Prague, a Crisis Prevention Centre in Vienna and the establishment of the Assembly of Europe based on the Council of Europe.[14] It is, however, relatively poorly equipped to coordinate and command any joint action. The North Atlantic Cooperation Council meeting of 4 June 1992, therefore, recognized NATO as an appropriate body for the CSCE to use on a case-by case basis.[15]

The problems of relying upon the EU for joint action have also been recognized and the role has been delegated to the WEU.[16] The WEU has the advantage of relatively few members which means that the achievement of a consensus for concerted action is easier. Its members have agreed to create a number of permanent institutions such as a Planning Cell and the WEU Space Centre to facilitate joint action. This decision has been reinforced by the designation of a number of military units for its use.[17] In addition, its members' cooperation within NATO has provided a bank of experience which can be drawn upon.

NATO, like the WEU, has the advantages of permanently established institutions and designated military forces committed to it. Its membership is more substantial and it includes the United States whose power projection capability is unsurpassed.[18] Moreover, the longevity of NATO's survival has enhanced its credibility.

Thus any institutional approach needs to centre upon the WEU and NATO as the institutional tool for collective action. In both of these the decision-making process relies on the collective decision of the member states and their individual interests. Therefore an analysis needs to concentrate upon the decision-making process and thus on the states themselves since Western Europe, at least in the short-term, remains a collection of sovereign states attempting to pursue their own national rather than corporate goals. They are thus susceptible to individual rivalries and division.

Within this collection of individual states, four distinct groups can be identified in terms of their policy towards, and participation, in military intervention. The first group, dubbed here the *Old Sheriffs* has been defined in terms of their ability to undertake and sustain independent military intervention politically and militarily. Their interests can be summarized in terms of the preservation of the *status quo* in Europe and the wider world by avoiding such action. The second group, the *Young Guns*, has been defined by its members' ability and potential desire to initiate military intervention in pursuit of their own nation interests without possessing the ability to complete such action independently. The third group, the *Extras*, are a collection of states who can neither initiate nor undertake military intervention. However, they are linked by the reorganization of their military respective forces to support intervention and their preparedness to contribute to such action. They are also identified by their position within both NATO and the WEU which allows them to arbitrate between the preceding two groups. The fourth group, the *Fringe*, is characterized by its inability to support or initiate military intervention or have any influence upon the decision-making of the other groups.

The Old Sheriffs

The first group currently comprises France and Britain. These two states are the only ones within the region with the capability to undertake military intervention on their own. Admittedly this capability is somewhat limited in comparison to that of the United States. However, both deploy a comprehensive range of intervention hardware supported by an appropriate level of command, control and communications capability. Furthermore, both states are unique within Western Europe in that they possess a strategic nuclear capability. More importantly they each occupy a permanent seat on the United Nations Security Council which provides them with the ability to justify any actions to a limited extent and prevent condemnatory action from the rest of the United Nations. In addition, both retain limited colonial territories for which they are responsible and which provide bases from which they can project military force.[19]

The possession of a nuclear deterrent and a permanent seat on the UN Security Council have provided Britain and France with the ability to influence matters to a far greater extent than their economic size would indicate. With the collapse of the Soviet Union and the broadening of security beyond mere military strength, both Britain and France have had to face the potential consequences of the end of the Cold War *status quo*.

Britain

During the Cold War British foreign and defence policy was concentrated upon dealing with the perceived threat posed by the Soviet Union. This led successive governments to emphasize Britain's membership of NATO, to preserve the *special relationship* with the United States and to retain a strategic nuclear deterrent.[20] The end of the Cold War and the collapse of the Soviet Union has found Britain with what has been described by William Wallace as: [a] Government which has no clear sense of its place in the world or its foreign policy priorities ...[21] This position is primarily due to internal conflicts within the Government. At a time when Willem Van Eekelen has argued that defence policy will return to its position as the servant of foreign and economic policy, in Britain foreign and economic policy have become diametrically opposed.[22] The British Foreign Secretary, Douglas Hurd has tended to adopt the van Eekelen line. *The Times* leader column noted: 'Mr. Hurd is clear that Britain, which exports twice as much of its gross domestic product as Japan, cannot neglect its interest in "a safer and more decent world": anarchy interferes with trade, generally involves appalling human rights abuse and unchecked, has a tendency to lead to wider conflict.'[23] Whilst Douglas Hurd went as far as saying

> [s]ome problems - state-sponsored terrorism, for example, or the proliferation of ballistic missiles - may prick our skin more than our consciences. But, if we really want a world that is more secure, more prosperous and more stable, then humanitarian problems can be just as threatening and must be seen not just as a moral issue, but as a potential security threat as well.[24]

This speech, however, was rapidly countered by the Secretary of State for Defence, Malcolm Rifkind, who referred to the national interest along more traditional conservative lines.[25]

Rifkind has found himself in a very difficult position. Britain's economic weakness and large public sector borrowing requirement has encouraged the Treasury to demand sweeping cuts in Britain's defence budget. In late 1993 reports in the press about alleged top-heaviness of the Royal Air Force in comparison to other air forces such as Israel's have highlighted the prominence being given to the need to make defence cuts.[26] This was confirmed by the Chiefs of the Defence Staff who are known to have used their right of access to the Prime Minister to ensure their views were heard.[27] The Chief of the Air Staff, Sir Michael Graydon, went as far as publicly airing this view before making a hasty retraction.[28] Consequently,

Malcolm Rifkind has been forced to make significant defence reductions beyond those announced in the Options for Change review.[29] The cancellation of the tactical air-to-surface missile is a recent example.[30]

The reorganization of defence policy has, however, left the Trident programme virtually untouched.[31] Not only has Trident been viewed by the Conservative Party as its sacred cow, but it has also traditionally been used as one of Britain's justifications for her permanent seat on the UN Security Council. Thus the bulk of Britain's defence cuts have fallen upon her conventional forces. With the advent of NATO's new strategic concept, a major reorganization of NATO's command structure has been undertaken.[32] This has resulted in Britain's loss of its one major command.[33] It led the British Government to successfully pursue command of the new Allied Command Europe Rapid Reaction Corps (ARRC) at Germany's expense and the commitment of a significant number of troops resulted. This led to the observation that

> [t]he ARRC presents great potential for a crisis in Britain's ability to sustain its current level of commitments. Having fought to take a leading role in the ARRC, Britain finds itself committed to commanding that force and to providing two divisions. The corollary of this commitment is that whenever the ARRC is deployed, British troops will be first on call. However, as any discussion of army overstretch makes clear, units allocated to the ARRC are likely to be committed to other roles. The first occasion on which the ARRC is called upon - which given a deteriorating security environment, could be in the near future - could also precipitate a crisis for the Government.[34]

To cover the high cost of the ARRC commitment Rifkind has had to achieve short term savings by delaying a number of re-equipment programmes including the replacement of the amphibious warfare ships thereby reducing Britain's seaborne projection forces.[35] As a result, the Ministry of Defence has been loathed to undertake further overseas commitments. Amongst its West European allies Britain was noticeable in failing to send ground troops to Somalia when the United States called for assistance.[36]

This position has been heavily criticized by the House of Commons Select Committee on Defence who concluded that

> [t]he United Kingdom's position in the world owes much to its defence expertise, and the level of national commitment to defence. **The maintenance of that position is at risk if the United Kingdom does not respond to the international peacekeeping requirement on a scale**

> **commensurate with membership of the Security Council, let alone the legitimate demands of UK public opinion.**[37]

The threat to Britain's permanent seat on the UN Security Council is of real concern. Whilst for budgetary reasons the British Government will attempt to minimize the level of future military deployments overseas, it is certain to continue to participate in the majority of UN or European sponsored actions in order to justify the retention of its permanent seat. This policy has been clear over Yugoslavia. It was noticeable that Britain was one of only two EU states to vote against the EU sending military forces as peacekeepers during the initial break-up of the Yugoslav Federation. Yet it later managed to pull together an infantry force for the escort of humanitarian aid in Bosnia.[38]

The problem of conflicting views on the future use of military intervention between the Foreign Office and the Treasury assisted by the Ministry of Defence is further confused by the Armed Services themselves. Whilst none appear to be particularly concerned about the relative merits of retaining this power projection capability, all are attempting to play on the perceived link between Britain's participation in United Nations peacekeeping missions and the preservation of her status as one of the permanent members.

Thus the Army has managed to reduce the level of its cuts by focusing on the problems of providing suitable infantry forces for UN missions given the necessity of internal security operations in Northern Ireland and manning the ARRC.[39] The Royal Air Force (RAF) has managed to protect its most important programme, the European Fighter Aircraft, by highlighting its role in providing air cover and support to any use of military force.[40] However, the long-term retention of No.2 Group within Germany appears doubtful. The relative success of both the Army and RAF is clear from the recent Defence Estimates whose cuts were primarily aimed at the Royal Navy.[41]

What is noticeably new within the Royal Navy is a move from a concern about destroyer and frigate numbers to one stressing the importance of core units. The Royal Navy appears to be returning to an emphasis upon the big ships. Thus only two days after the announcement of the 1993 defence cuts the Navy was reported to be considering the reintroduction of the large conventional carrier into its inventory.[42] The only justification for this and the replacement of the amphibious fleet can be the preservation of a naval power projection capability beyond the range of UK bases.

The return of inter-service fighting for scarce defence resources will lead to an emphasis by the individual services upon their power projection capabilities in order to substantiate themselves. However, the pressure from the Treasury for still further cuts can only lead to a diminution in the capability of the armed force. In retaining a limited power projection capability the British Government will allow itself the potential to utilize such a capability.

With the ultimate decision remaining with the Prime Minister and his Cabinet, the role of public opinion has an increasingly pro-active role to play. Relatively poor public interest in Somalia allowed the Government to make only a minor contribution whilst the recent *Operation Irma* indicated the responsiveness of the key decision-makers to public opinion.[43]

France

The other member of the *Old Sheriffs* group is France who now finds herself with a right-wing government and a left-wing President. Although the President has traditionally been responsible for foreign policy, this is likely to be increasingly challenged. Historically French post-war policy has been based on France's unique place in the world with the twin aims of leading European affairs and retaining an influence in world affairs. In Europe, France has been fortunate in its position as one of the four major victor states responsible for Germany the other three Great Powers allowed France to join them. This has provided a degree of political superiority over Germany which was further reinforced by the preservation of a strategic nuclear force. On the world stage France has retained its permanent seat on the Security Council and sought to retain a military presence world-wide via its dependent territories.[44]

However, since the end of the Cold War and following German re-unification this has all changed. France's aims of counter-balancing Germany and retaining a world role are under threat. The end of the Cold War has resulted in reduced importance being attached to the possession of nuclear weapons whilst reunification of Germany has resulted in a loss of French political superiority. Instead, the superior size of the German economy has led to a shift of the balance of power within Western Europe. Furthermore, the rapid transition of NATO from a Cold War Alliance to a potential military instrument of the CSCE has left France with little say in NATO at a time when Germany is having greater influence.[45]

This French problem of counter-balancing Germany in the next few years will have important implications for military intervention. The policy to date has been geared towards integrating Germany further within the European political and economic institutions for fear of any renationalization of German security and defence policy.[46] This accounts for the creation of the Eurocorps as a military force and France's support for Maastricht. Such integration has been beset by problems such as those of the European exchange rate mechanism.[47]

This has led France to seek a partial return to NATO. The new defence minister, François Léotard, has made reference to France adopting an approach similar to Spain which involves active participation in the various planning committees of NATO without an actual commitment of forces.[48] This would be one way to counter the growing German influence within NATO and have a say in the latter's decisions regarding its use of military force. However, the rapidity of NATO's reorganization of its command appointments has pre-empted any major French involvement. It is also noticeable that the traditional French calls for an end to the United States perceived dominance of NATO have become less evident. The French now view the US presence in Europe as a means of limiting German influence. Thus the French President overruled his Defence Minister's decision not to send troops to Somalia in order to give encouragement to the continued involvement of the US in world affairs.[49] French support for the WEU continues to be strong with emphasis being placed on the organization's future peace-making role.[50] Furthermore the WEU provides a safety net against a US withdrawal from Europe, French efforts have resulted in the WEU setting up a space centre training facility at Torrejon in Spain.[51]

France's view of itself as a world power continues and is clearly reflected in her defence budget. Unlike the majority of her neighbours, the French Government has not sought to make stringent force cutbacks but to continue the programmes they already have.[52] They have consequently chosen to stretch-out the programmes as a temporary means of covering the expenditure deficit that exists.[53] However, the military's performance in the Gulf War highlighted a number of weaknesses in France's intervention capability which have placed further demands on the country's overloaded defence budget.[54]

In marked similarity to Britain, France has found herself committed to a number of new deployments overseas in support of various UN missions resulting in considerable over-stretching of its forces.[55] Britain's example of withdrawing from some of its overseas bases and the double and treble-hatting of individual units has largely been ignored by France and the continued policy of the world view would seem to be unsustainable. Yet over the last year France has slightly increased her overseas garrisons whilst significantly increasing her involvement in UN missions.[56] Consequently the French Government have announced an increase in defence spending for next year of 3.6 per cent.[57] However, the French Government, like it's British counterpart, is still faced by one of the worst recessions in decades matched to increasing demands. It will, therefore, be forced to reduce its defence establishment further inevitably affecting the French intervention capability.[58]

Britain and France

As permanent members both countries will also face pressure from the international community for the provision of forces for United Nations tasks. For France this situation will be further exacerbated by her own on-going fears of Germany.[59] These will encourage her to follow German policy in an attempt to retain a degree of control over Germany and thereby become involved in interventions that are not in France's own national interest.

Perhaps the most ironic thing is the similarity of French and British interests. Conservative Euro-Sceptics and Gaullist diehards may reject such notions but the preservation of the *status quo* which they both want has a far greater chance of success through cooperation than from hostile rhetoric and independent actions.[60] However, mutual distrust and misunderstanding will not lead to another *entente cordiale* but to further disharmony.

The Young Guns

This group has been defined in terms of its ability to force the initiation of West European military intervention without either the military or political capability to sustain such action independently. Thus the group comprises Germany, Italy and Greece.

Germany

The reunification of Germany and the end of the Cold War has brought about a change in Germany's position *vis-à-vis* the rest of Western Europe. With a population of 79 million, the world's fourth largest economy, and geographically at the heart of Europe, Germany will inevitably play a leading role in future political, economic and strategic affairs.[61] Whilst the threat from the east has receded from Britain and France's point of view, concern still remains within Germany. Germany's immediate action after re-unification was to establish fresh relations with Poland, Hungary and Czechoslovakia in an attempt to help provide support for the new democratic regimes.[62] In addition, she has sought to maintain NATO and involve France more by encouraging the WEU. Germany was therefore a prime mover in the creation of the Eurocorps and a move towards closer European integration. This policy, together with the continued decline of the Anglo-American special relationship has given the United States encouragement to reduce its military presence in Europe further.[63] As a result the initial German moves towards France and greater European integration have been offset by a re-emphasis upon NATO and the United States. This view has been confirmed by defence sources in Bonn, for whom

> [i]f NATO were orientated toward foreign intervention, the alliance would offer Germany not only the indispensable US military infrastructure for long-range mobility but also the right framework for German forces to prepare themselves for rapid action in unpredictable foreign crises.[64]

German moves towards the need for future military intervention have been linked with it's moves towards achieving a permanent seat on the UN Security Council.[65] Any belief that Germany's economic might would entitle her to a permanent seat were dashed by the Gulf War where Germany's support for the Coalition was severely criticized. The lesson drawn by Germany's political leaders from the conflict was that economic support on its own was insufficient and that an actual military commitment was required if Germany were to receive due recognition for her help.[66] Thus in the immediate aftermath of the Gulf War Germany sent troops to Iran to assist in the distribution of humanitarian aid to the Kurds.[67] More recently Germany has begun the deployment of a much larger force to Somalia to help underwrite its application for a permanent seat on the Security Council.[68]

However, whilst the German leadership has sought to enhance Germany's say in military interventions it has reduced its ability to provide the requisite forces for such a policy. The huge financial costs of re-unification have presented Germany with a severe fiscal burden. To help meet this the Government has sought to make significant savings in defence. The *Bundeswehr* has been forced to reduce the state of readiness of a large number of units leaving few available for rapid deployment elsewhere.[69] Furthermore, programmes such as the Eurofighter 2000 are under severe threat of cancellation.[70] This will further hamper the deployment of suitably equipped military units in the intervention role.

This position is further exacerbated by the Social Democrats' attempts to block Germany's deployment of troops overseas.[71] Their unsuccessful action reflects public concern for the need to concentrate upon economic problems at home rather than on costly financial commitments abroad.

Thus on the domestic front Germany's position is against military intervention but her foreign policy goals include the achievement of a permanent seat on the UN Security Council. In the short-term at least, the domestic front appears to have the upper hand with the German announcement of the withdrawal of her troops from Somalia.[72]

Italy

The Italian Government, like the German, has as it's goal a permanent seat on the UN Security Council. Italy has also begun to contribute to United Nations operations, most notably in her former colonial territory of Somalia. Italy's position, however, is much weaker then Germany's or Japan's. Without the support of the United States as a sponsor, Italy is in no better a position than Brazil or India in achieving this goal.

Within Italy the dispatch of conscript troops to Somalia has proven to be very unpopular. This has been exacerbated by the disagreements between US and Italian military forces within Somalia and the UN campaign against the Italian commander, General Bruno Loi.[73] Furthermore, the internal crisis that marks current Italian politics means that their influence on military intervention in the short-term is similar to that of the *Extras* described below.

It is Italy's geographical position that will encourage it in future to call for collective pre-emptive action in response to problems in the Balkans. The Italian Government has already had to provide for refugees fleeing from Albania. The current problems in Bosnia could easily escalate leading to further problems on a far larger scale.

In addition, Italy's proximity to the North African coast means that it will be one of the first states to be threatened by the proliferation of ballistic missile technology in the region. Any real threat to the Italian mainland will encourage the Italian Government to seek support in the pre-emptive use of force to nullify such threats.

Greece

Greece is in an even more vulnerable geographic position than Italy *vis-à-vis* the Balkans. In particular, ethnic tensions within the former Yugoslav republic of Macedonia may well encourage a Greek reciprocal response to any Albanian intervention.[74] The current West European policy of containment looks exceedingly fragile and a Greek initiative could easily result in West European intervention.

Greek tensions with Turkey also remain over the Aegean Islands and the potential for war is invariably high in the region. This concern is evident by the large-scale Greek and Turkish rearmament programmes which have benefited from the redistribution of arms within NATO as a result of the CFE Treaty.[75] The United States has traditionally kept the peace between these two. If the United States continues its withdrawal from Europe then the West Europeans may have to fill this vacuum.

Andreas Papandreou's election as Prime Minister of Greece has caused widespread concern within the EU and NATO.[76] He waged his electoral campaign on an irredentist nationalist ticket referring to the need to restore Greek dignity and a non-negotiable line of defence.[77] Furthermore, Greek membership of the WEU provides a further platform for Greek nationalism to be emphasized at Turkey's expense.

Thus Germany, Italy and Greece all have the potential for initiating a West European decision in favour of military intervention. Whilst their aims may be different they can still pull in the same direction and thus reinforce the decision to intervene. Individually, they are all incapable of undertaking significant action but are all capable of initiating such action and leaving the rest of Western Europe to pick up the pieces.

The Extras

This group is defined by the preparedness of its members to participate in concerted European military intervention whilst possessing neither the ability to initiate such action nor to undertake such action independently. As members of both the EU and NATO the members of this group have a collective ability to arbitrate between the *Old Sheriffs* and *Young Guns* within these organizations. The members are also distinct in undertaking the most drastic reorganization of their respective military forces in favour of an interventionalist capability. All contributed naval forces to the recent Gulf War and have sizeable forces with various UN operations.[78] The group thus comprises Belgium, Denmark, the Netherlands and Spain.

Belgium

As part of the post-cold war defence reductions the Belgium Government have decided to end conscription and rely solely on volunteer recruitment.[79] This will facilitate the dispatch of troops abroad by reducing any domestic hostility to the use of conscripts. The army, in particular, has re-orientated its forces to the collective role by committing its sole division to the new Eurocorps and its Para-Commando brigade to NATO's Multinational division (Central) (MND (Cent)).[80]

Furthermore, Belgium's long-standing involvement in NATO's integrated command structure makes it a prime candidate for the *Old Sheriffs* or *Young Guns* to call upon for assistance. The Belgium Government has already shown itself ready to participate in UN missions with the deployment of infantry battalions to Somalia and Croatia.[81]

Denmark

The Danish Government perhaps surprisingly has gone one step further than the Belgians in deciding to create a 4,500 strong brigade staffed by volunteers for the purposes of out of area deployment.[82] However, Denmark is a noticeable exception in this group by its non-membership of the WEU and failure to commit any major units to the ARRC.[83]

Netherlands

Within this group the Dutch have gone the furthest in adapting its forces towards the role of military intervention. They have also decided to completely abolish conscription and have a regular army of 70,000.[84] Holland will also commit a brigade to MND (Cent) and reinforce its presence in the UK/NL Amphibious Force.[85] The Dutch have sought to improve their ability to deploy military force by air by the decision to purchase tanker aircraft and modernize its transport fleet.[86] Furthermore, the Dutch have deployed aircraft to Italy in support of Operation Deny Flight and Disciplined Guard, support troops to Cambodia and also a marine battalion.[87]

Spain

The Spanish, like the French, are not involved in NATO's integrated military structure. Spain has, however, decided to join the Eurocorps which indicates her efforts towards increasing her European credentials.[88] At the same time, Spain's geographical proximity to North Africa and her historical links with the region make her a prime candidate for the dispatch of any interventionist forces to the region. Furthermore, the location of the WEU's space centre in Spain will become of increasing importance to the members of the *Old Sheriffs* and *Young Guns* as they move towards the greater pooling of intelligence collection facilities.[89] Spain does have the problem of an army almost totally made up of conscripts which would severely limit its deployment capabilities. This was particularly clear when Spain was called upon to increase its force levels in Bosnia.[90]

Role and Influence

Whilst France and Britain are looking for a period of retrenchment and the preservation of the *status quo*, Germany, Italy and Greece will be conducting a far more adventurous policy. This will inevitably lead to a clash of opinion with France and Britain. Thus the balance held in the WEU and NATO by the Extras will be crucial in the short-term. In addition, as the European forces increase their moves towards integrated forces the ability of individual states to take action will be reduced since they will be relying upon others for the provision of full logistical support.

In the near future, the armed forces from the *Extras* appear to be the most suited towards military intervention if they were to receive the appropriate support from the other states. They do face the problem of a lack of inherent portability and logistical support but this could be overcome by support from France, Britain or the United States. Furthermore, the latter three would find the participation of the Extras in any military intervention politically advantageous since it would help to disperse any criticism levelled by the rest of the international community as well as helping to placate domestic concerns.

The Fringe

The last group encompasses all the West European states which have not been included in the other three categories. Its membership is defined by those states who lack the ability either to initiate, undertake or influence military intervention. Thus it includes Austria, Eire, Finland, Norway, Portugal, Sweden and Switzerland. The majority of these states have been active participants in UN peacekeeping operations. Their armed forces have been largely geared towards the task of Home Defence and are not suited to the task of military intervention to which they have shown little interest. It is noticeable that the Scandinavian countries are still concerned with a residual threat from the East and have therefore not undertaken the major defence cuts of other West European states.[91]

The role of the *Fringe* is, therefore, largely superficial. It is unlikely to be able to contribute any significant practical help towards a military intervention whilst its political influence is minor. The states of the *Fringe* are thus largely reduced to the role of bystanders in West European policy on military intervention.

The Future

The composition of the four groups has so far been based on a relatively short-term outlook. However, as time passes by there will be changes in individual state policy and in their relationship to one another. It is therefore necessary to establish some parameters which govern the movement of individual states between the groups.

The groups themselves will remain defined as at present with one exception. If the UN Security Council is reformed to include Germany then the membership of the *Old Sheriffs* is likely to include a state without a nuclear deterrent or significant military capability. Instead Germany's key role within Europe and its economic strength will lead the Old Sheriffs group to be defined purely in terms of the retention of the status quo with a much more limited military intervention capability than is possessed at present.

The *Old Sheriffs* may lose Britain to the *Extras*. The future of Britain's permanent seat is in some doubt whilst her continuing military reductions are severely weakening any independent intervention capability.[92] Britain's traditional close ties with the United States are in rapid decline and thus the role of arbiter between Western Europe and the United States has no future.[93] This decline is reinforced by the lack of government perception of Britain's place in the world.

The expansion of Europe eastwards by the various institutions has significant ramifications for the composition of the *Young Guns*. NATO is already discussing whether Poland, Hungary and the Czech Republic should be admitted.[94] In the long term, the further expansion of NATO and the EU seems certain. Any such expansion would present Western Europe with a variety of problems. Unresolved ethnic tension and border disputes threaten to lead to conflagration within Eastern Europe. Thus the majority of these East European states, if they succeed in becoming members of either the EU, WEU or NATO will gain automatic entry into the Young Guns group.

Italy is likely to become a member of the *Extras* whilst Denmark and Belgium seem likely to join the *Fringe*. Italy's attempts at raising its standing in the world are under threat from the continuing domestic political turmoil within the country. Increasing regionalism and extremism have encouraged politicians to focus on internal order rather than exterior threats. If this situation remains Italy's position within the *Young Guns* can only weaken and lead to a shift towards the *Fringe*. Belgium and Denmark's membership of the *Fringe* is also only tenuous. A continuation in defence reductions will encourage their exile to the Extras.

Conclusion

Clearly there is no uniform West European view regarding military intervention at present. There are three groups within Europe that have an interest in this aspect of governmental policy and they are at odds with each other. A consensus will only be achieved when the shift in the balance of power within the region is settled. At present the differences in view between the *Old Sheriffs* and the *Young Guns* are partially settled by the voting power of the *Extras* within the WEU and NATO.

This all has a number of implications for military intervention within the context of Western Europe. In the short-term whilst Germany seeks to obtain a permanent seat on the United Nations or if the situation in the Balkans escalates there is likely to be a much greater call for military intervention. However, if the United States is not involved in such an operation, the practical support of Britain or France will be necessary as West European military force capabilities are being reduced. Judging from recent experience the withholding of support is unlikely since both wish to maintain their status as Permanent Members of the Security Council and placate the *Young Guns*.

In the longer-term the expansion of Europe threatens to restrict the influence of individual states and a more collective policy within these groups is likely. The increase in the number of states and the lack of a common foreign and defence policy can only cloud the decision-making process further within the EU, NATO or WEU.

What is therefore most likely to occur is an increased incidence of military intervention by West European states under a compromised agenda. Such an agenda will almost certainly lead to problems of implementation and therefore be contrary to the ideals of what military intervention is about, i.e., the temporary use of overwhelming force. Thus the drawn out situations in Somalia and Bosnia are likely to be repeated more frequently as West European forces are deployed piecemeal in worsening situations.

Notes

1. House of Commons, Defence Committee, Fourth Report: United Kingdom Peacekeeping and Intervention Forces: report together with the proceedings of the Committee relating to the report, minutes of evidence and memoranda, House of Commons papers 1992-93 188, London, HMSO, 1993, p.v.

2. cf.Boutros-Ghali, Boutros, Agenda for Peace, New York, USA, UN, 1992.

3. Freedman, Lawrence, 'Recasting European Security' in Brassey's Defence Yearbook 1993, edited by the Centre for Defence Studies, King's College, London, Brassey's (UK) Ltd., 1993, p.12.

4. In a recent article Philip Sabin argues that whilst defence missions have expanded beyond protecting British territory they have also become more discretionary with frustration and embarrassment often being the sole result of any failure. Sabin, Philip A.G., 'British Defence Policy beyond 'Options for Change', in International Affairs, vol.69, no.2, April 1993, p.271.

5. cf.Delors, Jacques, 'European integration and security', in Survival, vol.XXXIII, no.2, March/April 1991, p.100.

6. The operations in Northern Iraq and Somalia were essentially military interventions with a humanitarian goal. Cambodia, Mozambique and Croatia have been essentially peacekeeping tasks along traditional United Nations lines whilst the intervention in Bosnia was in support of aid convoys.

7. IISS, Strategic Survey 1992-93, London, Brassey's for the IISS, 1993, p.209.

8. For a fuller examination of this argument see John Roberts article, 'Oil, the Military and the Gulf War of 1991', in The RUSI Journal, vol.136, no.1, Spring 1991, pp.11-16. In contrast Dilip Hiro in Desert Shield to Desert Storm: the Second Gulf War, London, HarperCollins*Publishers*, 1992, emphasizes the level of Kuwaiti overseas investment. Whilst Kenneth R. Timmerman in The Death Lobby: How the West armed Iraq, New York, USA, Houghton Mifflin Co., 1991 argues that it was to do with the West's over-arming of Iraq and the imbalance created in the balance of power in the region.

9. Eekelen, Willem van, 'WEU on the way back to Brussels', speech given at Chatham House on 22 September 1992, p.3., reprinted in WEU Press Review, no.161, 24 September 1992.

10. In the deployment to the Gulf and Somalia the West European countries were the first to follow the US in announcing the deployment of their forces.

11. The role of the media in influencing public opinion has been clearly evident in Britain with the recent airlift of wounded from Bosnia. Operation Irma, the aerial evacuation of a nuber of seriously wounded individuals from Bosnia was due largely to the media focus on the plight of one child.

12. 'Statement on the Defence Estimates 1993 - Defending Our Future', Cmnd.2270, London, HMSO, 1993, p.10.

13. Apart from its' current notoriety in the media at present, Sarajevo was also the site of the assassination of the Austrian Archduke Francis and his wife on 28 June 1914 which provided the spark that resulted in World War 1.

14. Hype-Price, Adrian, 'Future security systems for Europe' in Security and Strategy in the new Europe, edited by Colin McInnes, London, Routledge, 1992, p.50.

15. 'North Atlantic Council gets under way:European identity and peacekeeping', Atlantic News, no.2,429, 5 June 1992, p.1.

16. Western European Union Council of Ministersw, Petersberg Declaration, Bonn, Germany, 19 June 1992.

17. The forces committed to the WEU comprise:

Fr/Be/Ge/Sp	Eurocorps
UK/NL	UK/NL Amphibious Force
UK/Be/NL/Ge	MND (Central)

18. Note the scale of the United States contribution to the recent Gulf War. See Survival, vol.XXXIII, no.3, May/June 1991.

19. For example, the French were able to use their military bases Djibouti in support of their actions in the Gulf and Somalia whilst the British have made extensive use of their facilities at Gibraltar and Cyprus as staging posts.

20. Croft, Stuart and Williams, Phil, 'The United Kingdom' in Security with nuclear weapons? Different perspectives on national security, edited by Regina Cowen Karp, Oxford, Oxford University Press for SIPRI, 1991, p.147.

21. cf.Wallace, William, 'Britain's search for a new role in the world', in The Observer, no.10,531, 15 August 1993, p.16.

22. Eekelen, Willem van, op.cit., p.3.

23. cf.'Hurd's troubled world', in The Times, 29 January 1993.

24. cf.Hurd, Douglas, 'Foreign policy and international security', in The RUSI Journal, vol.137, no.6, December 1992, p.2.

25. Rifkind, Malcolm, 'Peacekeeping or peacemaking? Implications and prospects', in The RUSI Journal, vol.138, no.2, April 1993, pp.1-6.

26. Bellamy, Christopher, 'Why the RAF has so many, and Israel so few', The Independent, no.2,189, 25 October 1993, p.6.

27. Brown, Colin, 'Chief of Staff protest to major over cuts', The Independent, no.2,194, 30 October 1993, p.2.

28. Almond, Peter, & Jones, George, 'RAF chief apologises to Rifkind', in The Daily Telegraph, no.43,042, 10 November 1993, pp.1-2.

29. The Chancellor of the Exchequer's Autumn budget has resulted in further defence cuts of £1.8 bn over the next few years. Bellamy, Christopher, 'Extra front-line soldiers and tanks promised', in The Independent, no.2,222, 2 December 1993, p.13.

30. Barrie, Douglas, 'Nuclear conflicts', in Flight International, vol.144, no.4,393, 27 October - 2 November 1993, p.18.

31. The recent announcement of cuts in Trident warhead numbers appear to have more to do with the problems at the Aldermaston plant than a desire for arms control. Fairhall, David, 'Aldermaston plant delay a factor in decision to scale down warheads', in The Guardian, 16 November 1993, p.2.

32. Agreed at the NATO Heads of State and Government meeting in Rome, 7-8 November 1991, NATO Press Communique S-1 (91) 85, 7 November 1991.

33. 'Statement on the Defence Estimates 1993 - Defending our Future', op.cit., p.10.

34. cf.George, Bruce, & Ryan, Nick, 'Options for Change: a political critique', in Brassey's Defence Yearbook 1993, edited by the Centre for Defence Studies, op.cit., p.44.

35. House of Commons Defence Committee, op.cit., p.xiv.

36. Britain's contribution consisted merely of providing Hercules aircraft to support the airlift of humanitarian aid to the more remote regions of Somalia. Ibid., p.xxiii.

37. cf.Ibid., p.xxvi. In bold in original report.

38. Schmidt, Peter, The Special Franco-German Relationship in the 1990s, Chaillot Papers no.8, Institute for Security Studies, 1993, p.29.

39. The Army succeeded in having its strength increased by 3,000 men resulting in the retention of two infantry battalions. Statement on the Defence Estimates 1993 - Defending our Future, op.cit., p.11. The army also succeeded in ordering a further 259 Challenger 2 main battle tanks. Bellamy, op.cit., p.13.

40. Cook, Nick, 'The fight begins for the few', in Jane's Defence Weekly, vol.18, no.10, 5 September 1992, p.49.

41. The £1.05 bn reduction in the defence budget was primarily met by the decission to sell or mothball the Upholder class conventional submarines. Wood, Nicholas, & Evans, Michael, 'Backbench Tories draw the line on defence cuts', in The Times, no.64,689, 6 July 1993, p.1.

42. Elliott, Simon, 'UK plans for return of fast-jet carriers', in Flight International, vol.144, no.4,378, 14-20 July 1993, p.5.

43. Savill Annika, 'Sarajevo's symbol of agony flies in', in The Independent, no.2,124, 10 August 1993, p.1.

44. Venet, Daniel, 'The dilemma of French foreign policy', in International Affairs, vol.68, no.4, October 1992, p.656.

45. Schmidt, op.cit., p.8.

46. Ibid., p.12.

47. Eyal, Jonathan, 'France's facade begins to crumble', in The Independent, no.2,117, 2 August 1993, p.18.

48. Riding, Alan, 'France seeks a greater role in NATO', in The International Herald Tribune, 13 May 1993.

49. Buchan, David, & Rawsthorn, Alice, 'Minister *sans frontieres*', in The Financial Times, 22 January 1993.

50. Mauthner, Robert, 'WEU to be given military units for peacekeeping role', in The Financial Times, 21 June 1992.

51. The centre will initially use commercially available imagery which will later be replaced by that supplied by the Spanish-French-Itakian *Helios* programme. 'WEU: Torrejon Satellite Centre inaugurated', Atlantic News, no.2,521, 30 April 1993, p.4.

52. Schmidt, op.cit., p.8.

53. Lewis, J.A.C., 'Key projects threatened as France weighs up its options', in Jane's Defence Weekly, vol.20, no.4, 24 July 1993, p.19.

54. To fulfil its long-range transport deficit the French Government have purchased four Airbus A310-300s to replace the ageing DC-8s. 'France to buy two used A310-300s', in Flight International, vol.142, no.4,341, 21-27 October 1992, p.20.

55. France has temporarily hired additional tanker aircraft from the United States to support its deployments in Turkey and Saudi Arabia. 'France hires three tankers from US', in Flight International, vol.143, no.4,363, 20-26 January 1993, p.12.

56. IISS, The Military Balance, 1992-93 & 1993-94, London, IISS, 1992 and 1993.

57. Lewis, J.A.C., 'French spending rise secures major items', in Jane's Defence Weekly, vol.20, no.16, 16 October 1993, p.15.

58. Lewis, op.cit., p.19.

59. Thatcher, Margaret, The Downing Street Years, London, HarperCollins*Publishers*, first edition 1993, p.796.

60. Savill, Annika, 'Anglo-French spat masks wider policy harmony', in The Independent, no.1,987, 3 March 1993, p.10.

61. Van Orden, Geoffrey, 'The *Bundeswehr* in transition', in Survival, vol.XXXIII, no.4, July/August 1991, p.352.

62. Ibid., p.359.

63. Adams, James, 'That Special relationship', in The Sunday Times, 31 January 1993, pp.8-9.

64. cf.Flitchett, Joseph, 'Military sees new life in old Alliance', in The International Herald Tribune, 21 April 1993.

65. 'UN Security Council: Germany and Japan coordinate their requests for becoming permanent members', in Atlantic News, no.2,542, 9 July 1993, p.3.

66. Schmidt, op.cit, p.18.

67. Van Orden, op.cit., p.367.

68. Crawshaw, Steve, 'Germans reach Somalia', in The Independent, no.2,108, 22 July 1993, p.10.

69. Naumann, General Klaus, 'The role of the *Bundeswehr*, in a changing security environment', in The RUSI Journal, vol.137, no.5, October 1992, pp.13-14.

70. 'Germany reviews Eurofighter quota', in Flight International, vol.144, no.4,380, 28 July - 3 August 1993, p.4.

71. Gow, David, 'Bonn votes to send troops', in The Guardian, 3 July 1993, p.13.

72. 'Germans begin UNISOM pullout', in Jane's Defence Weekly, vol.20, no.23, 4 December 1993, p.5.

73. Johnston, Bruce, 'Italy's Somalia campaign reached high noon at Checkpoint Pasta', in The Sunday Times, no.8,813, 18 July 1991, p.21.

74. IISS, Strategic Survey 1992-93, London, IISS, first edition 1993, p.94.

75. IISS, The Military Balance 1992-93, op.cit., pp.13, 34 & 36.

76. Doyle, Leonard, 'EC and NATO wince at Papandreou victory', in The Independent, no.2,178, 12 October 1993, p.12.

77. Doyle, Leonard, 'Europe braced for return of Pasok', in The Independent, no.2,177, 11 October 1993, p.8.

78. For a complete order of battle for the Coalition forces see IISS, The Military Balance, 1991-92, London, IISS, 1991, pp.238-243.

79. IISS, The Military Balance, 1992-93, op.cit., p.33.

80. The Belgium commitment will be one mechanised division of 12,000 men. 'Eurocorps: Belgium decides to join' in Atlantic News, no.2,539, 30 July 1993, p.3. For the structure of both MND (Central) and NATO's RRC see IISS, The Military Balance, 1992-93, London, IISS, 1992, p.30.

81. IISS, The Military Balance, 1993-94, London, IISS, 1993.

82. 'Foreign service Army brigade to form', in Jane's Defence Weekly, vol.19, no.9, 27 February 1993, p.11.

83. IISS, The Military Balance, 1992-93, op.cit.

84. Atlantic News, no.2,513, 2 April 1993, p.2.

85. The Dutch have ordered an LPD to reinforce the capability of the UK/NL Amphibious Force. Lok, Joris Janssen, 'Royal Schelde chosedn for joint LPD team', in Jane's Defence Weekly, vol.19, no.21, 22 May 1993, p.12.

86. Hatch, Paul, 'World's Air Forces', in Flight International, vol.140, no.4,295, 27 November - 3 December 1991, p.57.

87. IISS, The Military Balance, 1993-94, London, IISS, 1993, pp.54-55.

88. Ing, David, 'Problems' for Spain despite its budget rise', in Jane's Defence Weekly, vol.20, no.18, 30 October 1993.

89. Doyle, Leonard, 'Security plans for brave new world of EU security', in The Independent, no.2,205, 12 November 1993, p.12.

90. Spain's army of 146,000 contains only 12,293 professionals. Hooper, John, 'Spain baulks at plea for 5,000 troops', in The Guardian, 10 May 1993.

91. For Finnish and Swedish defence policies see Jane's Defence Weekly, vol.20, no.18, 30 October 1993.

92. Savill, Annika, 'Britain off UN budget body', in The Independent, no.2,216, 25 November 1993, p.14.

93. Adams, James, 'Who do we believe as the special relationship is stretched', in The Sunday Times, no.8,827, 24 October 1993, p.17.

94. Marshall, Andrew, 'NATO denies bowing to Russian will', in The Independent, np.2,187, 22 October 1993, p.12.

5 Aspects of Intervention in the South

STUART CROFT AND ADRIAN TREACHER

Introduction

Violence in the South has been endemic, certainly since the traditional Great Powers began the process of decolonialization midway through the 20th century; the process began, of course, much earlier in Latin America.[1] Counts vary, but, according to one source, since 1945 '[t]here have been at least 80 wars ... killing somewhere between 15 and 30 million people'.[2] Clearly, the overwhelming majority of these cases have occurred in what subsequently became termed the developing world. This chapter attempts to identify some of the principal reasons which lie behind this seemingly endemic propensity to resort to violent intervention, be this through war or through other means, by breaking down the use of force into types, each with certain characteristics. Intervention is important in understanding the security politics of the South but, it will be argued, this is only true if intervention is defined in a wide sense; it is not enough to explain the high levels of violence by applying Northern interpretations of intervention, as these only have a limited relevance in the South.

While much of the violence is 'classical' state to state confrontation, this chapter will also highlight a distinctive Southern variation of intervention: that is, within a state. This chapter will, therefore, examine intervention in the South through the prism of three ideal types each of which will be examined in turn: Regional Power Intervention, Humanitarian Intervention and Internal Intervention. The complexity of the violence in the South will be demonstrated in that some of the case studies can be categorized by association with more than one of these ideal types.

This chapter is concerned only with intervention within the South. There is a great deal of literature on questions of the intervention of the Northern powers in the affairs of the South, whether this be for the creation of empires in the 18th and 19th centuries, the maintenance of those empires in the 19th and early 20th centuries, and the maintenance of economic interests or intervention to create or maintain allies in the South in the context of the Cold War confrontation. Only the latter of these forms of intervention will be of relevance to this analysis, which will focus on the much less well ploughed field of intervention by Southern states themselves. The Cold War superpower contest impacted on events in the South, but it was rarely the determining factor; the Superpowers may have provided the means for armed intervention, but the causes of intervention were distinctly Southern.

Traditional analyses in security studies would suggest that the most fruitful avenue of enquiry into the character of intervention would be to examine the nature of the national interests of the states involved. The use of the military instrument can be said to accord with rational calculations of the political gains that might be made either in terms of enhanced power, or in terms of greater security. For Clausewitz, resort to the military instrument is a rational policy option, one deeply embedded in political judgements.[3] For Morgenthau, politics is about the pursuit of power, and the use of the military instrument is one means to developing that power.[4] Thus, the study of military intervention is deeply rooted in the most traditional aspects of the study of international relations and security studies, connected with states, their motivations (national interests, the exercise of power and the development of security), and their relations (through balances of power).

Thus, building upon these perspectives, the first of the ideal types that will be examined will be termed Regional Power Intervention. This mainly focuses upon the actions of the most powerful states in a particular region, or of those states which wish to attain that status. States which have regional ambitions will often seek to realise them via the use of force. Threats to this actual or potential regional hegemony are forcibly removed.

Whereas traditional realists, such as Morgenthau, would stress the importance of intervention in terms of states expanding their power, Neo-Realists would see intervention more in terms of enhancing security. For Waltz, states use the military instrument because they exist in a world characterized by anarchy which leads, sometimes, to military intervention to enhance security.[5] Such defensive intervention could be as a kind of pre-emptive strike, to remove the target states' capability to carry out what the defensive state perceives to be an impending attack on its territorial or political integrity. Alternatively, armed intervention could occur as a riposte to actual military action against the state in question by foreign forces or a foreign state. Perhaps the most classic case of such defensive intervention by a regional power came in a Cold War, North-South context. For those who argued that the Soviet intervention in Afghanistan was not part of a communist plot to take over the world, the motivations of Moscow were rather more limited.[6] What would have been the consequences of *not* intervening? Might Islamicists have come to power, offering an alternative to Marxism-Leninism to the Muslims of Central Asia? Might pro-western forces have come to power, affording the United States and Pakistan forward intelligence bases? Or might the sheer instability of conflict in the country have led to the importation of terrorism, chaos and violence into the Soviet Union itself? One could, therefore, argue that the Soviet intervention into Afghanistan appeared to be defensive, rather than offensive, to the leadership in Moscow. How might such 'defensive' motivations have motivated state leaders in the South?

The second ideal type is Humanitarian Intervention. Such action is ostensibly intervention in a state with a view to relieving the physical suffering of the people within that state. Cosmopolitanists, or neo-Kantians, have argued that the military forces of states should be used in order to save the lives of people, rather than advance the interests of the nation.[7] However, humanitarian concerns have rarely been sufficient cause to prompt intervention. Often, military intervention, driven by other motives, has been 'dressed-up' as humanitarian concern. Hence, the relief of physical suffering has been used as the pretext for the military intervention in one state by the forces of another as the latter pursues its own interests. These could be the removal of the host state's political elite and its replacement by more acceptable leaders. It has been argued, for example, that the incursion by Ugandan forces in October 1978 into Tanzanian territory was the legitimating rationale that Dar Es Salaam had been seeking in order to bring about a change of leadership in that country, rather than being purely a Tanzanian desire to save the lives of Ugandans suffering under Idi Amin.[8]

The third ideal type will be termed Internal Intervention. This category examines those uses of military force that take place within states. One of the major characteristics of the South has been that the state has been much weaker, and much more vulnerable, than in the North. The problems of nation-building have proved to be great, and bloody, in Africa, Asia and Latin America. For example, the inability of the state and of the government to fully legitimize itself has led to widespread bloodshed for at least 20 years in Guatemala.

The term 'state' has other meanings in the South. The Maldives, a collection of small islands in the Indian Ocean with a population of only 200,000, is deemed to be a state. Similarly, Tuvalu is a state, although its population is only 10,000. By contrast Nigeria, a state with some 90 million people, comprises many different peoples with different cultures, traditions and languages. Rwanda is also deemed to be a state, although with the bloodshed of April 1994, the state descended into anarchy. Each of these examples is called a state, for each has an international legal identity; yet, they are unable to attain the levels of administrative coordination and control that Northern states take for granted.

The category of Internal Intervention is a key concept to understanding the use of military force in the South. Many governments in the South, whether for reasons of nation-building, or regime survival, deem elements within the state to possess a quality of 'otherness' that requires a military response. Sometimes this focuses on political opposition, sometimes on ethnic identity, while on other occasions the two cannot be distinguished. Unable to impose their power onto these 'others', military and political elites in the South often resort to imposing their will by force of arms. Thus, for those who would wish to take a broader view of security, Internal Intervention is a vital concept to explain the high level of violence in the South.

This chapter will now focus on these categories by examining each in turn.

Regional Power Intervention

In the first category, Regional Power Intervention, four case studies stand out. The first concerns India, with its increasing identification as a regional superpower. The second focuses on the Middle East, and specifically the Israeli-Syrian competition for influence in and control of Lebanon. The third has been the conflict and competition between Iran and Iraq. The final example is from South East Asia, examining the role and motives of both Vietnam and China in the region. Nigeria could also be cited as an example, as will be explained in a later section.

The first case study concerns India. As Robert Bradnock has noted, '[w]hile the philosophy of India's foreign policy has been formed by the ideology of non-alignment, its practice has also reflected an essentially pragmatic pursuit of national interests'.[9] Those national interests have led to the use of military force by India in South Asia. Under the terms of the

Indian-Sri Lankan peace pact of 1987, 50,000 Indian troops were deployed in Sri Lanka.[10] In November 1988, the Maldives were invaded by an army of mercenaries. Almost immediately, India responded with some 1,600 paratroopers who were able to rapidly defeat the invading force and return President Maumoon Abdul Gayoom to power.[11] In March 1989, apparently in response to the lapsing of a trade agreement, but in reality in response to the purchase of weapons by Nepal from China in August 1988, the Indian Army closed 13 of the 15 border crossings with Nepal, causing enormous economic austerity. 'New Delhi's desire for a more subservient Nepalese foreign-policy orientation clearly motivated its actions.'[12]

Such interventions were part of at least a 20 year period in which India had frequently resorted to the use of force. From 1971, when the Indian army's actions in East Pakistan led to the emergence of Bangladesh, to the assistance given to the Sri Lankan government against Sinhalese extremists in the same year, the incorporation of Sikkim into India in 1975, the extension of *de facto* protectorate status for Bhutan, and the use of the military again in Sri Lanka and later in the Maldives, successive Indian governments had strengthened the notion that India had set itself up as a willing regional policeman and that it had become the regional superpower of South Asia through the use of arms.

This is not to suggest that India has in any sense become an imperialistic or expansionist power. The government in New Delhi has had to face a series of external pressures which have led to the development of a sharper focus on Indian interests on the sub-continent: for example, the development of Islamic fundamentalism in Afghanistan, the growth of Tamil nationalism in Sri Lanka, and the Islamicisation of the politics of Pakistan, and, since the war of 1962, concern regarding the ever-present position of the Chinese giant to the north. India's security policy has to be defined in a particularly difficult region. India's actions in Sri Lanka and the Maldives, and in its competition with Pakistan, seem to suggest that stability in South Asia will be defined by unipolar hegemony. For example, the July 1987 Indian-Sri Lankan Pact allowing the Indian army to take on responsibilities in Sri Lanka also includes a commitment by the Sri Lankans to deny the use of the deep-water port of Trincomalee to any foreign navy.[13] As John Bray put it, 'India sees itself as a regional superpower, with Sri Lanka well within its sphere of interest.'[14] And yet strategically, from the perspective of New Delhi, South Asian security is dependent upon the nature of relations with China. But, in the world's largest democracy, the resort to violence has also been dependent upon the character of the government and Prime Minister. Rajiv Gandhi, for example, sought 'to compete with potential adversaries to find a more influential role for his country ... Not surprisingly, therefore, India under Mr Gandhi [was] keener than before to use its political as well as military muscle.'[15] This was true to such an extent that questions were being asked inside India as to whether he was promoting a 'Gandhi doctrine' which would establish a zone of interest following the example of the US Monroe Doctrine for the Western Hemisphere.[16] In contrast, Gandhi's successors - V.P.Singh, Chandra Shekhar, Narasimha Rao - have been beset by problems of domestic legitimacy and localized violence often generated by the Hindu supremacist party, the BJP. As the BJP has risen in power, it has challenged the secular nature of the India created by the Mahatma and developed by Nehru. With the legitimacy of India's governmental system and, indeed, societal base, under challenge, the assertiveness of India's external policies under, especially, Indhira and Rajiv Gandhi, has dramatically weakened.

Indian policy has, at least in part, been concerned with the extension of their influence and power in South Asia. In the Middle East, it is possible to argue that both Israel and Syria have sought to further both their influence and their security through the adoption of policies of military intervention in Lebanon. It is from the Middle East that a second example of intervention in support of the Regional Power explanation is drawn. In June 1982, Israel launched a full invasion of Lebanon, in part to attack those military forces that had been shelling Israeli territory from southern Lebanon. However, the invasion went much further than this. Israel sought to break Syrian and Palestine Liberation Organisation (PLO) influence in Lebanon, and to effectively disassociate the country from the Arab-Israeli conflict. Israel managed to break much of the PLO's military forces in the country, and also to push the Syrian Army into retreat as they moved into the country as far as Beirut. By breaking the power of both the PLO and the Syrians (the Syrian army was defeated, and Syria's air defences shattered), and by strongly supporting a new Lebanese government, the Israelis sought to recreate a fuller Lebanese sovereignty, albeit with many concessions to Israeli security concerns.[17]

Syrian intervention dated from 1976, when the army entered Lebanon, at the invitation of the government in Beirut, to prevent it from falling to a coalition of PLO and Druze forces.[18] The Syrian army quickly occupied the Beka'a Valley, which was to become central not only to Syrian policy in Lebanon, but also, more fundamentally, to Syrian security policy as a whole. With the loss of the Golan Heights to Israel in the Six Day War of 1967, the western part of Syria became very vulnerable, and occupation of the Beka'a, along with the north and east of the country, offered at least some strategic compensation.[19]

Throughout the latter part of the 1980s, the Israelis and Syrians maintained their positions of influence and control in Lebanon. During the

United Nations' war with Iraq over Kuwait, Israeli tanks moved back into the southern part of Lebanon in opposition to guerilla attacks on Israel itself.[20] Throughout the rest of the year, Israeli forces - both land and air - attacked guerilla forces in southern and central Lebanon. Although Lebanon and Syria signed an agreement which stated that Syria would defend Lebanese sovereignty, these further incursions did not lead to an Israeli-Syrian confrontation.[21] Both states had worked out tacit rules of behaviour that would allow each to act in its respective spheres of influence in Lebanon without coming into direct contact with one another. However, Israeli incursions continued in 1992, as Hizbollah, a pro-Iranian, pro-fundamentalist group that was essentially Lebanese in character, increased its attacks against Israeli territory.[22] These attacks led to a full strike by the Israelis in July 1993, named *Operation Accountability*. Israel launched massive attacks against Lebanese towns and villages. The damage was enormous. Hundreds were killed, and over 300,000 made homeless. Eleven years on from its last invasion, Israel was again making use of high levels of force in order to secure its northern territories from rocket attack. However, unlike 1982, the targets in 1993 were different. Whereas in 1982 the targets had been Palestinians, in 1993 the target was Hizbollah, it being the main focal point of Lebanese opposition to Israel's political presence in the country. Whereas the Palestinian tactics in the face of the Israeli onslaught had been to withdraw, Hizbollah's tactics were to seek confrontation. Israel sought to take advantage of this. By creating such carnage, the Israelis hoped to generate anti-Hizbollah feeling in Lebanon itself that would provide a pretext for both the Lebanese and Syrian governments to take measures against Hizbollah.[23] From open confrontation between Israel and Syria over the Lebanon in 1982, by 1993 there had grown a tacit understanding and cooperation against the new common enemy, Hizbollah.

The conflict between Iran and Iraq has appeared to many to be a classic confrontation between rival states, of the type that could be traced back to that between Athens and Sparta. The Iranians and Iraqis fought a bloody war between 1980 and 1988. The war, begun by the Iraqis, sensing that the military balance of power was in their favour following the victory of the Islamic revolutionaries in Tehran, was dominated for much of its course by desperate Iraqi rearguard actions, designed to protect the territory of Iraq itself from Iranian invasion.[24] The war was one of the most bloody in post-1945 history. Iran's military tactics seemed drawn from the practice of the First World War, with human waves sent repeatedly into Iraqi machine gun fire in order to try to swamp the defences. Iraq did not hesitate to use chemical weapons against its adversaries, less so against the Iranian forces, more brutally against Kurdish villages. And both countries fired many missiles against each other in the so-called war of the cities.[25] After eight long years of war, both sides accepted United Nations Security Council Resolution 598 in mid-1988, designed to lead to a restoration of the *status quo ante bellum*, and an end to the fighting.

In August 1990 Iraq invaded its neighbour, Kuwait.[26] In the aftermath of the United Nations' war with Iraq, armed resistance to the government of Saddam Hussein began in Kurdistan in the north of Iraq, and also in the south. Both of these areas in part bordered with Iran. The Iranians denied any role in the uprising, but the true situation was unclear. The Iraqis accused the Iranians of supporting and aiding the uprising with the deployment of Revolutionary Guards in Iraq, specifically in Basra, Nasiriyah and Amarah.[27] The Iranians claimed that this was not the action of Revolutionary Guards but, rather, opposition Iraqis who had been based in Iran.[28] In any case, these forces were speedily defeated by heavy Iraqi armoured forces. However, reports emerged of Iranian forces attacking the main opposition group to the Iranian government, Mujahideen e Khalq, in Iraq.[29] Such attacks continued into 1992 and 1993. In April 1992, the Iraqis managed to shoot down an Iranian F-4 Phantom north of Baghdad which had been attacking a Mujahideen base just 40 miles from the Iraqi capital.[30] In the summer of 1993, the Iranians attacked the Mujahideen e Khalq based in southern Iraq.[31] Resistance to Kurdish attempts at gaining independence were not limited simply to the aftermath of the Gulf War, however. In the summer of 1993, the Iranians launched a major offensive into Iraq against Kurdish forces.[32] Moreover, the Iranians were largely copying the Turks who, since the immediate aftermath of the Gulf War, and with implicit American support, had been attacking Kurdish targets in northern Iraq with impunity.[33] The weakness of Iraq has, thus, been used by its neighbours to further weaken their opponents based on Iraqi territory.

The final example of traditional military intervention relates to Sino-Vietnamese rivalry. Two of the communist regimes that emerged victorious from the Indo-Chinese wars against the French and the Americans were unable, in peacetime, to maintain the fraternal relations developed during wartime. Tensions between Vietnam and Cambodia worsened in the late 1970s for a variety of reasons: in videological terms, as the two ruling communist parties argued over the true path; in ethnic terms, as ethnic Vietnamese living in eastern Cambodia suffered particularly badly under Pol Pot, while the Khmer Rouge launched attacks over the border into Vietnam; in political terms, as those Khmer who had been trained by Hanoi were systematically murdered by Pol Pot; and strategically, as Hanoi looked to Moscow for patronage, while Phnom Penh looked to Beijing.[34] On 25 December 1978, Vietnam launched an attack on Cambodia that led to the overthrow, although not the destruction, of the ruling Khmer Rouge. Further explanations for this action will be examined later in this chapter. In retaliation for this Vietnamese action, Chinese military forces attacked several northern provinces of Vietnam in February 1979.[35]

The Chinese justified their action as a 'punishment' of the Vietnamese for their intervention in Cambodia. Undoubtedly, the defeat of the pro-Chinese Pol Pot was a significant setback for Beijing, for the Chinese had long sought to prevent the emergence of an Indo-Chinese political entity under Vietnamese control. The Chinese reaction to the extension of Vietnamese influence into Cambodia was particularly strong due to the Chinese failure to maintain a separate existence for Laos. In 1977, Vietnam and Laos had signed a Treaty of Friendship which effectively placed Laotian development under Vietnamese tutelage. Thus, the fall of Cambodia under Vietnamese influence completed, in only three years, the extension of Hanoi's power from North Vietnam, through the conquest of the South in spring 1975, to the whole of Indo-China.

However, it is important, in the context of the Chinese intervention into Vietnam, to realise that Sino-Vietnamese relations have been conditioned by over 2000 years of history. The name 'Vietnam' is itself Cantonese in origin, although there is dispute over whether it is best translated as 'Pacified South' or 'Southerly Dependencies of the Canton Region'.[36] China ruled Vietnam for over one thousand years to the middle of the 10th century. Subsequently, Vietnam had from time to time posed a security threat to China, whether it be through Vietnamese policy, (the last time being in the 1790s), or through the policies of others through Vietnamese territory (from the Mongols in the Middle Ages to the French, Japanese and, according to some, the Americans, in the 19th and 20th centuries). Vietnam's intervention in Cambodia, coming, as it did, only one month after the signing of a Treaty of Friendship between Vietnam and the Soviet Union, revived these security fears. Since the Mongols invaded China in the Middle Ages simultaneously from both Vietnam and Central Asia, traditional Chinese policy had been, as Western theorists of the balance of power would advocate, to avoid facing two allied threats to their territory. In 1979, the Vietnamese invasion of the last remnant of independence in IndoChina, plus Hanoi's alliance with Moscow, seemed to remind Beijing of its traditional concerns.

The Chinese intervention into northern Vietnam was, on the face of it, unsuccessful. The Chinese withdrew quickly, while the Vietnamese continued for several years to fight the Khmer Rouge in Cambodia. However, the use of the military instrument by China allowed Beijing to maintain a threat of further military action against Vietnam, a threat that was maintained until at least the dry season of 1984-5. Up to that time, large Chinese forces were maintained on the Vietnamese border, making occasional border raids, forcing Vietnam to maintain a large portion of its army facing China rather than fighting the Khmer Rouge in Cambodia.[37]

What is clear from these four examples is that there are different aspects to traditional military intervention. In the case of India, one state has used its military forces in its perceived national interests to further its influence in its immediate region. Yet, it is impossible to evaluate Indian assertiveness in South Asia without giving due consideration to Indian defensiveness *vis-à-vis* China. In addition, the exercise of Indian intervention has been related to the power of the Indian government domestically, and the rise of an internal challenge, the BJP, has lessened the scope for external action. In the Middle East, intervention by both Israel and Syria in Lebanon has changed, over the course of a decade, from competitive intervention to, implicitly at least, cooperative intervention. However, again, it is important to recognize the defensive element in the politics of both states. Although it may not appear to be the case to the people of Lebanon, Israeli policy has been motivated by the vulnerability of northern Israel to attack by guerillas from southern Lebanon; while, again at least in part, Syrian policy has been motivated by the post-1967 vulnerability of Damascus to Israel. The third example, Iran and Iraq, demonstrates the multiple nature of regional rivalries and the use of intervention. During much of the 1980s, both nations fought a bloody war in order to further their own interests in the region. In the aftermath of the war over Kuwait, both states continued this intervention by using their military forces against their political opponents based in the other state. Again, both offensive and defensive motivations (in this case, against ethnic opposition groups based abroad) predominated. Finally, the Chinese intervention against Vietnam demonstrates the importance of the historical dimension to intervention and, again, the relevance of defensive motivations.

Thus, traditional notions of using military force to further the national interest do not appear to be out of place when examining intervention in the South. The above case studies illustrate the importance of national interests and of domestic and historical factors in determining reasons for intervention, and also illustrate many different types of intervention: invasion, provision of 'peacekeepers', competitive and cooperative intervention, and intervention in the affairs of another state in order to destroy political opponents to a regime. These interventions may be interpreted as expansionist in power terms, drawing upon the traditional Realists, or more defensive actions by powerful states, as would be suggested by the Neo-Realists. However, unlike the second ideal type explanation, the interests of the state are paramount.

Humanitarian Intervention

Humanitarian Intervention represents the second category. It is applied to the use of military force by one or more states in the territory of another state with the expressed aim of alleviating the physical suffering there. But, as was hinted at earlier, humanitarian concerns, although often genuine, have rarely by themselves stimulated sufficient political will for military intervention to take place. Rather, the humanitarian card has been employed as a smokescreen for other motives behind any action. The humanitarian card has been used in an attempt to make dubious military activity appear acceptable, both internationally and domestically; as a source of convenient justification. This can be seen with reference to three case studies: the Tanzanian intervention in Uganda; the ECOWAS action in Liberia; and Vietnam's overthrowing of the Khmer Rouge.

When President Nyerere sent the Tanzanian army into neighbouring Uganda, towards the end of 1978 it was justified on humanitarian grounds. The brutal and widespread atrocities committed in President Amin's name inside Uganda were evident to all. However, the sense of outrage at what had been occurring inside Uganda had not been strong enough to stir foreign governments to impose diplomatic and economic sanctions, let alone undertake military action.[38] There was evident international relief at the passing of Amin's regime; enough to overlook the suspect nature of the Tanzanian intervention.

There could be no question that the Tanzanian government had been appalled at the brutal treatment of the Ugandan people by Amin. However, it would be unreasonable to see this outrage as an adequate motivation for the Tanzanian intervention. President Nyerere of Tanzania had constantly questioned the legitimacy of the Amin government, it having seized power in a military coup which overthrew the democratically elected regime of President Obote, particularly since Obote had been a close ideological and political ally. However, not only had Tanzania lost an ally, when Obote was displaced by Amin, but it had also gained a threatening and potentially dangerous neighbour. Indeed, the catalyst for the Tanzanian invasion had been an incursion into Tanzanian territory by Ugandan troops, reputedly in pursuit of deserters from the Ugandan army; thousands of local Tanzanians were left unaccounted for. National indignation was further fuelled by Nyerere's military advisors, who were anxious to avenge the embarrassment caused by the ease with which Tanzanian territory had been occupied.

Tanzania's action went well beyond both self-defence and Humanitarian Intervention. It did not represent an attempt at territorial aggrandizement, but nevertheless it still openly flouted international law.[39] Tanzania did not have a legal right to take an active role in the overthrow of an incumbent regime and to replace it with one more favourable to its own interests - Obote was eventually returned to office. Moreover, the bloodshed caused as a result of the Tanzanian invasion raises doubts even as to whether the action was justifiable on humanitarian grounds.[40]

West Africa recently experienced its own brand of humanitarian intervention, although this also rapidly transformed itself into a conflict of national interests. In December 1989, Liberia slid into civil war following an incursion by rebel forces based inside Ivory Coast. Bloodshed on a massive scale ensued and neighbouring states were soon weighed down by the burden of hundreds of thousands of Liberian refugees. The Liberian President, Samuel Doe, was toppled and then tortured to death. The violent disintegration of Liberia then spilled over into Sierra Leone. International intervention came in September 1990 when the 16-member Economic Community of West African States (ECOWAS) deployed a 7,000-strong peacekeeping force to Liberia. This force was called ECOMOG (ECOWAS Peacekeeping Monitoring Group) and immediately engaged itself in trying to facilitate an end to the war, and to supporting the interim government of national unity while democratic elections were held. This was, on the face of it, a humanitarian intervention, for the conflict had, by this time, degenerated into a three-way fight, and all were clear that something had to be done to stop the carnage and the suffering.

But again, the mantle of Humanitarian Intervention did not suffice as a full explanation for the action; indeed, it may not even go half way to explaining it. By October 1992, the ECOMOG force had been increased to 14,000. But, more ominously, the humanitarian remit had largely been forgotten. ECOMOG had now gone on the offensive and was openly participating in the civil war against Charles Taylor's NPFL (National Patriotic Front of Liberia). ECOMOG had supposedly been sent into Liberia as a mediator but it soon became a combatant, pursuing an overtly political role; neutrality gave way to open aggression.[41] Any humanitarian initiative quickly became unravelled.

Over 70% of the initial ECOMOG force (that is to say 5,000 troops) were provided by one state, Nigeria (with the balance of the 7,000 troops coming from Ghana, Gambia, Guinea and Sierra Leone - Mali and Senegal contributed to subsequent reinforcements). More Nigerian troops were sent in, as was a comparatively large contingent of the Nigerian Air Force; in addition, Nigeria was eventually to provide the commander of the ECOMOG forces. This dominant role was criticized by the Francophone members of ECOWAS who wanted far more emphasis placed on negotiation; these countries were also far more receptive to Charles Taylor's NPFL.[42] Indeed, reports from the United States's State

Department suggested that Francophone Burkina Faso was supplying Libyan-made arms to the NPFL.[43] Ivory Coast, similarly, appears to have been providing the NPFL with ordnance, logistic and manpower support.[44] Liberia was the stage for a bitter struggle for dominance within ECOWAS; the organization was fissured along Anglophone-Francophone lines. The peace process was subsumed by the respective regional interests and the personal ambitions of the political leaders.[45] Each state had a different agenda for the Liberian crisis. Above all, Nigeria saw the war as a test of what it perceived to be its regional hegemony, for it was determined that Liberia would not succumb to the NPFL and thus join the Francophone bloc inside ECOWAS.[46] There was a danger of the conflict becoming, essentially, a Nigerian-Liberian war.[47]

Tyrannical and barbaric rule is synonymous with the reign of Pol Pot's Khmer Rouge in Cambodia. The Vietnamese invasion of Cambodia in December 1978 and the removal of Pol Pot from office was thus heralded in Hanoi as a humanitarian victory. But, as an act of Humanitarian Intervention, this action proved to be as questionable as the previous two examples. Vietnam played the humanitarian card because it felt it would enable it to achieve its interests; namely, the installation of a staunchly pro-Hanoi regime in Phnom Penh. It had been counting on the depth of anti-Pol Pot feeling within the international community being sufficient to give Hanoi a free hand in determining Cambodia's domestic politics. The expansion of Vietnam's influence to cover its western neighbour was also intended as a key move in the strategical power game with China; reference to which has been made earlier.

The humanitarian rhetoric was denounced by much of the international community, as foreign governments attacked what they saw as an illegal act of aggression. Diplomatic and economic isolation was to follow for Hanoi. The puppet government, under Heng Samrin, which assumed power in Phnom Penh, had no more legitimacy than its predecessor. Nor was peace restored to the ravaged country. Hanoi had expected a swift unchallenged victory, but a long drawn-out war ensued between the Vietnamese army and the Khmer Rouge, and various other nationalist factions.[48] Although the situation soon became one of stalemate, Vietnam showed no sign of willingness to withdraw its troops. Having invested so much in the campaign, Hanoi was not about to retire without its minimum security requirements having been met.[49]

Whereas the first ideal type, Regional Power Intervention, focused on the state as its level of analysis, the second, Humanitarian Intervention, focused upon people. However, as has been seen, in the South-South context Humanitarian Intervention has been a concept heavily compromised by competing national interests. Yet, it would not be correct to leave the examination of intervention purely in terms of traditional notions of national interests. A specifically Southern dimension of intervention has frequently occurred within countries, when a ruling elite deem indigenous peoples to be endowed with that same quality of 'otherness' that justifies military intervention by one state in the affairs of another. This third ideal type focuses upon the weakness of the state in the South, and the frequent lack of legitimacy of governments. These twin, yet reinforcing, issues have been at the root of much violence in the South. It is to this area, to Internal Intervention, that the analysis now turns.

Internal Intervention

The final category, Internal Intervention, considers the use of the military instrument by governments not against their neighbours but, rather, against their own population. In such cases, military forces are used by political and military elites to intervene in political and security developments within the state, to prevent particular groups from obtaining, or maintaining, a particular position of political power. In this category, examples will be drawn from two regions: South Asia, and Latin America.

In a previous section, the argument was made that India's abilities to intervene militarily in the affairs of other, neighbouring, states has been dependent upon the nature of its domestic politics. This is a theme that merits further examination. It is certainly true that, from the early 1970s, India used its military forces outside its borders more frequently than almost any other state in the South.[50] However, such a picture would be incomplete without an examination of the rest of Indian interventionary policy, which has taken place *within* the Indian state. In Punjab, it has been estimated that some 16,000 people have been killed in violence from the beginning of the separatist unrest in the early 1980s. To provide some context, this number is roughly equal to the total number of deaths in both the 1965 and the 1971 Indo-Pakistan Wars.[51] Neither is this the only part of the country in which large numbers of people have died. There has been great violence in Assam, and also in Kashmir; 'New Delhi seems to hope that a measured but relentless use of force will keep the Kashmir valley within the Indian Union.'[52] In all three parts of India, separatist violence has been met with the deployment of the Indian army, and the implementation of repression.[53]

Internal Intervention in South Asia is not limited simply to India, however. In Sri Lanka, the civil strife has led to the deployment of the army in the north and east against the Liberation Tigers of Tamil Eelam, and in the south against the Maoist Janatha Vimukthi Peramuna. Moreover, in both areas, the army has been accused of breaches of human rights.[54]

In Burma, the national army has also been accused of intervening violently against the population. The level of violence perpetrated against groups within Burma has led to the growth of significant refugee camps: some 60,000 Karen in Thailand; 30,000 people from Kachin in China; and some 2,000 from Sagaing Division in India.[55] In addition, in 1978, 200,000 Muslims from Arakan had been forcibly driven over the border into Bangladesh in an operation called *Dragon King*. Widespread popular protests ran from May to September 1988 and were put down with great brutality; there was a bloodbath.[56] Army trucks, complete with machine guns, routinely patrolled the streets of Rangoon, picking up any young people they found.[57] With 10,000 troops stationed within Rangoon itself, the city was effectively under military occupation. Faced with internal opposition from groups hostile to the authoritarianism of the government, the Burmese regime increased the size of its army to over 300,000 in the late 1980s, and obtained sophisticated weapons from China. The military government of General Saw Maung, which assumed power in September 1988, immediately set out to consolidate its position by physically crushing all opposition; 'They seem intent on closing Burma up.'[58] The military was manoeuvring for a permanent hold on power. A diplomatic source even reported the extrajudicial execution of pro-democracy students.[59] Initially, the government launched offensives within Burma itself: for instance, 5-6,000 students were forced into refugee camps on the eastern border. Once the government had achieved its targets within the country, it turned to the refugees on its borders. On 20 and 21 December 1991, the Burmese army launched an attack into Bangladesh, killing and wounding Bangladeshi soldiers, overrunning a military base, and carrying weapons and stores back into Burma.[60] In late 1991 and early 1992, Burmese army units moved into Thailand in order to attack major Karen bases from the rear. On this occasion, they were met by the Thai air force.[61] In 1989 and 1990, however, the Thais had been prepared to ignore Burmese intervention. Having been a strong supporter of the Karens for some 40 years, the Thais moved closer to the Burmese in the late 1980s, facilitating the weakening of the anti-government forces in the east of Burma.[62] This was largely due to the granting by Rangoon of over 20 logging concessions to Thai timber companies; with cross-border trade officially sanctioned, the Thais needed to clear the Burmese rebels from the border area to ensure open access to the logging areas.[63]

Internal Intervention in Latin America has been a constant feature since the conquest and colonization of the region in the 15th century. Colonial rule had been centralized into the hands of the Spanish and Portuguese colonialists and, over time, into the hands of an elite that had little connection with the indigenous peoples and their culture. Independence was not won by the people; rather, it was achieved by this 'foreign' élite. In terms of political culture, much of this distinction has remained. In many of the countries of the region, massive violence was used during the 1970s, 1980s and, in some cases, the 1990s, either against those who were deemed to be subversives (the dirty wars in countries such as Argentina, Brazil, Chile and Paraguay), or against the Indian population that was deemed to be a threat (for example, in Guatemala and Peru).

Opposition to those deemed to have this quality of 'otherness' in Latin America has led to the massive use of violence. While many of the so-called 'dirty wars' had apparently ended by the early 1980s with the increasing return to democracy in Latin America (notably, of course, in Argentina and Brazil) in fact, levels of violence remained high. For example, in El Salvador, in the decade of the 1980s, over 70,000 people were killed in the course of the civil war between the government and the rebel Farabundo Marti National Liberation Front (FMLN) largely, although not exclusively, by the Salvadoran army and the right-wing death squads.[64] Notoriously immune from prosecution, in one infamous instance, in November 1989, the Salvadoran army - in this case from the elite American-trained Atlacatl battalion - kidnapped and executed six Jesuit priests.[65] A second example would be Chile, where both murder and terror, remained high under the rule of General Pinochet. In 1986, for example, after the attempted assassination of Pinochet, there were 'over 7,000 political arrests, 1,000 people wounded and 58 people killed by security forces ... and there were also 132 charges of torture.'[66]

During the 1980s, there was much debate over how much of the violence, especially in Central America, could be blamed upon outside sources. Those on the Left tended to blame the United States for excessive support of reactionary forces. For example, Piero Gleijeses has argued that

> Self-delusion will help the Americans to overlook their moral burden - 30,000 Nicaraguan dead and a country in ruins. We will tell ourselves that the Contra war would have occurred anyway and that it was Sandanista mismanagement that ruined the economy. But how many Contras ... would have fought without the United States to encourage and arm them? How many Contras would have fought without secure Honduran bases? And would the Hondurans have played this indispensable - if miserable - role without the United States to cajole, bribe and bully them?[67]

For those on the Right, violence in Latin America was in essence the responsibility of communists in the Soviet Union and Cuba. Revolution and arms had been exported against the peoples of Central and South America, and for many on the Right, the American response had been too weak. Despite American support of the Contras, and the 30,000 Nicaraguan dead, Joachim Maitre could assert that 'Nothing was done to prevent the communist takeover in Nicaragua, and nothing serious was undertaken to remove the 'Sandanistas' - totalitarian, anti-American, an undeniable threat to democracy in the Hemisphere - from power.'[68]

The implication of these Left-Right perspectives was that, once the Cold War had come to an end, the essential causes of violence in Latin America would also end. With communism an outdated political philosophy, American military influence would decline, and Central and South America would become more peaceful. Of course, this was partly true, particularly with the peace agreement in El Salvador, the ending of the Contra war in Nicaragua with the electoral victory of Violeta Barrios de Chamorro, and the end of the Pinochet period in Chile. However, although violent Internal Intervention in Latin America might have been exacerbated by Cold War tensions, many of the underlying causes were indigenous to the region. Fundamental disparities of wealth, worsening economic conditions, inflation and economic shock therapy policies led to upsurges of social violence. In the 1989-1991 period, hundreds were killed in riots over conditions and food prices in Argentina, Brazil, Dominica, Trinidad and Venezuela.[69] However, such riots have occurred elsewhere in the South, and even in the North (for example in Poland, leading to the formation of Solidarity). What has been distinctive about Latin America has been the continuation of ideological conflict without external support (Peru), the crumbling of the state in the face of criminal organizations (Colombia), and the war against indigenous peoples (Guatemala).

The Peruvian case has illustrated the self-contained nature of conflict in Latin America. The Sendero Luminoso, or Shining Path, has engaged in a long and bloody fight against the Peruvian government since 1980; defending, in their eyes, the indigenous population against government repression. The Shining Path developed an indigenous political ideology, based on Maoism, which forced the government to place over half the country under emergency rule and, despite the capture of its leader, Abimael Guzman, the war led the democratically elected, President Fujimori, to suspend large sections of the constitution. Large parts of the countryside have been regularly subjected to intimidation and terror by both the Shining Path and the army, with the latter frequently murdering the inhabitants of entire villages, and 'disappearing' people, in order to frighten the population into surrendering information about the Shining Path.[70] During this conflict, over 18,000 people have been killed.[71]

The second major conflict to survive the end of the Cold War was in Colombia. Violence in Colombia is endemic at many different levels. Guerilla groups continued to operate into the 1990s, despite efforts at political reintegration during the 1980s (especially following the truces with the M-19 - the *Movimiento 19 de Abril* - the Armed Forces of the Colombian Revolution, and the Popular Army of Liberation), and has been associated with para-military excesses against elements of the rural population. In 1988, Amnesty International criticized the military for deliberate acts of violence and murder for political purposes. Drug-traffickers expanded their areas of control and the value of their operations during the 1980s, and in the 1990s continued to operate separately from the state although, through intimidation and bribery, they have managed to gain influence in, and over, many aspects of the state, including parts of the military and the judiciary, notably in Medellin with the cartel of Pablo Escobar Gaviria. Finally, acts of violence by individuals and groups within society itself have become endemic in Colombia. Taken together, Gary Hoskin has argued that this means that '[i]n short, crisis has become a highly institutionalised component of the Colombian political system ... '[72] In many ways, it has been the violence associated with the criminal organizations that has been the most damaging, proving to be 'progressively destructive of law, security and the integrity of the political system.'[73]

The third Cold War, and post-Cold War, conflict has been in Guatemala. The level of political violence in Guatemala has, arguably, been higher in proportion to the size of the country (with a population of around eight million) than anywhere else in the world in the period from the late 1970s. The government has been dominated by the military, and when civilians have been allowed to act as president, it has been clear that their power has been dependent upon the military.[74] And the military has taken the task of implementing a policy of terror and murder in the countryside. Guatemalan society has been divided, more clearly than many other parts of Latin America, into two: Hispanic and Ladino (mixed race people who adopted Spanish cultural norms); and Indian, largely Mayan, comprising around 60% of the population. The army, government and landowners predominate amongst the former; peasants among the latter. The disparity between rich and poor, based on an unequal distribution of land, has created resentment particularly amongst the rural population. The army, still the most important institution in the country, has sought to stifle such resentment since the American inspired overthrow of the reformist Arbenz government in 1954. In the course of Guatemala's history since that time, well over 100,000 people have been killed.[75] Elections in 1990 and 1991, constrained by the parameters set by the army, were relatively poorly attended.[76] Despite a peace process to try to end the conflict, army violence, in March 1993, led to another flood of refugees leaving the El Peten region of Guatemala for Mexico.

These examples of Internal Intervention have demonstrated the willingness of many political and military elites in the South to sanction the use of force against citizens of their own country. The majority of cases briefly examined here have been ones in which armed force has been used against separatist movements: for example, in Assam, Kashmir and Sri Lanka. However, violence has also been used against elements of the population of a state simply because they do not belong to the dominant group - whether that be defined politically or ethnically - as defined by the ruling regime. In Sri Lanka against the JVP, in Guatemala, in Argentina, Brazil and Chile during the 1970s, and elsewhere armies have attacked those who have defined themselves, or been defined by others, as dissidents.

Conclusion

This chapter has attempted to evaluate armed intervention in the South from a Southern perspective. Admittedly, traditional notions of using military force to further the national interest do not appear to be out of place when examining intervention in the South, but this chapter has tried to demonstrate that intervention in the South cannot be solely attributed to the action of state against state. Even within the category of Regional Intervention, states, Israel and Syria, were acting against elements within a third country, Lebanon, rather than against the state itself; and the same was true of some of the violence between Iraq and Iran.

This chapter has sought, therefore, to broaden the use of the term 'intervention'. Traditionally, intervention has been interpreted to mean the use of force by one state in the affairs of another. This definition has been broadened in this chapter to meaning - the intervention of military force into political discourse. Without such a definition, this chapter would have been unable to assess Internal Intervention; and without the ability to examine the role of Internal Intervention, the analysis would have lost the ability to examine a great deal of violence in the South. If intervention is to be a useful tool in a broader approach to Security Studies, especially in the South, its definition must move beyond the inter-state level, and consider intra-state dynamics.

A significant conclusion that can be reached from this brief analysis of intervention in the South is that traditional patterns of conflict, although perhaps exacerbated or minimized by the effects of the Cold War, were not dependent on the East-West confrontation for their existence. However, much of the violence, at least in part, has been the legacy of Northern imperialism. It would, therefore, be incorrect to suggest that the end of the Cold War has had a decisive effect upon the nature of intervention in the South. Certainly, Southern rivalries were affected by the Cold War. The superpowers supplied 'friendly' states in the South, and sometimes became close allies. In the 1970s, the Soviet Union supported Somalia and the United States backed Ethiopia but, after revolutionary changes in the African countries, the superpowers happily swapped sides. The impact of the Cold War, therefore, was evident in military and political support. But it would not be correct to see the conflicts outlined above as *created* by the Cold War, nor dependent upon that conflict. Thus, the end of the Cold War has not prevented many conflicts from continuing. It is true that external support did make a decisive difference in certain cases, not least Iraq's ability to survive in the Iran-Iraq war. However, in general, the Cold War and its termination has not been the vital variable in assessing military intervention in the South.

Intervention in the South, then, can be seen through the prism of three ideal types. The first, Regional Power Intervention, suggested that states intervened in the affairs of other states to pursue their national interests. This could be for offensive reasons, or through defensive motivations; it could be cooperative, with other states, or unilateral. Many examples of this form of activity could be found in the South, whether on the part of India, Israel, Iran, or Iraq. The second ideal type, Humanitarian Intervention, suggested that military forces could be used to intervene in the affairs of another state not in order to further national interests, but in order to save the lives of people in the target country. However, upon analysis, it was difficult to find any case studies to support this ideal type. The Tanzanian intervention in Uganda, the Vietnamese in Cambodia, ECOMOG/Nigeria in Liberia - each may have had the effect of saving lives (and this is controversial in many cases), though it is difficult to suggest that this was the main motivating force. Although Humanitarian Intervention exists as an ideal type, it is a theory without practice in the South. The third ideal type, Internal Intervention, examined the use of violence within a state, by a ruling elite against others deemed to be enemies. In order to understand insecurity in the South, this perspective is absolutely vital. To ignore Internal Intervention in examining relations in the South would be to impose an ethnocentric perspective on the politics of much of the world. For the majority of people in the South, death and injury is more likely to come at the hands of the forces of their own country than that of other states. It is above all for this reason, that intervention in the South has an important added dimension compared to intervention amongst, and by, the Great Powers in world politics.

Notes

1. For these purposes, the South will be defined geographically in the conventional manner: those states and peoples south of the United States, the Mediterranean, Russia and Japan, excluding South Africa, Australia and New Zealand. These states and peoples have in common, broadly, a history of colonialism, a current situation of economic under-development, and, often, political instability associated with nation-building.

2. Brogan, Patrick, World Conflicts, London, Bloomsbury, second edition 1992, p.viii.

3. See the classic: Clausewitz, Carl von, On War, edited and translated by Michael Howard and Peter Paret, Princeton: Princeton University Press, 1984.

4. Particularly in the original version: Morgenthau, Hans, Politics Among Nations: The Struggle for Power and Peace, New York, Alfred Knopf, 1948.

5. His classic exposition is in Waltz, Kenneth N., Theory of International Politics, Reading, Mass., Addison-Wesley, 1979.

6. See, for example, the debate as expressed by Czempiel, Ernst-Otto, 'Germany-USA: Cooperation and Irritations', in Aussenpolitik, vol.33, no.1, 1982. See also, Bowker, Mike, & Williams, Phil Superpower Detente: A Reappraisal, London, Sagc for Chatham House, 1986, especially pp.234-255.

7. See, for example, Wheeler, Nicholas J., 'The Human Rights And Security Agenda: Beyond Non-Intervention?, in International Politics In Europe, edited by G. Wyn Rees, London, Routledge, 1993, pp.133-157.

8. See Thomas, Caroline, New States and Intervention, Aldershot, Gower, 1985.

9. Bradnock, Robert, India's Foreign Policy Since 1971, London, Pinter for Royal Institute of International Affairs, 1990, p.86.

10. Ibid, pp.75-7.

11. See Tripathi, Deepak, 'India's Maldives mission and after', in The World Today, vol.45, January 1989.

12. International Institute for Strategic Studies, Strategic Survey 1989-90, London, IISS, May 1990, p.174.

13. See Tripathi, Deepak, 'Sri Lanka's elusive peace', in The World Today, vol.43 no.11, November 1987, pp.186-7.

14. Bray, John, 'Sri Lanka: things fall apart?', in The World Today, vol.45, nos.8 & 9, August/September 1989, p.158.

15. See Tripathi, Deepak, The World Today, 1989, op.cit., p.4.

16. Sareen, Rajendra, & de Silva, Manik, de, 'Playing At Cops', in Far Eastern Economic Review, vol.42, no.46, 17 November 1988.

17. See Bowder, Geoffrey, 'Lebanon's struggle for survival', in The World Today, vol.39, no.11, November 1993, pp.443-449.

18. Korn, David, 'Syria and Lebanon: a fateful entanglement', in The World Today, vol.42, nos.8-9, August-September 1986, pp.137-142.

19. Vatikiotis, P.J., 'The crisis in Lebanon: a local historical perspective', in The World Today vol.40, no.3, March 1984, pp.85-92.

20. See: 'Israeli army moves north of Lebanon buffer zone', in International Herald Tribune, 8 February 1991.

21. See, for example, Jaber, Ali, 'Israeli tanks move into Lebanon on eve of treaty', in The Times, 22 May 1991; Gumicio, Juan Carlos, 'Israelis renew raids on Lebanon', in The Times, 5 June 1991; and Black, Ian, 'Israeli forces to stay in Lebanon', in The Guardian, 8 July 1991.

22. See, for example, Carney, Hugh, 'UN urges Israelis to end incursion', in The Financial Times, 21 February 1992; and Beeston, Richard, 'Israeli bombing raids strike at Hizbollah's Beka'a bases', in The Times, 22 May 1992.

23. See Richards, Charles, 'Hizbollah pays the price for its defiance', in The Independent, 28 July 1993; and Fisk, Robert, 'Israelis pound Lebanon by land, sea and air', and Helm, Sarah, 'Rabin's cool use of ruthless force', in The Independent, 29 July 1993.

24. See Chubin, Shahram, & Tripp, Charles, Iran and Iraq at War, London, IB Taurus, 1988.

25. See King, Ralph, 'The Iran-Iraq War: The Political Implications', in Adelphi Paper 219, London,IISS, 1987; and Karsh, Efraim, 'The Iran-Iraq War: A Military Analysis', in Adelphi Paper 220, London, IISS, 1987.

26. On these wars, see, for example, Dannreuther, Roland, 'The Gulf Conflict: A Political and Strategic Analysis', in Adelphi Paper 264, London, IISS, Winter 1991/92; and McCausland, Jeffrey, 'The Gulf Conflict: A Military Analysis', in Adelphi Paper 282, London, IISS, November 1993.

27. See the reports in Butt, Gerald, 'Iran fears for refugees fate in bloodbath of century', in The Daily Telegraph, 9 April 1991.

28. 'Rafsanjani admits Iraqi exiles in Iran stirred rebellion but denies Tehran took a hand', in The Guardian, 13 April 1991.

29. See, for example, Bruce, James, & Banks, Tony, 'Iranians fighting Iraqi forces', in Jane's Defence Weekly, 30 March 1991, p.465.

30. See Fisk, Robert, 'Iraqis down Iranian plane near Baghdad', in The Independent, 6 April 1992; and Cockburn, Patrick, and Haeri, Safa, Iran threatens more attacks against Iraq', in The Independent, 7 April 1992.

31. Mosteshar, Parichehre, 'Iranians raid guerilla bases in Iraq', in The Financial Times, 26 May 1993.

32. See Pope, Hugh, 'Tehran goes gunning for the Kurds', in The Independent, 23 June 1993; and Richards, Charles, 'Iran starts new attack on Kurds', in The Independent, 26 July 1993.

33. See, for example, Randal, Jonathan, 'Turkey bombs Kurdish bases in Iraq', in International Herald Tribune, 12 October 1991; Pope, Hugh, 'Onslaught against the PKK', in MEI, 23 October 1992, pp.11-12; and O'Toole, Pam, & Hirst, David, 'Iraqi Kurds angry at Turkish offensive', in The Guardian, 2 November 1992.

34. Rathborne, David, unpublished dissertation, Department of Political Science and International Studies, The University of Birmingham, 1994.

35. See Gordon, Bernard, 'The Third Indochina Conflict', in Foreign Affairs, vol.65, Fall 1986, pp.66-85.

36. For the former, see Gordon, op cit, p.68; for the latter, see Duncanson, Dennis, 'China's Vietnam war: new and old strategic imperatives', in The World Today, vol.35, no.6, June 1979, p.243.

37. The Chinese ended this policy in 1984-5 in part due to their policy of drastically reducing the size of their armed forces, in part due to their attempts to isolate Vietnam internationally with new moves towards Moscow. See Buszynski, Leslek, 'Vietnam's Asean diplomacy: the assertion of a *fait accompli*', in The World Today, vol.42, no.4, April 1986, especially pp.64-5.

38. See Thomas, op.cit.

39. Noreen Burrows wrote: 'support for the view that the Tanzanian action was illegal comes from virtually every instrument of international law since the Charter of the United Nations in 1945', Burrows, Noreen, 'Tanzania's Intervention in Uganda: Some Legal Aspects', in The World Today, vol.35, no.7 July 1979.

40. See Burrows, op.cit.

41. The United States' Assistant Secretary of State for Africa was quoted as saying: 'The feeling right now is we support the West Africans, but unfortunately ECOWAS is no longer a neutral party'. See 'US Ready to Seek UN Role in Liberia', International Herald Tribune, 12 November 1992.

42. See Dowden, Richard, in The Independent, 7 November 1992.

43. 'The Danger in Liberia', in The International Herald Tribune, 10 November 1992.

44. 'The New Model Civil War: Liberia Shows That All Can Join', in Defense And Foreign Affairs Strategic Policy, July-August 1992.

45. Peterson, Scott, '"No War - no peace" for fearful Liberia', in The Daily Telegraph, 17 August 1992.

46. Ibid.

47. 'The Danger in Liberia', in The International Herald Tribune, 10 November 1992.

48. Mahbubani, Kishore, 'The Kampuchean Problem: A Southeast Asian Perception', in <u>Foreign Affairs</u>, 1984.

49. Ibid.

50. One can argue about whether a true measure of this should be in terms of numbers of actions, length of such actions, or numbers of forces. However, on all of these counts, in the context of the South, India has been one of the most interventionary states.

51. See Gordon, Sandy, 'Resources and Instability in South Asia', in <u>Survival</u>, vol.35, no.2, Summer 1993.

52. Clad, James, '<u>Valley Of Violence Far Eastern Economic Review</u>, vol.148, no.21, 24 May 1990.

53. See Ganguly, Sumit, 'Ethno-religious Conflict in South Asia', in <u>Survival</u>, vol.35, no.2, Summer 1993.

54. Ibid, pp.96-8.

55. Lintner, Bertil, 'Centrifugal Forces', in <u>Far Eastern Economic Review</u>, 27 February 1992, p.16.

56. McDonald, Hamish, 'The Generals buy time', in <u>Far Eastern Economic Review</u>, vol.147, no.8, 22 February 1990.

57. Lintner, Bertil, 'A Darkening Scene', in <u>Far Eastern Economic Review</u>, vol.142, no.47, 24 November 1988.

58. Idem.

59. Idem.

60. See Lintner, Bertil, 'Burma's new front', in <u>Far Eastern Economic Review</u>, 9 January 1992.

61. 'Thais hit back at Burmese', in <u>The Times</u>, 17 March 1992.

62. See 'Thai-Burmese border tensions', in <u>International Defense Review</u>, May 1992.

63. Lintner, Bertil, 'Crossed Signals', in <u>Far Eastern Economic Review</u>, vol.144, no.24, 15 June 1989.

64. See Bland, Gary, 'The Prospects for peace in El Salvador', in SAIS Review, vol.10, no.2, Summer-Fall 1990, pp.191-209.

65. See Arnson, Cynthia J, & Forman, Johanna Mendelson, 'United States Policy in Central America', in Current History, March 1991, pp.99-100.

66. See Valenzuela, Arturo, & Constable, Pamela, 'Plebiscite in Chile: End of the Pinochet Era', in Current History, January 1988, p.30.

67. Gleijeses, Piero, 'Central America: Reflections on Victory', in SAIS Review, vol.10, no.2, Summer-Fall 1990, p.171.

68. Maitre, H. Joachim, 'Lost in the Peace Process', in Strategic Review, Fall 1989, p.8.

69. See Lowenthal, Abraham F., & Hakim, Peter, 'Latin American Democracy in the 1990s: The Challenges Ahead', in Evolving US Strategy for Latin America and the Caribbean, edited by L. Erik Kjonnerod, Washington DC, National Defence University Press, 1992, p.72.

70. See Werlich, David P., 'Peru: Garcia loses his Charm', Current History, January 1988, p.15.

71. See Lowenthal and Hakim, op cit, p.67.

72. See Hoskin, Gary, 'Colombia's Political Crisis', in Current History, January 1988, p.9.

73. Martz, John D., 'Colombia's Search for Peace', in Current History, March 1989, p.127.

74. See Piero Gleijeses, op.cit., especially pp.172-4.

75. See Lowenthal and Hakim, op.cit., p.67.

76. See Millet, Richard, 'Limited Hopes and Fears in Guatemala', in Current History, March 1991, pp.125-8.

6 United Nations and Military Intervention: a Study in the Politics of Contradiction

SHAHIN P MALIK AND ANDREW M DORMAN

> 'If the United Nations once admits that international disputes can be settled by using force, then we have destroyed the foundation of the organization and our best hope of establishing a world order.'
>
> Dwight D Eisenhower
> 20 February 1957

Introduction

The fall of the Berlin Wall, the re-unification of Germany and the collapse of the Soviet Union symbolized the end of the Cold War.[1] The resultant breakdown of the bi-polar system sent tremors reverberating throughout thc international system, the effects of which havc still to be fully felt. This has resulted in some concluding that we have now reached the end of history,[2] whilst in direct contrast a number of historians have highlighted the similarities between the situations in 1919 and 1989.[3] Samuel Huntington, however, suggests that we are now moving towards an era in which we will witness the 'Clash of Civilizations'[4] as the main source of conflict.

Within these profuse visions of what the post-Cold War means there has been the proposal of Presidents Bush and Gorbachev of a 'New World Order'(NWO) in which the rule of law and the principle of collective security would be upheld.[5] This has helped to bring about discussions of a sea of change in the role of the United Nations (UN) has been prominent. Alan James noted that '[i]t has been widely thought that, at last, the organization might play a leading role in the maintenance of international peace and security'.[6]

An initial rush of enthusiasm for the United Nations and its use have been clearly evident. Between 1991 and mid-1993 the international system witnessed an eightfold increase in the number of UN peacekeeping troops deployed and a quadrupling of the UN's peacekeeping budget.[7] This was paralleled by the proliferation in the type of operation undertaken to include crisis prevention, peace enforcement and the idea of humanitarian intervention in an on-going conflict.[8] These changes have not been without their problems, Adam Roberts has shown that: 'Almost every difficulty connected with the preparation, deployment and use of force has re-emerged in a UN context and does not appear to be any easier to address'.[9]

This raises the question of what is the future role of military intervention in the UN context. To answer this question the chapter has been sub-divided into three parts. The first part considers the two main interpretation's of the UN's future position within the international system, i.e. whether the UN will remain subject to the dominance of the wishes of the Permanent Members of the Security Council[10] (a realist approach) or whether it will have a more autonomous role along the lines envisaged by the idealist school of thought. The second part examines the case studies of Somalia and Bosnia, both of which have arisen in the post-Cold War world, to establish how the UN has acted and continues to act in the international system and also highlight the factors influencing the UN decision-making process. The third section applies the lessons of the case studies to the idealist and realist interpretations of the international system and attempts to draw some conclusions about the future role of the UN in military intervention.

Realism versus idealism?

The continuation of realism?

The end of the Cold War has brought two conflicting arguments into play which directly impinge upon the use of military intervention by, or in the name of, the UN. Both revolve around the relationship of state sovereignty and the role of intervention.[11]

The ideas emanating from the realist school reject the concept that any form of world government or organization is capable of enforcing rules upon either inter-state or intra-state behaviour in the anarchic world of the international system particularly over the use of force.[12] To a certain degree realism has recognized the limited need for international norms and conventions of behaviour that enable states to interact with one another. Here the UN has a role to play, but the state remains the key actor within the international system, and pursues its own 'national interest' however loosely defined, rather than any notion of collective goals.[13] For the realist, military intervention thus remains a tool of statecraft, to be used in the pursuit of the 'national interest'.[14]

In order to understand the realists' reasoning behind the UN's current and future roles in military intervention it is first necessary to examine the UN Charter to establish the mechanism of the UN's decision-making process before turning towards the consideration of the conduct of operations themselves. According to the UN Charter the first purpose of the UN is

> [t]o maintain international peace and security, and to that end: to take effective collective measures for the prevention and removal of threats to the peace, and for the suppression of acts of aggression or other breaches of peace, and to bring about by peaceful means, and in conformity with the principles of justice and international law, adjustment or settlement of international disputes or situations which might lead to a breach of the peace.[15]

Currently, responsibility to enforce this lies with the Security Council under Article 39 of the UN Charter which states that

> [t]he Security Council shall determine the existence of any threat to the peace, breach of the peace, or act of aggression and shall make recommendations; or decide what measures shall be taken in accordance with Articles 41 and 42, to maintain or restore international peace and security.[16]

The Security Council currently comprises 15 seats: five are held by the 'Permanent Members' and the other 10 are held in turn by the remaining members of the United Nations. For any resolution to pass through the Security Council it must receive 9 votes in favour with none of the Permanent Members exercising their power of veto. Thus, the Permanent Members have retained the right to prevent UN action that is contrary to their wishes. To the realist this veto power is the key condition for it ensures the continuation of the Permanent Members' domination of the UN decision-making process and allows them to protect their own interests. Furthermore proposals for the reform of the UN Security Council have to pass through the Security Council and can thus also be vetoed.

At present the UN has no standing armed forces of its own, instead relies on it's members to supply the appropriate forces when called upon to do so. The UN is thus dependent on the willingness of its members to supply military forces when requested, but it cannot enforce such a request.

For any significant operation to be undertaken without local assistance (i.e. the dispatch of significant numbers of troops beyond an adjoining border against some form of opposition) a power projection capability is required involving an advanced command, control and communications system and a significant logistical tail. This type of capability is maintained by relatively few states (e.g. the United States and to a lesser extent France, Britain and Russia). Thus the other members of the UN have to rely upon the active rather than tacit participation of one or more of these Permanent Members in order to undertake any intervention.

These forces are then funded by the United Nations from the budgetary contributions of all the UN members. The UN has historically always been short of funding[17] and the proliferation in UN missions since 1989 has exacerbated this problem and has provided another method of Great Power control upon UN activities as the major donor states.

Within the UN Charter provision exists for the utilization of a UN Military Staff Committee for the conduct of UN activities[18]. However, this body has remained dormant, and instead command of UN forces has tended to be delegated to a particular Great Power's military commander on the ground who consults, in theory at least, with the UN political representative on the ground or with UN headquarters in New York rather than with his own national government.[19]

A return to idealism?

The alternative perspective suggests a more idealistic approach and suggests that the international transformation that has taken place presents the UN with the opportunity to have a far greater say than it has had in the past.[20]

Eisenhower's view that the UN was the best hope for 'World Order' foreshadowed the ideas of the NWO envisaged by President Bush. Both nestle neatly into the idealistic vision. The UN operation against in Iraq indicated how the UN could successfully use military force to uphold the rule of law and that collective security could work if all the UN members were prepared to adopt a reciprocal guarantee of each other's security.

The United Nations Secretary General, Boutros Boutros-Ghali, noted that '[t]he time of absolute and exclusive sovereignty, however, has passed; its theory was never matched by its reality'[21] since according to Major General Lewis MacKenzie, formerly UN Commander Peacekeeping Forces, Sarejevo: '[h]umanitarian need has [now] overwhelmed that clause in the Charter that precludes interference in the internal affairs of another nation'.[22]

The primary task of the UN has always officially been to maintain international peace and security '[a]nd to that end to take effective collective measures for the prevention and removal of threats to the peace ...'[23] When drafted the ideas of a threat to international peace and security followed the narrow interpretation of security. With the end of the Cold War the restriction of security to the 'narrow school' by the countries of the North has become increasingly irrelevant and a broader interpretation of security has tended to be adopted.[24] This has been acknowledged by the British Foreign Secretary, Douglas Hurd, who concluded that

> [s]ome problems - state-sponsored terrorism, for example, or the proliferation of ballistic missiles - may prick our skin more than our consciences. But, if we really want a world that is more secure, more prosperous and more stable, then humanitarian problems can be just as threatening and must be seen as not just a moral issue, but as a potential security threat as well.[25]

Furthermore, whilst realism has traditionally argued against the ideas of a universal moral order[26] and the interference in another state's domestic affairs, the end of the Cold War has seen an upsurge in humanitarian intervention and concern for human rights matched to a continuing Great Power desire to have UN support to justify their actions to their own population. These factors bring into question some of the assumptions made by the realist school and raise the question whether there is a movement within the international system towards a form of world order and the permanent undermining of the Westphalian system.

To achieve this aim the Security Council would either have to be reformed to reduce the power of veto of the Permanent Members, or reform threatened thereby ensuring the compliance of the Permanent Members with the general view held within the UN. In either case some degree of UN control is required over military forces either by the creation of UN forces or the permanent commitment of military forces from member states to the UN.

In both case studies the intervention of military forces under UN auspices for humanitarian reasons would suggest that there is a shift towards the idealists' camp but the reality of the situation needs to be examined to see if there is a growing role for the UN in preserving 'World Order' using military intervention as an instrument of this objective.

Case Studies

Somalia

The power vacuum created by the fall of President Siad Barre in January 1991 led to a struggle for control between numerous clans in many parts of Somalia with the most intense fighting in the capital Mogadishu resulting in widespread death and destruction. Hundreds of thousands of civilians were forced to flee their homes resulting in the need for international emergency humanitarian assistance. The incoming Secretary-General Boutros Boutros-Ghali stated in January 1992 that '[n]owhere in the world is the leadership of the UN more needed than in the Horn of Africa'.[27]

The precedent legitimizing UN involvement in the internal affairs of a country in order to alleviate suffering had already been set. In April 1991 Security Council Resolution 688 declared that the repression by a government of its own people constituted a threat to international peace and security. This was in response to the massive influx of Kurdish refugees into southern Turkey and northern Iran as a direct consequence of Saddam Hussein's repression in Iraq.[28]

Somalia presented the UN with a similar challenge. Resolution 733 was adopted on 23 January 1992. It called upon states and international organizations to contribute to the efforts of humanitarian assisitance to the population in Somalia.[29] Initially, however, between January and March 1992 the UN, with the assistance of the Organization of African Unity (OAU) and the Arab League attempted unsuccessfully to negotiate a ceasefire between the warring factions. At the time General Mohamed Farah Aideed rejected the deployment of peacekeeping troops. In accordance with established procedures the Secretary-General did not call for any troops to be deployed unless all the parties consented. The result of UN inaction was an escalation in fighting. This presented the Organization with two fundamental problems. Firstly, the practical issue of delivering humanitarian assistance with the civil war raging and thousands of Somalis dying. Secondly, the legal question of whether the UN had the right to intervene in the domestic affairs of a state.

The legal problem was oversome when the UN, Aideed and the other warring factions came to an understanding which led to the legitimization of UN deployment. The numerous, though unsuccessful, ceasefires did at least contribute to the process through which Aideed agreed to UN deployment. First, in February 1992, UN negotiators managed to get the warring factions to agree to the distribution of emergency food and medical aid to Mogadishu.[30] Second, on 2 March 1992, in an important concession, Aideed told the UN that he would accept military observers to monitor a ceasefire between the warring factions.[31] Nigeria's President, Ibrahim Babangida, as OAU Chairman, played a leading role in brokering the ceasefire which led to Aideed's concession. Previously Aideed had rejected any form of outside intervention stating that the problems of Somalia were a domestic matter.

Following on from this, in his report to the Security Council, the Secretary-General had made it clear that the crisis in Somalia posed a threat to international peace and security under Article 1 of the UN Charter since '[t]he countries of the region - Djibouti, Ethiopia, Kenya and the Sudan - some more than others, are beset by problems that are largely common to all. As a result, the exacerbation of conflict in one of the countries of the region could have serious consequences in one or more of the others'.[32] In addition, as has already been seen, the precedent for UN involvement in the internal affairs of a member state had been set.

As a consequence Resolution 751 of 24 April 1992 established the UN Operation in Somalia (UNOSOM) with the mandate to '[f]acilitate an immediate and effective cessation of hostilities and the maintenance of a ceasefire throughout the country in order to promote the process of reconciliation and political settlement in Somalia and to provide urgent humanitarian assistance'.[33] It also approved, in principle, the deployment of UN security forces to escort humanitarian aid to where it was needed. It was not until 14 September 1992, however, that the first group of security personnel (500 Pakistani peacekeepers) arrived in Mogadishu. This resulted in significant criticism of the United Nations because the delay had left the aid agencies completely exposed to the mercy of the warring factions.

The Pakistanis' mission was to secure Mogadishu airport, safeguard food shipments and escort aid convoys to their destinations. The Pakistanis were pinned down at the airport, however, by Somali clans. They failed to secure the airport let alone escort aid convoys. This was essentially due to them being inadequately armed for the situation and the constraints imposed by the United Nation's traditional rules of peacekeeping which allowed the use of force only in self-defence.

Political stability and security continued to be major concerns of the UN. By November 1992 the situation had deteriorated considerably. In reality Somalia, as a nation state, had ceased to exist. It lacked a central government with which to negotiate. The fighting between the two main factions in Mogadishu and amongst numerous other groups within the rest of the country severely constrained and threatened the humanitarian goal of UNOSOM. It was clear that anarchy reigned in Somalia.

The widespread media attention given to the looting of humanitarian aid corresponded with the end of the US Presidential elections which allowed President Bush to react to a shift in public opinion over the issue and focus on foreign policy again (see Wyn Bowen's chapter). Consequently, the US presented Boutros Boutros-Ghali with a plan that proposed the deployment of up to 30,000 troops, many of them American, in order to facilitate aid distribution. The goal was to stabilize the military situation in Somalia before letting the UN Secretary-General take responsibility.

Deteriorating conditions led the UN to accept the US offer to command a Unified Task Force (UNITAF). Resolution 794 was passed on 3 December 1992. The Security Council

> alarmed by the deterioration of the humanitarian situation ... [and] ... at continuing reports of widespread violations of international humanitarian law ... including reports of violence and threats of violence against personnel participating lawfully in impartial humanitarian relief activities ... authorizes the Secretary-General and Member States ... to use *all necessary means* to establish as soon as possible a secure environment for humanitarian relief operations in Somalia ...[34]

Operation Restore Hope began in early December 1992 with an initial welcome for the American led intervention force. This resulted in a positive impact upon the security situation and allowed the effective delivery of humanitarian assistance.[35] The illusion of success led to the announcement of a three month transitional period during which control was to return to UNOSOM II from UNITAF. It was soon realized, however, that the effort made by UNITAF to establish a secure environment was far from complete.

This was indicated by the growing rift between the UN Secretary-General on the one hand and the US on the other. The US viewed the mandate of *Operation Restore Hope* as limited to that of opening supply routes and to preparing for the hand over to UNOSOM II. The Secretary-General, however, had a wider interpretation including the use of the American led coalition to disarm the roaming Somali warring factions. The US showed a great reluctance to make the commitment for what seemed to be an almost impossible task.[36]

In addition, it was clear that Somalis were becoming increasingly hostile towards the UN. Armed chaos continued to be the underlying problem. At the end of March 1993 UNOSOM II was established amid a growing feeling within the UN, that unless the new operation in Somalia was provided with enforcement powers the job of establishing a secure environment for humanitarian relief would continue to be seriously hampered by the armed factions. Resolution 814 of, 26 March 1993, reflected the feeling that the UN mandate needed to be widened.[37] As a consequence the Security Council requested the Secretary-General to 'direct the Force Commander of UNOSOM II to assume the responsibility for the consolidation, expansion and maintenance of a secure environment throughout Somali ... and ... to organize a prompt, smooth and phased transition from UNITAF to UNOSOM II'.[38]

To make matters worse atrocities began to be committed. First, Aideed's forces ambushed and killed 24 Pakistani peacekeepers on 5 June 1993 who later killed 20 Somalis including civilians who had been used as human shields by Aideed's forces. At the same time US forces went on the offensive in Mogadishu.[39] This event acted as a catalyst which led to a sudden shift from humanitarian intervention to more forceful peace enforcement. Under this more aggressive mandate the objectives of UNOSOM II were dramatically widened. New attempts were made to implement a 'comprehensive programme for disarmament'.[40] Also the UN Security Council quickly identified the attackers as being supporters of General Aideed.[41] Paragraph 5 of Resolution 837 significantly reaffirmed that the Secretary-General was authorized, under Resolution 814, to take 'all necessary measures against all those responsible for the armed attacks ... including to secure the investigation of their actions and their arrest and detention for prosecution, trial and punishment ...'[42]

In the subsequent manhunt for General Aideed himself, UN forces, heavily reliant on the US, launched attacks on buildings controlled by Aideed's supporters.[43] This new objective had the effect of sucking the UN into an urban war which it had no prospect of winning. The problem was that, under Resolution 837, the UN forces were required by the Secretary-General to arrest General Aideed: this essentially eliminated any chances of a negotiated settement. In addition, UN action had two further adverse effects. Firstly, it resulted in an escalation of the conflict between UN forces and Somalis. This had the result of alienating the civilian population since it exacted a heavy toll in lives without significant success. Secondly, UN policy seriously divided those carrying it out. The Italians refused to get heavy-handed and as such asked the US and the United Nations to suspend combat operations in an attempt to reduce tension. At the time Italy's defence minister, Fabio Fabbri, said: 'We must consider the overall objective of the Somali mission. We suggest a cooling-off period to reduce tension, the suspension of combat operations and a renewed effort to restore dialogue'.[44] For its part the UN's head of peacekeeping operations in New York, Kofi Annan, insisted that the Italian commander in Somalia, General Bruno Loi, be withdrawn.[45] It was now clear that there was a fundamental disagreement over the UN's role in Somalia. The US wanted to continue with the war whereas the Italians called for a return to the original purpose of protecting humanitarian relief.

Other UN contingents were also not happy about the situation. Troops from Islamic countries were uncomfortable with the massive American strikes which killed innocent people in a fellow-Muslim country. France was unhappy that it had not been represented in the overall command structure of UNOSOM II. Consequently, it announced in late August that it would withdraw from Somalia by the end of January 1994. This lack of coordination between various contingents and a poor overall command structure clearly contributed to UNOSOM II's failure.[46]

The feud between the UN and the Italians highlighted some other problems faced by the UN in Somalia. By October 1993 it was clear that the UN/US pursuit of Aideed was not going to be successful. The subsequent retreat from the mandate of looking for Aideed showed that this policy had been inappropriate from the start. The US, therefore, sent out signals that the military hunt for the general was effectively over. Robert Oakley, the US envoy to Somalia said that 'President Clinton has recognised that over time the policy has become distorted ... obviously the situation is getting worse for Somalia rather than better'.[47] The US also announced that it was to withdraw its troops from Somalia by the end of March 1994. Numerous US casualties were paramount in reshaping public opinion which, in turn, forced the administration to end its operation. The subsequent withdrawal of 600 US Rangers confirmed that US policy had shifted from the manhunt in favour of a political settlement with Aideed and other clan leaders.[48]

The planned withdrawal by the US and European contingents confirmed, however, that UN intervention in Somalia had not only failed to achieve its objectives but it also placed UN relief operations into further jeopardy. As the US and European contingents planned their withdrawal there were fears that Somalia would slide back into anarchy; renewed civil war was a distinct possibility. Subsequent responsibility, for the success or failure of the UN operation, came to depend largely upon the Pakistani and Indian contingents who remained.[49] These remaining UN troops, however, lacked the equipment and capabilities of the retreating US and European contingents. The ambush of 5 June 1993 of Pakistani troops highlighted this serious shortcoming.

New rounds of secret talks were entered into between the various warlords in mid-January 1994. The UN stayed out. It became apparent that the Somalis themselves were looking for ways to bring peace to their country - particularly as the international contingents were planning to leave.[50] A possible solution was the division of the country into semi-autonomous regions along clan lines. Following this meeting there was some optimism that the new peace agreement between Mogadishu's warlords would hold. There were no indications, however, that the war between the Somalis and the UN would also end. This reinforced the widely held belief that the UN had essentially become part of the problem in Somalia.

The extent of the failure of the UN's coercive strategies was indicated by Security Council Resolution 897. Unanimously adopted on 4 February 1994, the Resolution envisaged a restricted role for UN troops stationed in Somalia. The UN role was now to monitor voluntary disarmament by willing factions with an emphasis on reconstruction. The UN force was also to be scaled down considerably to a maximum of 22,000 troops. In addition, the resolution stressed that the UN was to end its mission in Somalia by March 1995 regardless of any fears of a resurgence in violence.[51] Essentially, the resolution was a tacit admission that the UN had to retreat from its aggressive and combative peacemaking operations of the previous two years. As the Americans left Somalia they bolstered the strength of the Pakistani troops, who were to control the streets of Mogadishu, by leasing 80 armoured personnel carriers, 30 tanks and attack helicopters.[52] Subsequently, the US was harshly accused by Pakistan of leasing outdated and inferior equipment to the UN.[53] Furthermore, Pakistan stated that it would have to consider security questions before deciding whether to keep its 5,000 soldiers in Somalia. The escalating violence and banditry which coincided with the US and European withdrawal contributed greatly to the uncertainty felt by the largely Pakistani, Indian, Egyptian and African contingents.

Although UN military intervention did bring an end to famine and a respite for the majority of the population from the anarchy and civil war, it is largely viewed to have been a failure. There are three main factors which explain the UN's inability to end the civil war. Firstly, the US refusal to disarm militias during *Operation Restore Hope* was a major error. The disarming should have begun in late 1992 when the international contingents enjoyed support throughout the country. Secondly, the lack of a unified command structure and a failure to coordinate UN actions raised the levels of resentment amongst many of the peacekeeping contingents. Thirdly, the hunt for general Aideed was a mistake. The UN would have done better had it placed a greater emphasis on political negotiation between the warring factions rather than looking for Aideed for over three months. For those who hoped that the UN operation in Somalia would be a blueprint for future operations dealing with disorder and conflicts it has not been a wholehearted success.

Bosnia

Alongside the optimism created by the idea of the NWO the unleashing of forces previously strangled by the Cold War's long arm led to new sources of instability. One of these was the disintegration of Yugoslavia, into a number of states resulting in a number of protracted and bloody conflicts, particularly in Bosnia-Hercegovina.

The crisis in Bosnia is important as it has shown how unrealistic the rhetoric surrounding the idea of the NWO has been. The disintegration of Yugoslavia resulting in the conflict in Bosnia must be analysed in two stages. The first stage lies within the context of a policy of containment followed by the UN, European Community (EC) and NATO towards Serbia and by the setting down of commitments to military action by NATO on behalf of the UN. However, the conduct of military action did not take place until the second stage with the actual enforcement of the *No-Fly Zone* and the carrying out of limited air strikes against Serbian positions.

During the first stage, numerous declarations called for an emphasis on the principle of collective security but Bosnia showed that the Security Council was paralysed by the conflicting national interests and objectives of its Permanent Members.

Initially, the crisis began when the Croatian and Slovenian Republics declared their legislation as being supreme over federal law on 26 and 27 September 1990, respectively. Serbian reluctance to give up its political dominance of the federal structure to a loose federation of sovereign states led to unilateral steps by Slovenia and Croatia towards declaring independence on 25 June 1991. On 27 June, the armed forces of the central authorities (JNA) attacked the provincial Slovenian militia. Soon after, hostilities broke out in Croatia.[54] The Croats, were well aware that 600,000 Serbs in Croatia would not be left unprotected by the Serbian authorities in Belgrade.

In accordance with Article 52 paragraph 2 of the UN Charter the Dutch Foreign Minister Hans van den Broek informed the EC that there was agreement with the UN that the EC and the Conference on Security and Cooperation in Europe (CSCE), in their capacity as regional bodies, would handle the crisis.[55] Nevertheless, as events showed, neither the EC nor the CSCE were ready for the crisis. Central to their efforts to solve the Yugoslavian crisis has been the attempts to reach a consensus on foreign and military policy when Europe had 'no agreed military means of carrying out a common security policy' let alone an agreed foreign policy.[56]

The rapid EC-UN recognition of Slovenia and Croatia as nation states, in an attempt to stabilize the situation and prevent the escalation of the conflict, and for the sake of political expediency precipitated the Bosnian crisis and provided a pretext for the Bosnian Serb extremists to use military force in the name of a 'Greater Serbia'. Here the EC's need to preserve an image of unity allowed Germany to take a lead and recognize the republics.[57] Confusion within the various European security institutions inevitably led to the UN taking over the organization of peace keeping forces in Yugoslavia. Committed UN involvement began when the then Secretary-General, Javier Perez de Cuellar, appointed Cyrus Vance as his Special Representative. He became responsible for securing a ceasefire. The EC continued participation, however, initially through Lord Carrington whose responsibility was to make possible a 'negotiated political solution' of the conflict through an ongoing peace conference.[58]

Initially UN peacekeeping forces were deployed in the Serb dominated enclaves in Croatia. At the time Sarajevo, the then peaceful capital of Bosnia, was used as the base for this operation.[59] The drive for recognition by the other republics appeared to force the Bosnian presidency to recognize that the only way to preserve the borders of the republic was to seek international recognition. The subsequent referendum held in Bosnia on 1 March 1992 showed that almost 63% of the electorate opted for independence: however, there was a major Serb boycott. This result dealt a blow to Serbia's plans to keep Bosnia within the Yugoslav federation.[60] The poll results led the EC to go ahead and recognize Bosnia as an independent state on 6 April 1992.

Another important factor was that the EC and UN had insisted that the internal boundaries of the former Yugoslavia could not be changed by force or without the consent of the parties concerned.[61] This implied a united security guarantee for the Bosnians. NATO had made this clear that 'all attempts to change existing borders through the use of force or a policy of *fait accompli* are unacceptable; we will not recognize any unilateral change of borders, external or internal, brought about by such means'.[62]

It is important to consider the legal implications of the recognition of Bosnia within the context of the UN Charter. The rhetoric surrounding the rule of law and collective security in the post Cold War period is well documented. Had the Permanent Members followed their own rhetoric about the NWO then Humanitarian Intervention, as a distinct part of military intervention, would have been more forcefully implemented at an earlier stage.

Under Article 52.2 the Security Council passed Resolution 713 expressing support for EC/CSCE collective efforts thus providing regional arrangements with the opportunity to settle the local crisis.[63] However, the lack of progress with the EC sponsored ceasefire agreements, combined with the practice of 'ethnic cleansing' particularly in Serb-dominated areas, led the Security Council to hold Serbia responsible for the aggression. The first step by the UN was the indirect acknowledgement of the existence of Bosnia-Herzegovina as an independent state. Resolution 752 of 15 May 1992 demanded that 'all forms of interference from outside, as well as any attempts to change the ethnic composition of the population, cease immediately and that those units of the Yugoslav People's Army and elements of the Croatian Army ... be withdrawn, or be subject to the authority of the Government of Bosnia ...'[64]

Resolution 755 of 20 May 1992 admitted Bosnia-Herzegovina to membership of the UN. This backed up the earlier recognition by the EC and had the effect of internationalizing the problem, by opposing any Serbian idea of a Greater Serbia.[65] In addition, the UN Security Council passed Resolution 757, which effectively held Serbia responsible for the continuation of the conflict. The UN, therefore imposed 'comprehensive mandatory sanctions'.[66]

Subsequent media reports showed that rather than subsiding the fighting actually intensified. Nevertheless, the Security Council passed Resolution 770 on 13 August 1992 which fell significantly short of providing authorization for explicit military intervention.[67] The Resolution reiterated the need for a non-military political solution even though it did recognize that the situation in Bosnia constituted a threat to international peace and security. Going by the NWO rhetoric one might have expected much tougher action to preserve the territorial integrity of Bosnia-Herzegovina. Resolution 770 merely called upon states to provide troops under a mandate to use *all necessary means* to ensure the delivery of humanitarian relief supplies to Bosnia. It is clear that the resolution reflected the Permanent Members reluctance to become involved in the complex war.

The continuous efforts by the UN/EC negotiators to achieve a political settlement to the crisis themselves reinforced the ideas that there existed a lack of will on the part of the Permanent Members to get militarily involved. The main objectives of the London Peace Conference of 26-28 August 1992, for instance, were merely (a) to negotiate a political settlement to the dispute (b) to ensure the rapid flow of humanitarian relief and (c) to make the ceasefires stick in the former republic.[68] It is clear that such settlements had little effect on the fighting on the ground. In addition, it is difficult to see how the objectives of the conference could have been fulfilled without being backed up by some threat of intervention.

Continued ethnic cleansing by the Serbs appears to have created a general feeling of wanting to 'punish' them. In response, the UN passed Resolution 786, on 10 November 1992 imposing a *No-Fly Zone* over Bosnia.[69] This was an indication of the superfluous nature of the negotiations and therefore the provisions of Chapter VII were the only remaining option. Nevertheless, critics of the move were quick to point out that the enforcement action would inevitably be aimed at Serbia, it being the greatest violater. The risk of loss of partiality which these critics feared was realized when subsequent UN action was interpreted by Dr Karadzic, the Bosnian Serb leader, as one-sided punishment.

The town of Srebrenica, one of the last Bosnian Government strongholds in Eastern Bosnia, presented serious problems to the UN. Serb advances made it necessary to evacuate Muslims from the town; however, such action undermined the Bosnian Government's hold on the region and provided the West's critics with the argument that the UN was aiding 'ethnic cleansing'.[70] The April 1993 Serb massacre in Srebrenica, once again, raised the debate over whether military intervention was needed: 'The mood of the world is beginning to say that the democracies must intervene, even if it is not in their direct interest.'[71] It also reintroduced the debate over whether the arms embargo on the Bosnian Government should be lifted.

Whilst the roles of the United States, Britain and France have been particularly criticized in all the debates surrounding military intervention and the arms embargo (see Chapters 3 and 4 of this book) the influence of Russia has received less attention. Historically Russia has been a strong supporter of the Serbs under the influence of the Pan-Slav movement.[72] In part UN action in Bosnia had, therefore, rested upon the Russian withholding of its veto in the Security Council. A move towards more effective military action or the lifting of the arms embargo would have heightened tensions within the Security Council. This was clear in the timing of the resolution to enforce the *No-Fly Zone* until after a crucial referendum involving Boris Yeltsin on 25 April.[73] This clearly shows how the Security Council can become paralyzed as the direct result of a failure on the part of the Permanent Members to reach a consensus. Furthermore, it indicates that national interests remain an important factor for the Permanent Members.

Following the setting up of the *Safe Areas* and the enforcement of the *No-Fly Zone* there was a definite shift in UN and NATO policy. Resolution 824 of 6 May was adopted as the direct result of continued Serbian assault on Bosnian Government strongholds, such as Zepa. The Resolution stated the Security Council was

> [d]etermined to ensure peace and stability throughout the country, most immediately in the towns of Sarajevo, Tuzla, Zepa, Gorazde, Bihac, as well as Srebrenica ... Convinced that the threatened towns and their surroundings should be designated as safe areas, free from armed attacks and from any other hostile acts which endanger the well-being and the safety of their inhabitants ...'[74]

However, despite the implicit threat contained in Resolution 824 UN action, initially, merely provoked Serbian action against Gorazde. In addition the disarming of Bosnian Government forces within the safe areas was regarded by many UN sources as being '... deeply unfair, as the Serbian side kept their arms ...'[75]

As a result of the escalation of war between the Bosnian Government and the Bosnian-Croats, which further aggravated an already highly confused situation, the Security Council attempted to identify the aggressors in direct contradiction to its traditional impartial policy. The Bosnian war was clearly made up of several conflicts which encouraged the Permanent Members to hesitate in their actions. Those who have argued, therefore, that there cannot possibly be a single solution to such a multi-layered problem have a fair point. It is quite possible that applying military intervention to such a problem would not only have aggravated the situation but also have destroyed the already damaged reputation of the UN. It is also clear that military intervention would not have been successful unless there was a clear political goal behind the action. Cowan has pointed out that intervention could only be 'an aid to be used in support of a viable peace plan'.[76] This begs the question whether such a viable peace plan existed.

In early January 1993 Cyrus Vance and Lord Owen introduced a plan based on territorial division of Bosnia. This envisaged a de-centralized state of 10 autonomous regions 9 of which would have been dominated by a particular protagonist and joined together in a quasi-federal state.[77] It remains difficult to understand how such a plan could have worked with ethnic minorities existing in each region. The plan clearly created a split between the Americans and the EC/UN team. The US criticized the plan for rewarding ethnic cleansing whilst requiring a large interventionary force in Bosnia to preserve its unitary status and to protect the minorities. Furthermore, the regions left in the control of the Bosnian Muslims were of dubious viability and would have required an extension of the UN mandate to protect them.

Clearly in the first stage of the Bosnian conflict the Permanent Members failed to agree a common solution and aggression was rewarded. The rule of law based on Permanent Member guarantees to smaller states, as envisaged in the Charter, was not upheld. The failures of the UN were the result of a combination of the conflicting interests of the Permanent Members.

The second stage of the conflict, however, has been characterized both by the enforcement of the *No-Fly Zone* and the use of limited air strikes against Serbian positions surrounding a number of *Safe Areas*. The *Safe Areas* concept, initially dismissed by UN officials as a catastrophe, was, nevertheless, a necessary compromise for the US and the EC states so that they could put up a unified front. The US had wanted to end the Vance-Owen plan as they were not prepared to provide troops to implement it.

The Europeans on the other hand agreed to the safe areas concept since they wanted the US to drop its insistence of arming the Bosnian Government.[78]

The official purpose of the *Safe Areas* policy was to save lives while working towards a political settlement. The success, however, overwhelmingly depended upon whether the UN was prepared to carry out the provisions of Resolution 824, mandating the use of force, if necessary, to enforce the peace. Consequently the continued reluctance on the part of the UN to translate into action what had been said on paper helped to undermine the policy. Ignoring the Resolution the Bosnian Serbs, in particular, continued their assaults on Bosnian Government held areas including those regions designated as UN *Safe Areas*.[79] However, the conflict was further complicated by the eruption of fighting between the Croatians and Muslims who had previously been allies.

With the collapse of the Vance-Owen plan it appeared that EC governments were about to 'wash their hands' of Bosnia.[80] This was illustrated by two facts. The first was the danger to the UN peacekeeping role in Bosnia. General Philippe Morillon, the UN commander, threatened to pull out because UNPROFOR was facing increased aggression and mounting casualties whilst retaliation by UN troops, even in self defence, posed a serious danger to UN impartiality and credibility.[81]

Secondly, the extent of UN political failure in Bosnia was illustrated by the fact that once the Vance-Owen plan had collapsed the Croatian and Serbian leaders, Franjo Tudjman and Slobodan Milosevic, respectively, agreed to divide up Bosnia into three states at the expense of the Bosnian Government. Rather than condemn such a plan the EC negotiator, Lord Owen pressed the Bosnian Government to accept.[82] What is clear is that, had the Bosnian Government accepted the plan, it would have left it with an entity far too small to be economically viable and totally dependent upon its enemies for contact with the outside world.

The position of the Bosnian Government became even more precarious when the Croatian and Serbian militias combined forces to begin offensives against the stronghold of Maglaj in central Bosnia.[83] In addition, there were reports that the Serbs and Croats had agreed not to fight each other around the Neretva valley along which ran the only government controlled road into Central Bosnia. The implications of this Croat-Serb alliance reached not only the Bosnian Government but also affected the UN significantly. As the threat of international intervention subsided the UN was repeatedly humiliated, even going as far as to negotiate with local forces over road blocks and tolls. It was clear that the UN mission was badly hampered. Of the 8,800 tons of food required each week the blockades were allowing only 3,000 tons to get through to the beseiged areas. According to UNHCR officials Bosnian Croat and Serb militias were preventing aid convoys to pass on to the *Safe Areas*. The extent of UN failure was indicated by Thorvald Stoltenberg's (UN mediator in the war) warning to the Security Council on 15 July 1993, that the United Nations may have to stop its humanitarian efforts.[84]

Both the EC and the UN brokered numerous ceasefires which failed to achieve the desired results. When they were ignored threats of force were issued. These threats were not, however, followed through. At this stage the UN ought to have intervened militarily in order to open the roads to Mostar, Srebrenica and Gorazde. When nothing was done the blame was placed at the feet of the EC and the UN. It appeared that partition of Bosnia into three ethnically based statelets was inevitable.

Even the EC's push for sanctions against Croatia, in response to the latter's support of the Bosnian Croatians, was poorly received. Described as being 'too little ... too late,'[85] experts, at least at that time, believed that such action would lead to serious problems for the UN's humanitarian effort, particularly as many of the UN personnel were based in Croatia. This was reflected in the change of policy by the Americans from initially proposing the lifting of arms embargoes and the use of air strikes to protect Muslim enclaves, to the resignation that the only remaining option was to attempt to force the Bosnian Government into participating in peace talks aimed at dividing up the Bosnian state.[86]

All that was needed was for the Bosnian Government to accept defeat and settle for the creation of three ethnically based statelets.[87] Nevertheless, the UN humanitarian effort did not end. There are a number of factors which explain why this was so. Firstly, the orders to the Bosnian Serb, Croat and Government forces to stop the fighting on the ground were ignored by the various militias. The Bosnian Serbs had, by the start of August 1993, captured the strategic high ground surrounding Sarajevo. Consequently, the fate of the Bosnian capital and other beseiged areas contributed decisively to the continuation of UN efforts. In addition, this advance by the Serbs led to the failure of the talks at Geneva.[88]

Second, the costs of the escalation of fighting could not be ignored by the United Nations. Human lives were being lost daily. Had the UN withdrawn it would have appeared that the organization was appeasing aggression. As a consequence its reputation and credibility as a moral authority would have suffered a serious setback.

Third, the Bosnian Serbs tested the resolve of the UN by openly attacking an important French base at Zetra in Sarajevo. The attack provided the UN with a reason to provide air cover to protect UN peacekeepers in Bosnia.[89] A NATO air force was assembled in Italy to protect UN troops. Although NATO allies agreed that air strikes may be necessary they failed to reach agreement over just how much air power was to be used. The British and French resisted American pressure for a full-scale bombing campaign[90] because of concern for the safety of their ground troops. As a consequence UN commanders won an important victory against Washington. This was the right to decide, along with NATO, which targets to bomb. General Francis Briquemont (the then commander of UN forces in Bosnia) was fearful that air strikes would have led to retaliation by the Bosnian Serbs. Therefore, NATO's decision to draw up options for air strikes against the Bosnian Serbs around Sarajevo and other areas of Bosnia was a political signal rather than the start of a new stage in operational planning.

Nevertheless, the belief that the threat of air strikes was beginning to have an effect on Bosnian Serbian actions were put forward by the US. The fact that the Bosnian Serbs withdrew from Mounts Igman and Bjelesnica, around Sarajevo, in August 1993, prompted the US to support the proposition that the withdrawal was the direct result of the threats.[91] Fighting on Mount Igman was to be renewed shortly after however.

It remained impossible to see an end to the war, however, even though the Bosnian Serb guns around Sarajevo fell silent for a while. This was essentially due to the attempts by all three militias to continue to change the ethnic boundaries of any future republics by military means while delaying negotiations in Geneva.

The peace negotiations in Geneva failed to achieve a political settlement based upon a three-way ethnic split. The difference between the various factions were great enough to prevent such an agreement. According to Lord Owen, all the sides wanted more territory than either of the others was prepared to give.[92] In addition, Bosnian Government hardliners believed that it was in their interests to continue fighting as they were relying on the UN and NATO to carry out air strikes against their enemies.

Renewed threats of air strikes by NATO came in early January 1994. A number of factors help explain this decision. First, the Bosnian Serbs along with the other warring parties had regularly prevented the UN from carrying out its peacekeeping mandates. This was having the effect of seriously frustrating the UN's humanitarian efforts in numerous regions. In the Muslim enclave of Srebrenica, for instance, the Serbs had, for long, refused to allow Dutch UN troops to replace the Canadians. Second, the Bosnian Serb siege of Sarajevo made the most pressing place for the UN to act where the media attention was concentrated. Thirdly, the lifting of the Serbian siege of the airport at Tuzla was essential if much needed humanitarian aid was to get through to besieged *Safe Areas* in the north and east of Bosnia. Fourthly, there was a continued breach by both the Serbs and the Croats of the *No-Fly Zone*.

These four factors were central in explaining the renewed threats by Nato to bomb Serb positions. The final decision to carry out air strikes, however, rested with the United Nations. The Secretary-General, nonetheless, remained reluctant to give the order for air strikes because of the concern that they would lead to the break down in the political negotiation process. Opposed to the idea of NATO air strikes, Boutros-Ghali regularly informed the Security Council that 'there were not enough United Nations peacekeepers on the ground to carry through an effective military operation in the aftermath of Nato air strikes'.[93]

It was also clear that those countries with ground troops in Bosnia regarded reprisals against their soldiers as a serious enough possibility. The British Prime Minister, John Major, for instance, assured the Commons that the safety of more than 2,000 British troops in Bosnia would be a paramount factor in any decision.[94] In addition, Malcolm Rifkind, the British Secretary of State for Defence, stated: 'We ourselves are not enthusiastic about it. There has to be very special circumstances before the use, for the first time, of such a powerful means of force'.[95]

The special circumstances did, however, arise which made it necessary for air strikes to be carried out. Firstly, the mortar attack on a market in Sarajevo, which killed 68 civilians on 5 February 1994, acted as a catalyst. It clearly moved Western public opinion against the Bosnian Serbs and in favour of military action. Secondly, the Bosnian Serbs' flagrant disregard of the UN threatened to undermine the UN's position within the international system entirely. This the Permanent Members of the Security Council could not accept. Thirdly, the solidarity of the NATO allies, particularly, Britain, France and the US appeared seriously threatened and their own credibility and unity were now at stake.[96] Fourthly, the UN had authorized NATO and the EC to attempt to solve the Bosnian crisis under Article 52.2 of the UN Charter. It was important, therefore, for the UN, for NATO and the EC to appear to be taking tougher measures if future moves towards the use of regional arrangements were to continue.

One factor, however, which threatened to undermine the UN's threats of air strikes was the internal political situation in Russia. Boris Yeltsin was placed in a difficult position since he could not afford to be seen to be deserting his fellow Slavs - the Bosnian Serbs. Although Russia had no legal grounds for opposing air strikes, since all the relevant UN Resolutions were in place, it was necessary to assure Yeltsin that the West had 'no intention of becoming embroiled in the war in Bosnia-Herzegovina'.[97] Yeltsin's fears that NATO air strikes on the Bosnian Serbs would fuel the popularity of the Russian far right led to the commitment of Russian troops on the hills around Sarajevo and the Serbs withdrawing.

Instead, the Bosnian Serbs began to challenge the UN *Safe Areas* of Gorazde. Air strikes only achieved limited success, however. Indications for this were shown by the latters' advance on Gorazde. Despite limited attempts at enforcing Bosnian Serb withdrawal they continued their advance into the town. The Gorazde crisis left the UN with only two choices: effectively to do nothing or to escalate the pressure on the Bosnian Serbs backed up by the threat of more ambitious and damaging air strikes. Although significantly late the decision was taken to carry out air strikes against Serb positions in order to force them to withdraw from the UN safe area.[98] It is clear that there was no realistic alternative to bombing the Bosnian Serbs around Gorazde.

Conclusion

From the case studies it is evident that the UN's position *vis-à-vis* military intervention is an amalgam of contradiction with no clearly defined solution. Whilst humanitarian intervention has become an issue that can no longer be ignored by either the UN or individual Great Powers, there is an increasing reluctance amongst the Great Powers to become embroiled in military interventions beyond the confines of their national interests.

The news coverage of the recent Gulf War highlights the improvements made in modern broadcasting.[99] This has now given the media the ability to deliver real-time broadcasts from virtually anywhere in the world directly to the living room of the general public outside of the governmental control.[100] This has had, and will continue to have, an affect upon how governments react to events.[101] Foreign policy success or failure influences elections but more importantly, it causes opinion polls to fluctuate. For the politicians of the advanced industrialized West, and also for Russia such things cannot be ignored especially, in a time of recession.

The case studies highlight this point but also the contrasting influence within the Western Great Powers over the acceptability of casualties. For domestic reasons the United States, and to a lessor extent its West European allies, can no longer afford to accept significant levels of casualties upon operations outside of their narrowly defined national interests. This, in part, explains the growing US interest in the use of regional bodies to provide troops for UN operations rather than the Permanent Members.[102] Thus a movement in UN operations is evident which involves the increasing use of troops from the South, equipped and supplied by the states of the North, to undertake military interventions on the UN's behalf. The intervention in Rwanda clearly demonstrates how this trend has developed from the lessons of Somalia.[103]

The reluctance of the Permanent Members to get involved in further military interventions outside of their national interests has been reinforced by the financial cost of such action. As the major financial contributors to the UN they have already been required to meet the cost of the increase in UN operations. The US Congress has been particularly hostile to further UN operations[104] whilst the economic plight in Russia has helped to ensure that, along with the US, she remains a major debtor to the US.[105]

However, set against this Great Power reluctance to become involved has been concern for the preservation of the Westphalian system. The interest of the Great Powers in UN intervention may be declining but they are not prepared to accept the undermining of the UN by other states. The Iraqi invasion of Kuwait and the division of Bosnia-Herzegovina by force were both violations of state sovereignty and had the potential for destabilization of the balance of power within the respective regions.[106] In both cases the Great Powers have eventually resorted to military force in an attempt to remedy the situation.

Thus the role of the UN will not be that envisaged by those from within the idealist school of thought. Instead the UN's role in military intervention will be dictated by the national interests of its Permanent Members in line with the realist school. This does not mean the objectives of the idealists will remain unrealized. For individual, and occasionally collective reasons, the Great Powers will want to uphold the UN's role in military intervention. We are thus likely to witness a greater UN role in military intervention but by stealth rather than from any agreed policy due to the need to preserve the UN's symbolic position in anarchic world order.

Notes

1. For a good analysis of the implications of the fall of the Berlin Wall see Armstrong, David, & Goldstein, Erik, 'A World Transformed?', in The End of the Cold War, edited by Armstrong and Goldstein., London, Frank Cass & Co. Ltd., 1990.

2. Fukayama, Francis, 'The End of History?', in National Interest, no.16, 1989, pp.3-18, idem, The End of History and the Last Man, Harmondsworth, Penguin, 1992, p.6.

3. Armstrong & Goldstein, op.cit., p.10.

4. cf.Huntington, Samuel P, 'The Clash of Civilizations', in Foreign Affairs, vol.72, no.3, Summer 1993, p.22.

5. Russett, Bruce, & Sutterlin, James S., 'The UN in a New World Order', in Foreign Affairs, vol.70, no.2, Spring 1991, p.69. Note also Gorbachev's speech to the United Nations General Assembly, 7 December 1988, UNGA, A/43/PV.72.

6. cf.James, Alan, 'The United Nations', in The End of the Cold War, op.cit., p.183.

7. Weiss, Thomas G., 'Intervention: Whither the United Nations?, in The Washington Quarterly, vol.17, no.1, Winter 1994, p.118.

8. Goulding, Marrack, 'The Evolution of United Nations Peacekeeping', in International Affairs, vol.69, no.3, July 1993, pp.451-464.

9. cf.Roberts, Adam, 'The United Nations and International Security', in Survival, vol.35, no.2, Summer 1993, pp.3-30, p.3.

10. The Permanent Members are Britain, China, France, Russia (formerly the Soviet Union) and United States.

11. See Weber, Cynthia, 'Reconsidering statehood: examining the sovereignty/intervention boundary', in Review of International Studies, vol.18, no.3, July 1992, pp.199-216.

12. See, for example, Waltz, Kenneth N., Man, the State, and War, New York, Columbia University Press, 1959; Bull, Hedley, The Anarchical Society: a study of order in international politics, London, MacMillan, repr.1991; Morgenthau, Hans J, Politics among Nations: the struggle for power and peace, New York, A.A. Knopf, fourth edition 1967. For a critique see Tickner, J. Ann, Gender in International Relations, New York, USA, Columbia University Press, 1992, particularly chapter 2.

13. See Kissinger, H., 'Foreign Policy is about the National Interest', The International Herald Tribune, 25 October 1993, p.5.

14. See Holsti, K.J., International Politics: a framework for analysis, New Jersey, Prentice-Hall International Inc., fifth edition, 1988, particularly chapter 5, 'Foreign Policy Objectives', pp.118-139.

15. cf.UN Charter, Article 1.

16. cf.The reference in Article 39 to Articles 41 & 42 refers to actions which may be taken by the Security Council in the event of a threat to peace and actual acts of aggression.

17. Pick, Hella, 'Members must pay overdue bills for blue berets, warns Boutros-Ghali', in The Guardian, 5 April 1994, p.9.

18. UN Charter, Articles 45-47.

19. For the problems this has caused see, for example, Bellamy, Christopher, 'Generals battling the bureaucracy', in The Independent, no.2,272, 31 January 1994, p.15. See, Grove, Eric, 'UN Armed Forces and the Military Staff Committee', in International Security, vol.17, no.4, Spring 1993, p.183.

20. Rosenau, James N., The United Nations in a Turbulent World, International Peace Academy occasional Paper Series, Lynee Rienner Publishers, London, 1992, pp.8-9.

21. cf.Boutros-Ghali, Boutros, An Agenda for Peace, New York, USA, 1992, p.9.

22. cf.MacKenzie, Major General Lewis, 'Military Realities of UN Peacekeeping Operations', in The RUSI Journal, vol.138, no.1, February 1993, pp.21-24, p.23.

23. cf.UN Charter, Article 1.

24. For a discussion of the nature of security and the problems surrounding it see, for example, Buzan, Barry, People, States and Fear: the National Security Problem in International Relations, Brighton, Wheatsheaf Books Ltd., 1983; and Booth, Ken (ed.), New Thinking about Strategy and International Security, London Harper Collins *Academic*, 1991.

25. cf.Hurd, Douglas, 'Peacekeeping or Peacemaking? Implications and Prospects', in The RUSI Journal, vol.137, no.6, December 1992, p.2. This view was rapidly refuted by the Secretary of State for Defence: Rifkind, Malcolm, 'Peacekeeping or peacemaking? Implications and prospects', in The RUSI Journal, vol.138, no.2, April 1993, pp.1-6.

26. See Vincent, R.J., 'Western conceptions of a universal moral order', in British Journal of International Studies, (now known as Review of International Studies), vol.4, April 1978, pp.20-46.

27. cf.United Nations Information Centre News Summary, 11 July 1991.

28. Security Council Document, S/RES/688 (1991), 5 April 1991.

29. Security Council Document, S/RES/733 (1992), 23 January 1992.

30. 'Aid to Somalia', The Independent, 17 February 1992.

31. Richard, Dowden, 'Somali Warlords stop fighting to ponder UN truce', The Independent, 3 March 1992.

32. cf. Boutros-Ghali, Boutros, 'The situation in Somalia: Report of the Secretary-General', Security Council Document: S/23693, 11 March 1992, p.4.

33. cf.Security Council Document, S/RES/751 (1992), 24 April 1992.

34. cf.Security Council Document, S/RES/794 (1992), 3 December 1992.

35. 'Further report of the Secretary-General submitted in pursuance of Paragraphs 18 and 19 of Resolution 794 (1992)', Security Council Document, S/25354, p.12,

36. Bolton, John R., 'Wrong turn in Somalia', in Foreign Affairs, January-February 1994, vol.73 no.1, p.61.

37. Security Council Document, S/RES/814 (1993), 26 March 1993.

38. Security Council Document, S/RES/814 (1993), 26 March 1993.

39. Dowden, Richard, 'UN troops died trying to take Somali radio station', in The Independent, 8 June 1993.

40. The objectives of UNISOM II also now include the neutralization of broadcasting and other propaganda mechanisms which incite violence and therefore prevent further violations of the ceasefire. cf.'Report of the Secretary-General', Security Council Document, S/26022, 1st July 1993, p.5.

41. 'US bombs Somali warlord's arms cache after attacks', in The Independent, 7 June 1993.

42. cf.Security Council Document, S/RES/837, 6 June 1993.

43. Roberts, James, 'UN forces pound Somali Warlord's lair', in The Independent, 13 June 1993.

44. Lorch, Donatella, 'Italy asks UN to halt Somali combat', in The Guardian, 13 July 1993.

45. Dowden, Richard, 'UN Somalia effort crumbles amid raids and bickering', in The Independent, 15 July 1993.

46. Makinda, Samuel M., 'Somalia: from humanitarian intervention to military offensive', in The World Today, vol.49, no.10, October 1993, p.186.

47. cf.Hartley, Aidan, 'Aideed militia complain about US show of force', in The Independent, 13 October 1993.

48. Brodie, Ian and Fletcher, Martin, 'US denies Aideed deal over troop withdrawal', in The Times, 20 October 1993.

49. Lorch, Donatella, 'Somalia backslides into lawlessness', in The International Herald Tribune, 11 January 1994.

50. Kiley, Sam, 'Somalia's warlords hold secret talks to avert bloodshed', in The Times, January 14 1994.

52. Security Council Document, S/RES/897 (1994), 4 February 1994.

52. Peterson, Scott, 'US leaves Somalia in grip of banditry', in The Daily Telegraph, 24 March 1994.

53. 'Pakistan Criticizes US Somalia Gear', in The International Herald Tribune, 14 March 1994.

54. Weller, Marc: 'The International Response to the Dissolution of the Socialist Republic of Yugoslavia', in American Journal of International Law, Vol.86, No.3, July 1992, p.570 and 574.

55. Atlantic News, No. 2,368, 9 November 1991, Brussels; Also, Article 52.2 of the UN Charter states that States should 'make every effort to achieve pacific settlement of local disputes through such regional arrangements or by such regional agencies before referring them to the Security Council', UN Charter.

56. cf.'Moves on Balkans Conflict reveal an EC that's as Fractious as Ever', in The International Herald Tribune, 26 April 1992.

57. For criteria on recognition of new states see Atlantic News, No. 2,380, 18 December 1991, p.3. Also for account on German pressure being applied on the EC for the early recognition of Slovenia and Croatia see 'A critical briefing on the conflict in Yugoslavia', in Yugofax, no.10, 3rd February 1992.

58. See Weller, op.cit., pp.581-582 for an account on the Vance missions and further EC actions under Lord Carrington.

59. For an analysis of the initial UN operation see MacKenzie, op.cit.

60. 'Bosnia claims Independence Poll Victory', in The Financial Times, 2 March 1992.

61. Dempsey, J., 'EC tries to keep war out of Bosnia', in The Financial Times, 21 February 1992.

62. cf.'Rome Declaration on Peace and Cooperation', Atlantic News, Europe Documents, No. 1,744, 13 November 1991, p.7.

63. Security Council Document, 713/RES/(1991), 25 September 1991.

64. cf.Security Council Document, 752/RES/(1992), 15 May 1992.

65. Security Council Document, 755/RES/(1992), 20 May 1992. Resolutions 753 and 754 of 18 May 1992 admitted Croatia and Slovenia to membership of the United Nations.

66. Security Council Document, S/RES/757/(1992), 30 May 1992.

67. Security Council Document, 770/RES/(1992), 13 August 1992.

68. Binyon, Michael, & Judah, Tim, 'Major tells Serbia to stop grabbing land', The Times, 27 August 1992.

69. Security Council Document, S/RES/786/(1992), 10 November 1992.

70. Judah, Tim, 'UN Rescues lorries turned away empty by Muslims', in The Times, 7 April 1993.

71. cf. Judah, ibid. Comment by David Howell, Chairman of the House of Commons Foreign Affairs Committee.

72. Huntington argues that Bosnia lies on a fault line between the Western Christian, Orthodox Christian and Muslim worlds that means a clash is inevitable as these civilizations move towards greater internal integrity. Huntington, op.cit.

73. Davies, Patricia Wynn, 'Fate of Srebrenica spurs call for Serbia blockade', in The Independent, 17 April 1993. Also see Bone, J, 'UN delays Belgrade sanction as *No-Fly Zone* takes effect', in The Times, 13 April 1993. The United Nations adopted Resolution 820 on the 17th of April 1993 but the sanctions did not come into effect until 26 April. See Security Council Document, S/RES/820 (1993), 17 April 1993.

74. cf.Security Council Document S/RES/824 (1993), 6 May 1993.

75. Tanner, Marcus, 'West sets the stage for a human tragedy', in The Independent, 8 June 1993.

76. cf. Cowan, Edward, Military Intervention in the former Yugoslavia, International Security Information Service Briefing no.33, 1993.

77. Idem.

78. Savill, Annika, 'Chequered pedigree of a compromise', in The Independent, 8 June 1993. Also see Marshall, Andrew, 'EC-US split on Yugoslavia bursts into open again' in The Independent, 10 June 1993. Mr. Warren Christopher (the US Secretary of State) emphasized that he supported the Vance-Owen peace process but not the plan itself. In addition he insisted that this was because of a lack of support for the map of 10 new Bosnian provinces for which the plan provided.

79. Tanner, Marcus, 'Gorazde begs for help to end Serbian Siege' in The Independent, 15 June 1993.

80. cf.Palmer, John, 'Owen urges EC summit to safeguard Muslims', in The Guardian, 21 June 1993.

81. See for example Block, Robert, 'Life or death dilemma for UN troops', in The Independent, 12 June 1993. British soldiers fired on Croatian militiamen attacking a private Muslim aid convoy on its way to the besieged town of Tuzla. Two Croatians were killed. Daly, Emma and Castle, Stephen, 'Morillon threatens to pull out after Spanish officer is killed', in The Independent, 13 June 1993.

82. Sheridan, Michael, 'Bosnians under strong pressure to accept reality', in The Independent, 25 June 1993.

83. Tanner, Marcus, 'Croats and Serbs launch joint attack', in The Independent, 28 June 1993.

84. Pringle, Peter, 'UN aid to Bosnia may have to end, mediator says', in The Independent, 16 July 1993.

85. cf.Block, Robert, 'The time for evenhandedness has passed', in The Independent, 20 July 1993.

86. Usborne, David and Block, Robert, 'Muslims face stark choice: join talks or accept defeat', in The Independent, 25 July 1993.

87. 'The folly of betraying Bosnia', in The Independent, 26 July 1993.

88. Sheridan, Michael, 'Talks fail as Serbs take high ground',in The Independent, 5 August 1993.

89. Tanner, Marcus, 'Ceasefire is first casualty as Serbs bombard UN base', in The Independent, 26 July 1993.

90. Adams, James & Giovanni, Janine di, 'US and Britain agree to bomb Serb supplies', in The Sunday Times, 1st August 1993.

91. Reeves, Phil & Savill, Annika, 'Squabble exposes Bosnia tensions', in The Independent, 19 August 1993.

92. Sheridan, Michael, 'War in Bosnia to go on as peace talks collapse', in The Independent, 2 September 1993.

93. Ottaway, David, 'Boutros-Ghali Opposes Bosnia Air Strikes', in The International Herald Tribune, 20 January 1994.

94. Fairhall, David, 'UN chief to study NATO Bosnia threat', in The Guardian, 13 January 1994.

95. cf.Idem.

96. Fletcher, Martin, 'US poised to intervence against Bosnian Serbs', in The Times, 9 February.

97. cf.Webster, Philip & McElvoy, Anne, 'Major aims to underline limited role of air strikes', in The Times, 14 February 1994.

98. Starr, Barbara, 'Serbs feel force from Nato's CAS missions', in Jane's Defence Weekly, vol.21 no.15, 16 April 1994, p.3.

99. See Taylor, Philip M., War and the Media: Propaganda and persuasion in the Gulf War, Manchester, Manchester University Press, 1992; also Simpson John, From the House of War, London, Arrow Books Ltd., 1991; Brown, Ben, & Shukman, David, All Necessary Means: Inside the Gulf War, London, BBC Books, 1991.

100. For personal accounts see Lewis, Tim, The Human Shield, Bath, The Bath Press, 1991.

101. Note John Major's role in *Operation Irma*, see Savill, Annika, 'Sarejevo's symbol of agony flies in', in The Independent, no.2,214, 10 August 1993, p.1.

102. Pringle, Peter, 'Boutros-Ghali tries to muster African force for Rwanda', in The Independent, no.2,352, 4 May 1994, p.12.

103. Pringle, Peter, 'West snubs UN plea for action', in The Independent on Sunday, 1 May 1994, no.222, p.12.

104. Pringle, Peter, 'Can good come from this hell?', in The Independent, vol.2,353, 5 May 1994, p.20.

105. See Taylor, Paul, 'The United Nations system under stress: financial pressures and their consequences', in Review of International Studies, vol.17, no.4, October 1991, pp.365-382.

106. See the chapter by Otte, Thomas G., Dorman, Andrew M., & Bowen, Wyn Q., 'The West and the future of Military Intervention', in New Perspectives, edited by John MacMillan & Andrew Linklater, London, Pinter Publishers, 1995.

Section IV
Military Intervention: Continuity and Change

Military Intervention: Conclusions and Reflections

THOMAS G OTTE

'Cum igitur animum ad Politicum applicaverim,
nihil quod novum, vel inauditum est'.

Spinoza, *Tractatus Politicus*, I.4.

The introduction offered an *ideal type* definition of military intervention[1]; it offered the identification and abstraction of the essential characteristics and features of military intervention and the basic 'logic' on which its efficacy as an instrument of statecraft and its role as a function of the international system rests. It aimed at describing what is 'objectively possible' and at a 'causally adequate' explanation, thus enabling us to 'understand' the phenomenon of military intervention.[2] The analyses contained in this book have, guided by this *ideal type* definition, established new facts and have provided new insights into the matter. On this basis it is, therefore, possible to formulate generic knowledge to supplement or amend the *ideal type* definition of military intervention.

Military Intervention as a Function of the International system

Following an observation by Hedley Bull it was argued in the introduction that the phenomenon of military intervention is a 'built-in feature of the international system'.[3] The term 'international system' is, of course, somewhat misleading. It refers to a quasi-systemic configuration which, however, 'does not constitute a single form with relatively fixed features, but rather a single condition within which many variations can be arranged'.[4] This single condition is the prevailing state of international anarchy, defined as the absence of an overarching, norm-imposing global government.[5] In an international system which is composed of sovereign states, i.e. states which refuse to recognize a higher authority, the essential nature of the states inevitably defines the nature of the whole system.[6] Still, this quasi-Hobbesian imagined, pre-contractual state of nature among sovereign states is mitigated by certain societal elements such as international law, defined as a 'body of customary and conventional rules which are considered legally binding'[7] by most sovereign states, and other generally acknowledged norms of international behaviour.[8] Yet, as in Locke, in the absence of a central authority, it is for the individual members of the 'society' to judge for themselves and to enforce those elements.[9] Despite the undeniable process of erosion of sovereign statehood in international affairs by the growth of non-governmental actors the international system remains essentially a states system with an essentially anarchical character. In the *anarchical society*, therefore, 'self-help' is the necessary principle of action.[10] 'Self-help' basically implies the decentralization of security. In addition, the notion of state sovereignty entails the exclusive responsibility of states for their own security - even within alliances.[11] In the modern international states system security is therefore decentralized as well as indivisible. Self-preservation, the maintenance of their independence and security, is therefore the minimum 'national interest'[12] or 'core interest'[13] guiding the actions of states. As was argued in greater detail in the introduction, whenever two states are in regular contact they exist within a 'system'. In a complex process of interaction and interdependence the actions of one state affect the perceptions and calculations of the other states, who then arrange themselves accordingly in a certain systemic structure.

One of the outstanding features of the modern international system, in each of its historical configurations,[14] is what may be called the *antinomy* of international relations, i.e. its 'hierarchical anarchy'. 'Hierarchical anarchy' entails the specialization of different states (or 'system units') in different tasks in accordance with their capabilities.[15] Furthermore, the inherent 'logic' of systems is to strive for their own maintenance and, thus, for stability. Historically, the maintenance of order and stability in international politics has rested with the Great Powers: this has always been their specialized 'task'.[16] Their principal responsibility derives from the unequal distribution of power and capabilities among the states that constitute the international system. This contribution to international order can take different forms, and the use or the threat of force is only one of them.[17] In this respect, military intervention is not only an instrument of statecraft at the disposal of global or regional Great Powers pursuing their individual national interests; it is more than a 'built-in feature of international politics',[18] it is above all a function of the international states system, a mechanism to be set in motion by the Great Powers whenever order and stability or the overall global or regional balance of power are seen to be under threat, or whenever universally recognized norms of international conduct have been blatantly disregarded. From this military intervention derives its legitimacy.[19]

The analyses and case studies contained in this book clearly underline the essential character of military intervention as a function of the international system. Austria's intervention in Naples was necessitated, and therefore supported, or at least condoned, by the other Great Powers out of general balance-of-power considerations.[20] Similarly, the 'indirect' US intervention in Guatemala was acquiesced in, at least partially, because it helped to maintain American predominance in Latin America and thus the overall Cold War equilibrium between East and West.[21] A more recent example on a regional rather than global level is the tacit 'understanding' between Syria and Israel on rules of behaviour which allows each to act in her respective sphere of influence in the Lebanon without endangering the delicate power-political status quo in the Middle east.[22] The military interventions in Venezuela and at Suez, by contrast, failed above all because they fulfilled no clearly discernible order function.[23]

However, the functionality of military intervention with respect to international order notwithstanding, it is by no means inevitable or automatic. On the contrary, as was argued in the introduction and as the case studies have shown, military intervention is of an essentially *political* nature, and, moreover, it is complex and highly context dependent. Military intervention fulfils and international order function, but it still has to be politically decided upon; and, like the political sphere in general, it cannot be reduced to the interaction of quantitative factors, which would abolish politics altogether.[24]

The End of the Cold War: Military Intervention in a 'New' World Order

The end of the bipolar world order marked a *Zeitenwende* of far-reaching and fundamental consequences. The 'great sea-change'[25] is still under way, and the softened-up structure of the international system has not, as yet, hardened again into a new mould. At the beginning of a new era in international politics a new uncertainty dominates political thinking. Indeed, in view of the violent eruption of so many conflicts all over the globe, after having laid dormant since time unknown[26], has led many, political observers and practitioners alike, to look back with nostalgia to the 'remarkably stable and predictable atmosphere of the Cold War'.[27] Under the auspices of the East-West confrontation during the Cold War, the anticipated global apocalypse acted as a systemic constraint on many of the conflicts, which have since then erupted. The logic of nuclear bipolarity embraced all possible conflicts, which, once erupted, would have had global implications. Thus, the systematically immanent instrumental rationality of the (old) nuclear armed world order conditioned a significant reduction in the complexity of world politics.

Five years into the post-Cold War era, this simplification seems to have come to a violent end. The outbreak of numerous regional conflicts is subject to no apparent systemic rationality. In the light of the - so far - turbulent post-Cold War years, one may well wonder whether the Cold War was not after all an exception to the rule of international relations. The new era is still without a clearly discernible profile. But it has clearly opened new perspectives on international affairs. Many international theorists have begun a quest for the 'longe durée' (Fernand Braudel) in international relations, i.e. permanent factors influencing foreign policy formulation, but which are based on principles quite distinct from those of Cold War bipolarity. This new uncertainty, caused by the passing of the international system through a period of systemic transition and geopolitical interlude, is being reflected in the vocabulary of international relations theory. Like international politics itself, the systemic, quantitative, and pseudo-scientific terminology developed under the impression of the Cold War[28] is in the process of gradual transformation as well. In the immediate aftermath of the Cold War, for that one short 'unipolar moment'[29], when a new world order seemed to emerge from the ruins of the order of Yalta, 'Endism'[30] seemed to be on the verge of becoming the prevailing intellectual fashion. According to this particular form of 'secondary historicism' Western values had triumphed in a world in which everything had become the West. History - with a capital (Hegelian) H -, it was argued, had come to an end.[31] However, history habitually mocks the prophets of 'Endism' and makes them yesterday's fools. Thus, the 'rebirth of history' (M.Glenny), in turn, has led many writers to substitute Cold War functionalism with a 'secondary "Historismus"'[32]. And, indeed, the bizarre resurrection of the ghosts of particularism, the reinvention of the nation, and the resurgence of traditional concepts of political culture and different forms of civilization, often religiously defined, especially, but not only, in Eastern Europe seem to substantiate this view.[33] In this respect 'the present is shaped by yesterday as much as by tomorrow'.[34] The new era contains both elements of continuity and of change. The final shape of the new order in world politics cannot yet be foretold. But a number of features of the post-Cold War international system have already become clearly discernible, and some predictions can safely be made. All of these have a bearing on the problem of military intervention.

First of all, on a systemic level, the end of the Cold War has led to the re-emergence of all those imperatives of international order and security which, though never invalidated, had been reduced in their importance during the Cold War. With the break-down of the bipolar, nuclear armed world order the constitutive element of the Westphalian international system, state sovereignty, has come to the fore again. The ever more frequent occurrence of territorial disputes and the proliferation of new nation states clearly demonstrate that the state has again become the focus of international order. Inspite of transnational erosion and international integration the state remains the basic element of international order and security, and thus an international actor in its own right and a sphere of internal and external protection of its citizens.[35] This protection, however, can only be guaranteed within a clearly defined territorial entity; similarly, universal human rights can only be realized within the legal framework provided by the state.[36]

The renewed importance of such traditional, quasi-archaic elements as state sovereignty and territoriality was clearly demonstrated in the Gulf War, Iraq's attempted 'etatocide' of Kuwait was a clear violation of one of the fundamental principles of international politics, i.e. the inviolability of state sovereignty, as well as a threat to the stability of the region. Hence, the West's decision to reverse the Iraqi occupation of Kuwait. The fact that the war was halted once Kuwait was freed and the aggressor's territoriality and stability was perceived to be endangered, further underlines the renewed importance of these elements in the new post-Cold War era.

The principles of territoriality and regional stability based on state sovereignty clearly seem to enjoy priority in international affairs.[37] On the other hand, though, the growth of United Nations humanitarian missions as in Cambodia, Somalia, and lately in Bosnia highlights a new, humanitarian dimension of post-Cold War international politics.[38] Although, as Stuart Croft and Adrian Treacher have shown in this book, a healthy scepticism with regard to the humanitarian motivations of state governments is not at all misguided, internationally sanctioned military interventions on humanitarian grounds have clearly become an issue in an international system which is more integrated than ever before. In particular Western governments and the United Nations have repeatedly found themselves forced to take such action to preserve their status, and often in response to media and other public pressure.[39]

Humanitarian intervention, defined as a forcible action without the prior invitation or consent of the target state for the specific purpose of protecting fundamental human rights[40], represents a sub-species of military intervention. The concept of military intervention, as developed in the introduction to this book, is broad enough to accommodate both the more traditional concern with national security and international power and humanitarian motivations. The humanitarian dimension does not significantly alter the essential characteristics of 'traditional' military intervention; humanitarian intervention is but military intervention with a humanitarian objective.

However, the renewed importance of such archaic, or even atavistic, elements as nation, statehood and territoriality, on the one hand, and the new humanitarian dimension, on the other, represent two divergent trends in post-Cold War international politics. There is an obvious tension between these two trends. In fact, it may well be argued that there is an 'aporia', an inescapable dilemma, in the relations between human rights and the imperative of territoriality. As the cases of Somalia and Bosnia-Herzegovina have shown, intervention is feasible only in territorially clearly defined units. Humanitarian action in divided or even disintegrating territorial units, engulfed in a civil war, by contrast, is fraught with great dangers and the high risk of complete failure.

Moreover, this tension reflects the historical and now destabilized fault line between integrative and disintegrative forces in world politics.[41] The reunification of Germany and the collapse of the Soviet Union have significantly shifted the political coordinates of Europe. Both events have created a volatile situation in Central and Eastern Europe, where old national and ethnic rivalries are re-emerging; and, above all, both events have created a 'power vacuum' (Vaclav Havel) into which other Great Powers will push. Both developments have profound implications for the possible future interventionist behaviour of various governments and the future of intervention in the international system.

The most obvious effect of the dissolution of the Cold War order concerns Russia herself. Ever since the end of the old Soviet Union in December 1991, Russia has been engaged in a search for her national identity, as exemplified by broadly two main schools of thought. The fierce political controversy between what may be called the 'Atlanticists', advocating a Western style civil society, and the 'Eurasians', who maintain Russia's distinct uniqueness, has led to considerable confusion and lack of coherence in Russian foreign policy.[42] Whatever the final outcome of the internal Russian foreign policy debate, the indications are strong that Russia will continue to regard the entire geopolitical space of the former Soviet Union as a zone of Russia's vital interests, to be secured if necessary by means of intervention.[43]

However, the collapse of the Soviet Union also has wider implications which directly affect the problem of intervention. Since 1989 world politics is passing through a period of systemic transformation which, it may be safely predicted, will lead to multipolarity[44], thus further underlining the character of the international system as a 'multiverse' of states. In the course of modern history, there has been a continuous process of the rise and fall of Great Powers.[45] Whether a state will attempt to attain Great Power status depends largely, though not exclusively, on structural constraints pressing it to become a Great Power.[46] The strive for Great Power status has to be underpinned by economic, technological, and military capabilities, which are an indispensable precondition of national security in the anarchical 'self-help system'.[47] The current period of systemic transition affords an opportunity to and exerts pressure on a number of eligible states to become a Great Power.

One of the inferences that can be drawn from Wyn Bowen's and Andrew Dorman's contributions to this book is that Great Power status is linked to the capability to at least initiate and participate in a military intervention. This applies to established Great Powers as much as to those countries eligible for Great Power status. In Europe, Germany, in many ways bound to lead on account of her population strength, her economic power, and her geographical position, is already beginning to exert her potential leadership in European security affairs. Her prominent role in bringing about European recognition of the Yugoslav successor states and in providing economic aid to Eastern Europe are a first indication that the extent of her geopolitical interests is expanding. On the other hand, though, Germany's insufficient political and military support for the Gulf War allies has shown that without a convincing military capability she will not succeed in her attempts to obtain a permanent seat on the UN Security Council, the ultimate recognition of her de-facto Great Power status. In the Far East, there is a similar development with Japan poised to take on a more prominent international role.[48]

The rise of both these nations is widely held to be a threat to Britain's and France's permanent membership of the UN Security Council. They are the only European countries who currently have a comprehensive, though in comparison to the United States limited, intervention and power projection capabilities. For the foreseeable future the governments of Britain and France face a difficult task. While they have to match their military commitments with their economic capabilities, they will have to continue to participate in UN or NATO/WEU sponsored military actions in order to maintain their present international position.[49]

The position of the United States in this period of change is, by contrast, quite different. Only the United States possesses imposing strength in all categories (economic, technological, and military) of Great Power capabilities. For the time being, she enjoys unrivalled pre-eminence in international affairs. Yet with the evaporation of a direct threat to US national security and an ever more pressing domestic agenda America's security outlook is somewhat confused. However, although the Clinton administration's foreign policy doctrine is still being developed, it appears more than likely that the United States will continue to employ the instrument of military intervention whenever American strategic or humanitarian interests are threatened.[50]

Throughout the Cold War, under the auspices of the global ideological conflict, the United States and the Soviet Union were engaged in an elaborate 'game' of interventions and proxy wars in the periphery. After the collapse of nuclear bipolarity a 'new game' of intervention has begun. But, in contrast to the past, this 'new game' will be characterized by a broader concept of military intervention, which embraces both traditional notions of the national interest and humanitarian concerns, and, secondly, by the proliferation of potential interveners. Military intervention, therefore, will remain an instrument of statecraft and thus a constant feature of international politics.

Military Intervention as an Instrument of Statecraft

Throughout history, policy-makers have found military intervention to be a useful instrument amenable to a wide variety of political ends. No doubt, under certain circumstances, the employment of limited military force to maximum political effect may present a tempting policy option. The case studies presented in the second section of this book enable us to understand better the difficult task political decision-makers face when confronted with the option of military intervention in a particular situation. The case studies show that military intervention is highly context dependent. In each of the exemplary interventions analyzed here a complex of contextual variables affected the policy options. The complex configuration of each individual case has to be taken into account when policy-makers contemplate the option of military intervention.

The careful analysis of the cases referred to enables us to identify four major contextual factors which give each situation a distinct character.

(1) Whether or not military intervention is used depends on the given conflict of interests between the target state and the potential intervener. As was argued in the introduction, the target state presents a politcal problem for the intervener. However, the case studies have shown that military intervention is a highly inflexible instrument; it is a zero-sum game in which all parties involved either win or lose. The risk of ultimate failure is significantly higher in this strategy than in any other forms of compellant

threats. Once launched, as was explained in greater detail in the introduction, a military intervention cannot be reversed: it is a one-way road. Policy-makers will therefore have to weigh cautiously the interests involved in the conflict and they will have to make sure that all other means of conflict solution cannot be applied in the given situation.

(2) As was just explained, military intervention is a highly inflexible instrument. It is aimed at the re-establishment of the intervening party's power over the target state. A speedy return to the pre-conflict pattern of bilateral relations between the two is therefore essential. But this means that the intervener operates under great pressure of time; he has to achieve his stated objective swiftly, or else run the risk of failure. In a protracted conflict there is always the possibility that the opponent will grow militarily stronger or that other powers will intervene on his side either diplomatically or militarily. Given the essential inflexibility of military intervention, the decision to employ this instrument of statecraft always embraces the potential risk of escalation. Military intervention is a one-way road, and it can turn out to be either the 'King's highway' or a cul-de-sac.

(3) Military intervention is most of all an instrument of politics. It, therefore, needs careful diplomatic preparation. The wider international context of the conflict at hand has to be considered, in particular the possible implications of an intervention for other Great Powers. This can help to avoid an unintended escalation of the conflict. If the intervener succeeds to isolate the target state internationally and to win international support for the action, both prior the actual operation, his chances of ultimate success are all the more higher.

(4) International support for a contemplated military intervention is clearly needed; it adds legitimacy to this action and puts additional pressure on the target state. However, as some of the case studies have pointed out, multilateral interventions may suffer from a lack of coordination and a lack of common purpose. The decision for intervention, its implementation, and its final outcome may depend on strong, effective, and well-coordinated top-level political leadership. Indeed, the evidence offered by the case studies would suggest that unilateral military interventions have a higher chance of success than multilateral ones.

In addition to these four contextual factors which have to be taken into account, there are four general conditions for the successful use of military intervention as an instrument of statecraft. However, it should be well understood that none of these conditions as such can be regarded as sufficient for the ultimate success of an intervention. Politics is as much a science as it is an art, and it can not be reduced to the interaction of quantitative factors; political reality defies theoretical schemes that do not reflect it but try to superimpose an artificial rationalization.[51] In world politics, in particular, the force of the accidental and unpredictable, what Herbert A.L. Fisher once called 'the play of the contingent and the unforeseen'[52], must never be neglected. The success of military intervention depends above all on the sound political judgement of the policy-makers.[53] Hence, there can be no practical manual for the successful use of military intervention. It has to be understood that the four general conditions listed below only favour military intervention.

(1) The need of international support for an intervention has already been explained. But some of the case studies also suggest that adequate domestic support is essential for the successful employment of military intervention.

(2) The case studies also suggest that the clarity of the intervener's stated political objective is an essential factor. Only if the objectives and demands are stated clearly and consistently can the conflict of interests be diagnosed adequately and possible difficulties in winning international support be avoided.

(3) In the introduction it was explained that an asymmetry in terms of military power is an essential feature of military intervention. However, in addition, for an intervention to be successful there also has to be an asymmetry of motivation as this enables the intervener to achieve his stated objective more swiftly.

(4) Closely linked to the last point is the need for the intervener to create a sense of urgency for complete compliance. By launching a swift blow and inflicting maximum damage with limited force the target state has to be forced to decide between complete and unconditional compliance or further escalation. There remains, however, a risk which the intervener cannot fully control.

Military intervention, to repeat a point made earlier, will probably remain an instrument of statecraft. But it is an unwieldy and incongruous instrument, the use of which requires careful deliberation, circumspect preparation, and, if decided upon, decisiveness. If used lightly, military intervention is bound to back-fire and to damage the intervener's wider political interests and his standing in the international arena. It should never be forgotten that military intervention is a political instrument and as such an 'ultima ratio'.

Notes

1. See: Weber, M., 'The Fundamental Concepts of Sociology', in: idem, The Theory of Social and Economic Organization, edited by T. Parsons, New York: Free Press, 1964 (pb), p.89f.; idem, Economy and Society, edited by G. Roth and C. Wittich, Berkeley-Los Angeles: University of California Press, 2nd ed.1978, vol.i, p.4f.

2. Weber, Economy and Society, op.cit., p.5f.

3. cf.Bull, H., 'Conclusion', in: idem (ed.), Intervention in World Politics, Oxford: Clarendon, 1984, pp.181-195, p.181.

4. cf.Buzan, B., Peoples, States and Fear: An Agenda for International Security in the Post-Cold War Era, New York-London: Harvester Wheatsheaf, 2nd ed.1991, p.174.

5. Buzan, op.cit., pp.147ff.; Morgenthau, H.J., Politics Among Nations: The Struggle for Power and Peace, New York: A.A.Knopf, 4th edition 1967, pp.4ff.; Bull, H., 'Society and Anarchy in International relations', in: H. Butterfield & M. Wight (eds.), Diplomatic Investigations: Essays in the Theory of International Politics, London: Allen & Unwin, 3rd edition 1969, pp.40ff.; idem, The Anarchical Society: A Study of Order in World Politics, London: Macmillan, Repr.1991, pp.46ff.; Wolfers, A., Discord and Collaboration: Essays on International Politics, Baltimore: Johns Hopkins Press, 1962, pp.25ff.; Waltz, K.N., 'Political Structures', in: R.O. Keohane (cd.), Ncorcalism and Its Critics, New York: Columbia University Press, 1986, p.80f.; Northedge, F.S., 'The Nature of Foreign Policy', in: idem (ed.), The Foreign Policy of the Powers, London: Faber & Faber, 1969 (pb), p. 10f.

6. Morgenthau, Politics Among Nations, op.cit., pp.299ff.; Northedge, F.S., The International Political System, London: Faber & Faber, Repr.1981, pp.134ff.; Craig, G.A. & George, A.L., Force and Statecraft: Diplomatic Problems of Our Time, New York-Oxford: OUP, 1983, pp.150ff.

7. cf.Oppenheim, L.F.L., International Law: A Treatise, vol.i, Peace, edited by Sir H.Lauterpacht, London: Longmans, 5th ed.1937, pp.150ff.

8. Bull, Anarchical Society, op.cit., pp.127ff.; Wright, Q., Problems of Stability and Progress in International Relations, Berkeley-Los Angeles: University of California Press, 1954, pp.251ff.

9. Bull, Anarchical Society, op.cit., p.48f.; idem, 'Society and Anarchy', op.cit., p.49; see also Malik & Dorman chapter 6 in this book.

10. Waltz, K.N., 'Anarchic Order and Balances of Power', in: Keohane (ed.), Neorealism and Its Critics, op.cit., pp.98-131, p.108; idem, Theory of International Politics, Reading, MA: Addison-Wesley 1979, pp.118ff.; Howard, M., 'Military Power and International Order', in: International Affairs, xi/3, (1964), p.405f.

11. Howard, ibid.; Hudson, G.F., 'Collective Security and Military Alliances', Butterfield & Wight (eds.), Diplomatic Investigations, op.cit., pp.176-80; Northedge, The International Political System, op.cit., p.151f.

12. Morgenthau, Politics Among Nations, op.cit., p.8f, 36, and 541; idem, 'Politics Among Nations. The Mainspring of American Foreign Policy: The National Interest vs.Moral Abstraction', in: American Political Science Review, xliv/4, (1950), pp.833-54; see also his: 'The Organic Relationship between Ideology and Political Reality', in: G.Schwab (ed.), Ideology and Foreign Policy: A Global Perspective, New York-London: Cyrco Press, 1978, pp.117-23.

13. Northedge, The International Political System, op.cit., pp.194ff.; for a different view see: Putnam, R., 'Diplomacy and Domestic Politics: The Logic of the Two-Level Games', in: International Organization, xlii/3, (1988), pp.427-60; Snyder, J., Myths of Empire: Domestic Politics and International Ambition, Ithaca, NY-London: Cornell University Press, 1991, pp.19ff.

14. Craig & George, Force and Statecraft, op.cit., Pt.I; Hinsley, F.H., Power and the Pursuit of Peace: Theory and Practice in the Relations between States, Cambridge: CUP, Repr.1982 (pb), pts.II and III; idem, 'The Rise and Fall of the Modern International System', in: Revue of International Studies, viii/1, (1982), pp.1-8.

15. Waltz, Theory of International Politics, op.cit., p.111; idem, 'Political Structures', op.cit., pp.87ff.; Morgenthau, Politics Among Nations, op.cit., ch.ix.

16. Bull, Anarchical Society, op.cit., pp.205ff.; Waltz, Theory of International Politics, op.cit., p.131f.; see also: Berridge, G.W. & Young, J.W., 'What is "a Great Power"?', in: Political Studies, xxxvi/2, (1988), pp.224-34; Holbraad, C., The Concert of Europe: A Study in German and British International Theory, 1815-1914, London: Longmans, 1970; Dehio, L., The Precarious Balance: The Politics of Power in Europe, 1494-1945, London: Chatto & Windus, 1962.

17. Bull, ibid.; O'Neill, R., 'The Use of Military Force: Constant Factors and New Trends', in: Adelphi Papers, No.236, The Changing Strategic Landscape, Pt.II, pp.3-17; Northedge, F.S., 'The Resort to Force', in: idem (ed.), The Use of Force in International Relations, London, 1974, pp.11-35; Howard, 'Military Power and International Order', op.cit., pp.397ff.

18. Bull, 'Conclusion', op.cit., p.181; see also the introduction to this book.

19. Oppenheim, International Law, op.cit., vol.i, para 135ff.

20. See chapter 1.

21. See chapter 2 contribution.

22. See chapter 5.

23. See chapters 1 and 2.

24. Morgenthau, H.J., Internationale Rechtspflege, ihr Wesen und ihre Grenzen, Leipzig: R.Noske 1929 (= Ph.D.thesis Frankfurt 1928), esp. ch.III.2.7 on 'Der Begriff des Politischen', pp.59 ff.; also: idem, A New Foreign Policy for the United States, New York: F.A. Praeger 1969, p.140f.

25. Pinto, D., 'The Great Sea-Change', in: Daedalus, cxxi/4, (1991), pp.129-50; Hyde-Price, A., European Security beyond the Cold War: Four Scenarios for the Year 2010, London: Sage for the Royal Institute of International Affairs, 1991, pp.46ff.

26. Judt, T., 'The Past is Another Country: Myth and Memory in Postwar Europe', in: Daedalus, cxxi/4, (1992), pp.83-118.

27. Former US Secretary of State Lawrence Eagleburger, as quoted in: Waltz, K.N., 'The Emerging Structure of International Politics', in: International Security, xviii/2, (1993), p.44; see also: Mearsheimer, J.J., 'Back to the Future: Instability in Europe after the Cold War', in: ibid., xv/1, (1990), pp.5-56.

28. On the shortcomings of these theories, already apparent at the time, see: Morgenthau, A New Foreign Policy, op.cit., p.140f.

29. cf.Krauthammer, C., 'The Unipolar Moment', in: G.Allison & G.F.Treverton (eds.), Rethinking America's Security: Beyond Cold War to New World Order, New York: Norton 1992, pp.295-306; see also: Layne, C., 'The Unipolar Illusion: Why New Great Powers Will Rise', in: International Security, xvii/4, (1993), pp.5-51; Rosecrance, R., 'Regionalism and the Post-Cold War Era', in: International Journal, xlvi/3, (1991), pp.373-93.

30. Huntington, S.P., 'No Exit: The Errors of Endism', in: National Interest, No.17, (Autumn 1989), pp.3-11.

31. Fukuyama, F., 'The End of History ?', in: National Interest, no.16, (Summer 1989), pp.3-18; idem, The End of History and the Last Man, New York: Free Press, 1992, esp. pp.39ff.

32. The somewhat inelegant German term 'Historismus' was given preference here over the usually used term 'historicism' as the latter's meaning has been pre-empted by Benedetto Croce and above all by Karl R.Popper. For examples see: Mearsheimer, 'Back to the Future', op.cit.; Minc, A., Le Nouveau Moyen Age, Paris, 1993; Freedman, L., 'Potential European Instability: An Historical Perspective', in: RUSI Journal, cxxxv/2, (1991), pp.65-70; Hunter, R.E., 'The Future of European Security', in: Washington Quarterly, xiii/4, (1990), pp.55-68.

33. Berlin, I., 'Two Concepts of Nationalism', in: New York Review of Books, 21 November 1991, p.5f.; Judt, T., 'The Old New Nationalism', in: ibid., 20 May 1994, pp.44-51; Schlesinger, J., 'New Instabilities, New Priorities', in: Foreign Policy, No.85, (1991-2), pp.3-24; Van Evera, S., 'Hypotheses on Nationalism and War', in: International Security, xviii/4, (1994), pp.5-39; Snyder, J., 'Nationalism and the Crisis of the Post-Soviet State', in: Survival, xxxv/1, (1993), pp.5-26; Posen, B., 'The Security Dilemma and Ethnic Conflict', in: ibid., pp.27-47; Gottlieb, G., 'Nations Without States', in: Foreign Affairs, lxxiii/3, (1994), pp.100-12;

Huntington, S.P., 'The Clash of Civilizations ?', in: Foreign Affairs, lxxii/3, (1993), pp.22-49.

34. cf.Otte, T.G., 'Continuity and Change: NATO's Role after the Cold War', in: Arms Control, xiii/2, (1992), p.234.

35. Morgenthau, Politics among Nations, op.cit., pp.493ff.; Arendt, H., The Human Condition, Chicago: Chicago University Press, 1958; Dahrendorf, Lord R., Reflections on the Revolution in Europe, London: Chatto & Windus, 1990, pp.4ff.

36. Dahrendorf, ibid.

37. International Institute for Strategic Studies, Strategic Survey, 1992-93, London: Brassey's for IISS, 1993, pp.7ff.

38. Arend, A.C. & Beck, R.C., International Law and the Use of Force, London-New York: Routledge, 1993, pp.112ff.; for the older discussion of this issue see: Akehurst, M., 'Humanitarian Intervention', in: Bull (ed.), Intervention in World Politics, op.cit., pp.95-118.

39. See chapters 3,4 & 6.

40. See: Arend & Beck, International Law and the Use of Force, op.cit., p.113; also: Oppenheim, International Law, op.cit., vol.i, p.155, para.137.

41. Gaddis, J.L., 'Toward the Post-Cold War World', in: Foreign Affairs, lxx/2, (1991), pp.102-22; idem, 'The Cold War, the Long Peace, and the Future', in: Diplomatic History, xvi/2, (1992), pp.234-46.

42. IISS, Strategic Survey, 1992-3, op.cit., pp.67ff; Allison, R., Military Forces in the Soviet Successor States, London: Brassey's for IISS, 1993 (=Adelphi Paper No.280), p.21f.; Dannreuther, R., 'Russia, Central Asia, and the Persian Gulf', in: Survival, xxxv/4, (1993-4), pp.92-112; MacFarlane, S.N., 'Russia, the West and European Security', in: ibid., vol.xxxv/3, (1993), pp.3-25, pp.7ff.; Arbatov, A.G., 'Russia's Foreign Policy Alternatives', in: International Security, xviii/3, (1993), pp.5-43, esp. pp.8-14.

43. Allison, op.cit., p.24f.; Pope, H., 'Russians claw back control of unstable Transcaucasus', in: The Independent, 1 July 1993, p.13; McElvoy, A., 'Moscow pledges not to use nuclear arms first', in: The Times, 4 November 1993, p.12; see also: Kipp, J.W., 'Russian Military Doctrine and Military Technical Policy: An American Military Historian's Perspective', in: Contemporary Strategy, xiii/1, (1994), pp.25-41.

44. Layne, 'The Unipolar Illusion', op.cit., pp.35ff.; Waltz, 'The Emerging Structure of International Politics', op.cit., pp.50ff.; Jervis, R., 'The Future of World Politics: Will It Resemble the Past?', in: S.M. Lynn-Jones & S.E. Miller (eds.), America's Strategy in a Changing World, Cambridge, MA: MIT Press, 1992, pp.3-37.

45. Dehio, The Precarious Balance, op.cit.; Thompson, W.R., 'Dehio, Long Cycles, and the Geohistorical Context of Structural Transition', in: World Politics, xlv/1, (1992), pp.127-52; Kennedy, P.M., The Rise and Fall of the Great Powers: Economic Change and Military Conflict from 1500 to 2000, London: Fontana, 1989 (pb), p.xvif.; Bull, Anarchical Society, op.cit., pp.200ff.; Hinsley, Power and the Pursuit of Peace, op.cit., pp.153ff.

46. Waltz, Theory of International Politics, op.cit., p.131f.; Morgenthau, Politics among Nations, op.cit., pp.109ff.

47. Waltz, ibid., pp.107 and 131; Kennedy, Rise and Fall of the Great Powers, op.cit., p.xxii; for an alternative view see: Maull, H.W., 'Germany and Japan: The New Civilian Powers', in: Foreign Affairs, lxix/5, (1990-10), pp.91-106.

48. Friedberg, A.L., 'Ripe for Rivalry: Prospects for Peace in a Multipolar Asia', in: International Security, xviii/3, (1993-4), pp.5-33; McCarthy, T., 'Asia's New Great Game', in: The Independent, 18 January 1994, p.16.

49. See chapter 4.

50. See chapter 3.

51. Morgenthau, A New Foreign Policy, op.cit., pp.140ff.; Aron, R., 'What Is a Theory of International Relations ?', in: idem, Politics and History: Selected Essays, transl.and edited by M. Bernheim Conant, New York: Free Press, 1978, pp.166-85, and 'History and Politics', in: ibid., pp.237-48.

52. cf.Northedge, 'The Nature of Foreign Policy', op.cit., p.9; see also: Fisher, H.A.L., Political Prophecies, Oxford: Clarendon Press, 1919.

53. Weber, M., 'Politics as a Vocation', in: H.H.Gerth & C. Wright Mills (eds.), From Max Weber: Essays in Sociology, London: Routledge & Kegan Paul, 6th ed.1967, p.127f.; Arendt, H., Between Past and Future, London: Faber & Faber 1961, pp.220ff.